Virtuous Bodies

AAR
AMERICAN ACADEMY OF RELIGION

RELIGION, CULTURE, AND HISTORY SERIES

SERIES EDITOR
Jacob N. Kinnard, Iliff School of Theology

A Publication Series of
The American Academy of Religion
and Oxford University Press

ANTI-JUDAISM IN FEMINIST RELIGIOUS WRITINGS
Katharina von Kellenbach

CROSS CULTURAL CONVERSATION
(Initiation)
Edited by Anindita Niyogi Balslev

ON DECONSTRUCTING LIFE-WORLDS
Buddhism, Christianity, Culture
Robert Magliola

THE GREAT WHITE FLOOD
Racism in Australia
Anne Pattel-Gray

IMAG(IN)ING OTHERNESS
Filmic Visions of Living Together
Edited by S. Brent Plate and David Jasper

CULTURAL OTHERNESS
Correspondence with Richard Rorty, Second Edition
Anindita Niyogi Balslev

FEMINIST POETICS OF THE SACRED
Creative Suspicions
Edited by Frances Devlin-Glass and Lyn McCredden

PARABLES FOR OUR TIME
Rereading New Testament Scholarship after the Holocaust
Tania Oldenhage

MOSES IN AMERICA
The Cultural Uses of Biblical Narrative
Melanie Jane Wright

INTERSECTING PATHWAYS
Modern Jewish Theologians in Conversation with Christianity
Marc A. Krell

ASCETICISM AND ITS CRITICS
Historical Accounts and Comparative Perspectives
Edited by Oliver Freiberger

VIRTUOUS BODIES
The Physical Dimensions of Morality in Buddhist Ethics
Susanne Mrozik

AAR
AMERICAN ACADEMY OF RELIGION

Virtuous Bodies

The Physical Dimensions of Morality in Buddhist Ethics

SUSANNE MROZIK

OXFORD
UNIVERSITY PRESS
2007

OXFORD
UNIVERSITY PRESS

Oxford University Press, Inc., publishes works that further
Oxford University's objective of excellence
in research, scholarship, and education.

Oxford New York
Auckland Cape Town Dar es Salaam Hong Kong Karachi
Kuala Lumpur Madrid Melbourne Mexico City Nairobi
New Delhi Shanghai Taipei Toronto

With offices in
Argentina Austria Brazil Chile Czech Republic France Greece
Guatemala Hungary Italy Japan Poland Portugal Singapore
South Korea Switzerland Thailand Turkey Ukraine Vietnam

Published by Oxford University Press, Inc.
198 Madison Avenue, New York, New York 10016

www.oup.com

Library of Congress Cataloging-in-Publication Data
Mrozik, Susanne.
Virtuous bodies : the physical dimensions of morality
in Buddhist ethics / Susanne Mrozik.
p. cm. — (American Academy of Religion
Religion, Culture, and History series)
Includes bibliographical references and index.
ISBN 978-0-19-530500-5
1. Śāntideva, 7th cent. Śikṣāsamuccaya.
2. Body, Human—Religious aspects—Buddhism.
3. Buddhist ethics. I. Title.
BQ3247.M76 2007
294.3'92—dc22 2006034982

9 8 7 6 5 4 3 2 1

Printed in the United States of America
on acid-free paper

Acknowledgments

It is a great pleasure to acknowledge the many people who have contributed to this book. I began my research on the book when I was a graduate student at Harvard University. It is thus fitting to open by acknowledging the pivotal role my teachers have played in shaping my intellectual sensibilities. I thank my advisor, Charles Hallisey, for many years of outstanding teaching and mentoring. His own research on Buddhist ethics is the inspiration behind this project. My debt to him is inestimable. I also thank Diana Eck, Stephanie Jamison, and Margaret Miles for their extraordinary teaching and scholarship.

In addition to these wonderful teachers, I have also had many wonderful conversation partners. I am grateful to Carol Anderson, Stephen Berkwitz, Karen Derris, Damchö Diana Finnegan, Janet Gyatso, Paul Harrison, and Carolyn Podruchny for reading drafts of the book. My debt to Karen Derris is especially great, since she read and commented on multiple drafts of the book over a period of many years. I have benefited greatly from her expertise in Buddhist ethics. I am also especially grateful to Paul Harrison for sharing his research on the *Compendium of Training.* Paul kindly read through the entire manuscript once it was finished, offering corrections and suggestions for its improvement. He has been a very generous conversation partner. I also wish to thank Jonathan Silk and Jens Braarvig for giving me a copy of the sole extant manuscript of the text, Kim Plofker and David Pingree for interpreting the colophon of another fragmentary manuscript of the text, and Jacob

Kinnard, Marylin Rhie, and Sonya Quintanilla for art historical assistance. Jacob Kinnard is also the editor of Oxford University Press's Religion, Culture, and History series, in which this book appears. I thank him, Christine Dahlin, Daniel Gonzalez, Cynthia Read, and Julia TerMaat for all their efforts on my behalf.

A number of scholars have taken the time to read through portions of the *Compendium of Training* and related Sanskrit materials with me. I thank Biswanath Banerjee, Tom Burke, M. G. Dhadphale, Stephanie Jamison, Mahinda Palihawadana, Jogesh Panda, and Asanga Tilakaratana. Especially I thank W. S. Karunatillake, who read almost the entirety of the *Compendium of Training* with me over the course of two years. Additionally Maria Heim, Steven Heim, and Andy Rotman have been astute consultants on problematic Sanskrit and Pāli passages. Jay Garfield and Holly Gayley have provided invaluable help with the Tibetan materials, as has Mark Blum with the Chinese materials.

There are also many others who contributed in diverse ways to this book. I thank my colleagues in the religion department of Mount Holyoke College—Jane Crosthwaite, Lawrence Fine, John Grayson, Michael Penn, and Amina Steinfels—for providing such a congenial setting in which to complete my research. I also thank Anna May Dion, Laurie Dion, Janet Ewing, and Aleefia Somji for assistance at the college. Additionally, I am grateful to Julia Jean for kindly offering to type for me when injuries prevented me from doing so myself.

Several institutions have provided financial support for my research, including the U.S. Educational Foundation in India, the American Institute of Indian Studies, Harvard University, and Mount Holyoke College. I am also indebted to Snehadri Shekhar Chakraborty, Uma Das Gupta, Tissa Jayatilake, Martin Kämpchen, the Dekeva family in Darjeeling, the Karunatillake family in Eldeniya, the Mukherjee family in Santiniketan, and the Wikremarachchi family in Colombo for their help and hospitality during my stays in India and Sri Lanka.

Finally, I think my parents for their support throughout these many years of research and writing.

I gratefully acknowledge permission from Blackwell Publishing to reprint portions of my article "Cooking Living Beings: The Transformative Effects of Encounters with Bodhisattva Bodies," which appeared in the *Journal of Religious Ethics* 32:1 (Spring 2004): 175–194; The Gale Group to reprint portions of Liz Wilson, "Ascetic Practices," in *Encyclopedia of Buddhism*, ed. Robert E. Buswell, Jr., vol. 1 (New York: Macmillan Reference, 2004); Oxford University

Press to reprint portions of Ronald Inden, "Introduction: From Philological to Dialogical Texts," in *Querying the Medieval: Texts and the History of Practices in South Asia*, ed. Ronald Inden, Jonathan Walters, and Daud Ali (Oxford: Oxford University Press, 2000); Rowman & Littlefield Publishing Group to reprint portions of Mark Tatz, trans., *Buddhism and Healing: Demiéville's Article "Byō" from Hōbōgirin* (Lanham, Md.: University Press of America, 1985); the State University of New York Press to reprint portions of Paul J. Griffiths, *On Being Buddha: The Classical Doctrine of Buddhahood* (Albany: State University of New York Press, 1994); and the University of South Carolina Press to reprint portions of Steven Kemper, "Wealth and Reformation in Sinhalese Buddhist Monasticism," in *Ethics, Wealth, and Salvation: A Study in Buddhist Social Ethics*, ed. Russell F. Sizemore and Donald K. Swearer (Columbia: University of South Carolina Press, 1990).

Contents

Virtuous Bodies

I

Introduction to the *Compendium of Training*

A person who generates the aspiration to attain awakening (*bodhicitta*) and worships at the *stūpa*, or shrine, of the Teacher [i.e., Buddha] is never blind or lame even in vast numbers of eons.[1]

A Focus on Bodies

This book offers a new approach to the study of Buddhist ethics by asking what we can learn about Buddhist ethics if we make body the focus of ethical inquiry.[2] More often studies of Buddhist ethics place heartmind at the center of investigation, defining ethical development as the cultivation of desired affective and cognitive qualities such as compassion and wisdom.[3] By making body the focus of ethical inquiry, I hope to demonstrate that ethical development also includes the cultivation of desired physical qualities such as the serene appearance and deportment of monastics. Buddhist traditions admit no easy or absolute separation between the physical and moral dimensions of living beings. Body and morality are inextricably linked. Thus Buddhist literature is replete with descriptions of living beings who literally stink with sin, are disfigured by vices, and, conversely, are perfumed or adorned with merit and virtues. The close relationship Buddhists posit between body and morality means that the formation of ethical persons is conceived of as a process of both physical and moral transformation, affecting the entire complex of body, feelings, and thoughts.

Although body and morality are inextricably linked in Buddhist ethical discourse, studies of Buddhist ethics rarely devote much attention to bodies. There are various reasons for this oversight. The tendency of the more culturally authoritative strands of modern Western thought to posit a sharp distinction between body and mind is likely in part to blame. Buddhist ethical discourse itself, however, directs our attention to heartmind. Specifically it directs our attention to *cetanā*, a term usually translated as "intention," "motive," "volition," or "will," but more recently by Damien Keown as "moral psychology."[4] It is well known that Buddhist traditions place great weight on taking into account the intentions or motives of a person in evaluating his or her actions.[5] *Cetanā* is such an important issue in Buddhist ethics that karma is specifically defined as volitional action.[6] Thus a person earns good karma, or merit (*puṇya*), and bad karma, or sin (*pāpa*), in accordance with the good or bad intentions he or she had in performing that action. For instance, some negative karmic debt may accrue to me if I inadvertently run over a dog with my car (particularly if I have been careless), but the karmic consequences will be far less grave than had I done so on purpose. Hence studies of Buddhist ethics often quote the following canonical statement: "It is intention [*cetanā*], O monks, that I call karma; having willed, one acts through body, speech, or mind."[7]

Given the importance of *cetanā* in Buddhist ethics, it is perhaps not surprising that studies of Buddhist ethics privilege heartmind over body. This book will demonstrate, however, that Buddhist attention to heartmind does not preclude an equal attention to body. Both body and heartmind figure prominently in Buddhist ethical discourse. Taking an early medieval Indian Mahāyāna Buddhist text as a case study, this book explores the important and diverse roles Buddhists have ascribed to bodies in the ethical development of living beings. The text, written in Sanskrit, is the *Compendium of Training* (*Śikṣāsamuccaya*). According to Buddhist tradition, it was composed in north India in the seventh or eighth century by a scholar-monk named Śāntideva. The *Compendium of Training* is, as its title implies, a compendium or compilation of Buddhist teachings. It quotes extensively from approximately one hundred Buddhist sources in order to describe the training (*śikṣā*) of bodhisattvas. Bodhisattvas are living beings who seek liberation in order to become capable of liberating others from the suffering inherent in saṃsāric existence, that is, in the endless cycle of birth, death, and rebirth. Because Buddhists believe in rebirth, the path to liberation, which is defined in Mahāyāna Buddhist terms as the experience of awakening or buddhahood, may take countless lifetimes. Bodhisattvas dedicate all of their lifetimes to the happiness and well-being of others. They thus represent one of the highest ethical ideals in Buddhist traditions. In Mahāyāna Buddhism, the bodhisattva path is open to all Buddhist practitioners, lay and monastic. Nevertheless, the *Compendium of Training* regards a monastic lifestyle as most conducive to concentrated practice. Thus the text is primarily, although not exclusively, addressed to monastic bodhisattvas. Additionally, even householder bodhisattvas are at times exhorted to adopt monastic attitudes such as detachment from sensual pleasures, including sex with one's own spouse. The *Compendium of Training*'s preference for a monastic bodhisattva lifestyle flies in the face of modern popular representations of Mahāyāna Buddhism as a lay-oriented tradition. The *Compendium of Training* is one of many South Asian Mahāyāna texts that advocate a monastic, rather than lay, bodhisattva lifestyle.[8]

The *Compendium of Training* places bodies front and center in bodhisattva training, especially monastic bodhisattva training. The philosopher and historian Michel Foucault has illumined the physical effects of a wide range of disciplinary practices, from those found in modern prisons to those enjoined by ancient Greek and Greco-Roman philosophers.[9] The *Compendium of Training* prescribes many different kinds of disciplinary practices for bodhisattvas, including study of scriptures, confession liturgies (*pāpadeśanā*), forms of meditation, codes of ethical conduct, and observance of monastic etiquette and deportment. As Foucault would argue, these disciplinary practices were intended to have physical as well as moral effects. For example, observance of monastic etiquette and deportment produces bodhisattvas with serene features and gestures as well as serene feelings and thoughts. The *Compendium of Training*'s bodhisattva ideal is an embodied ideal. The effects of bodhisattva practices are as manifest in the features, postures, and movements of bodies as they are in the experience of particular affective and cognitive states. Thus bodhisattva practices are intended to produce virtuous bodies as well as virtuous heartminds.

Given the close relationship between physical and moral transformation, bodies serve in the *Compendium of Training*, as they do more broadly in Buddhist ethical discourse, as markers of moral character. For example, in the quotation at the start of this chapter the absence of certain disabilities serves as a physical marker of past virtuous actions. The fact that bodies serve as markers of moral character is, however, but one of several reasons why bodies are front and center in the *Compendium of Training*'s description of bodhisattva training. Perhaps the most important reason why bodies figure so prominently is that the text assumes that certain kinds of bodies, especially the virtuous bodies of bodhisattvas, can have profoundly transformative effects on other living beings. The *Compendium of Training* teaches bodhisattvas how to cultivate bodies in present and future lifetimes whose very sight, sound, and in some instances even touch and taste, transform other living beings in both physical and moral ways. For instance, animals who eat bodhisattva corpses are reborn as gods in heaven; humans who touch the living bodies of bodhisattvas are no longer tormented by lust, anger, and delusion. Throughout the text, the *Compendium of Training* draws attention to the physically and morally transformative power of bodhisattva bodies. Bodhisattvas use their bodies as much as their heartminds to transform living beings. The *Compendium of Training* thereby foregrounds the role bodhisattva bodies play in the bodhisattva ideal of liberating others from the suffering of saṃsāric existence.

Goals of the Study

This book has two broad goals. First it corrects the common misperception in scholarship on Buddhism and Buddhist ethics that South Asian Buddhists (with the exception of practitioners of Vajrayāna or Tantric Buddhism) ascribed little value to bodies. Bodies are frequently characterized in South Asian Buddhist literature as impermanent, foul, and without any intrinsic and eternal essence. Scholars have thus often concluded that bodies were of limited concern to most South Asian Buddhists. There are two problems with this assumption. First, a negative discourse on bodies does not bespeak a lack of interest in bodies. To the contrary, it bespeaks a deep fascination with bodies, a point I argue in chapter 5. Second, there is more than one kind of discourse on bodies in Buddhist literature. Alongside a negative discourse that represents bodies as impermanent, foul, and without intrinsic and eternal essence, we find a positive discourse that underscores the inextricable link between body and morality. This positive discourse highlights the critical role bodies play in the ethical development of oneself and others. I call the negative discourse on bodies an "ascetic discourse," and the positive discourse on bodies a "physiomoral discourse." Both are present in the *Compendium of Training*. One of the challenges of this book is to examine how both ascetic and physiomoral discourses contribute to the *Compendium of Training*'s larger goal of producing bodhisattvas with virtuous bodies as well as virtuous heartminds. In this text the ascetic discourse is always in service of the physiomoral discourse, because the goal of the text is to produce bodhisattvas whose bodies as well as heartminds benefit other living beings.

It should be noted that one well-known form of body discourse is altogether absent from the *Compendium of Training*. It does not discuss the three-body (*trikāya*) doctrine. The three-body doctrine is a sophisticated scholastic discourse on the nature of a buddha's body. Perhaps surprisingly for a text penned by the scholar-monk Śāntideva, the *Compendium of Training* does not discuss this most famous of Mahāyāna scholastic body discourses. There is not a single reference to the *trikāya* doctrine in the entire text. Instead, the *Compendium of Training* reveals the presence of other kinds of body discourse in medieval South Asia, including a physiomoral discourse, which links body to morality and links physical transformation to moral transformation. The text is a training manual for bodhisattvas. Its primary concern is to teach bodhisattvas how to cultivate virtuous bodies as well as virtuous heartminds. It is less concerned with describing the precise nature of a buddha's or bodhisattva's body than it is with describing the physically and morally beneficial effects bodhisattva bodies have on other living beings. Analysis of this text's body discourse thus requires a different interpretive framework than that of the three-body doctrine.

The second aim of the book is to explore the ethical implications of the *Compendium of Training*'s discourse on bodies for both medieval and contemporary audiences. The book is motivated as much by a desire to learn *from* medieval Indian Buddhist ethics as it is by a desire to learn *about* medieval Indian Buddhist ethics. This approach—and its very formulation—bespeak the influence of Charles Hallisey, who describes the experience of studying Buddhist literature as one in which ideally we learn to listen to and think alongside this literature.[10] Similarly, Ronald Inden challenges positivist readings of medieval South Asian literature, urging scholars to

> establish a dialogical or interdiscursive relationship with the texts we study. Instead of looking at them as dead monuments, as mere sources of factual information or the expression of a creative and exotic genius that we can only appreciate in itself for itself, or as the accidental expression/sedimentation of some larger structure or context, we want to see them as living arguments both in their historic usages and by virtue of our reenactment of their arguments, in our own present. We want to see what we can learn from these texts that pertains to our own time and its problems.[11]

By exploring the ethical implications of an early medieval Buddhist discourse on bodies for contemporary as well as medieval audiences, the book seeks to make a place for the *Compendium of Training* in the living arguments of the present. A growing number of scholars have argued that we should take the corporeal specificity of human beings as the starting point for ethical inquiry.[12] Feminists, in particular, have been extremely suspicious of ethical theories that presume a generic universal subject, because that subject is frequently implicitly male. This book introduces a medieval Indian Buddhist perspective on bodies to current work in this area. The *Compendium of Training* underscores the corporeal specificity of ethical ideals. There is a bodily dimension to morality and a moral dimension to bodies. The text displays a fascination with bodily differences and the ways in which such differences affect the ethical development of oneself and others.

Yet, if the *Compendium of Training* displays perspectives resonant with those of some current scholars as well as religious practitioners, it also displays perspectives that many of these would regard as highly problematic, notably its hierarchical ranking of bodily differences. Humans are superior to animals, high castes to low castes, men to women, and so forth. Analysis of the *Compendium of Training* thus entails both a hermeneutics of recovery and suspicion, suggesting how a complex, brilliant, and yet often problematic discourse on bodies can offer intellectual resources to contemporary scholars and practitioners committed to a vision of human flourishing that values human differences.

Methodological and Theoretical Perspectives

This study of the *Compendium of Training* is based on a close reading of Cecil Bendall's 1897–1902 edition of the sole complete extant Sanskrit manuscript, with reference to a copy of the manuscript itself.[13] While there are some problems with Bendall's edition, for the most part these are not critical to the interpretation of this study. Exceptions, in the form of emendations to Bendall's edition, are duly recorded in the notes. This study is in sympathy with Gregory Schopen's suggestion that we study texts in their historically attested form.[14] Therefore the book leaves aside questions of the original authorial version of the text as well as the original date of composition. It also leaves for other scholars an analysis of the Tibetan and Chinese recensions of the *Compendium of Training*, although, as will be evident from my notes, I have occasionally consulted the Tibetan when faced with a particularly problematic Sanskrit passage. A Tibetan translation was made in the beginning of the ninth century and was subsequently revised at the end of the eleventh century.[15] A Chinese translation was made in the Northern Song dynasty between 1058 and 1072.[16] Some scholars have insisted that the Tibetan translation in particular is crucial to a "correct" (or corrected) reading of the Sanskrit text.[17]

Again, this study of the *Compendium of Training* is a study of a text in its historically attested form. It does not attempt to "correct" the Sanskrit manuscript. Instead it attends to the details and nuances of its Sanskrit language in order to understand how and why bodies figure so prominently in its conception of the bodhisattva ideal.

The book is methodologically informed by three broad areas of study. First, it draws upon the research of historians and anthropologists of South Asia such as E. Valentine Daniel, Ronald Inden, McKim Marriott, and Ralph W. Nicholas, who have argued that South Asians frequently posit a close relationship between body and morality.[18] Speaking of Bengal, Inden and Nicholas state that there is "no absolute separation between natural and moral orders or material and spiritual orders."[19] The assumption that body and morality are closely linked is at such a sufficient level of generalization in South Asia that it is ubiquitous in Sanskrit literature. Although it is beyond the scope of this study to engage in systematic comparison of South Asian perspectives on bodies, the study nevertheless situates the *Compendium of Training* within broader patterns of ethical thought and practice in South Asia.

Second, the book is in conversation with recent scholarship on bodies. Over the last few decades scholars in diverse fields have shown increasing interest in this topic. Michel Foucault's work has had a particularly strong influence on many academic disciplines, including that of the history of religions. His studies of the "technologies of power" (e.g., *Discipline and Punish*) and the "technologies of the self" (e.g., *The Use of Pleasure* and *The Care of the Self*) have made it impossible to ignore the corporeal effects of diverse forms of disciplinary practices—whether these practices are imposed upon one by others, as is the case with technologies of power, or are self-imposed, as is the case with technologies of the self. Of particular relevance to this book is Foucault's research on the technologies of the self. He defines the technologies of the self as those disciplinary practices individuals intentionally adopt in order to transform themselves into ideal ethical subjects. Bodhisattva practices are disciplinary practices in the Foucauldian sense of the term. Individuals who are committed to the bodhisattva ideal self-consciously adopt these practices in order to transform themselves into ideal ethical beings, that is, bodhisattvas. The *Compendium of Training* is quite explicit about the intended physical effects of its disciplinary practices. It seeks to shape bodies as much as heartminds. This book explores how the *Compendium of Training* uses Buddhist (and especially monastic) disciplinary practices to cultivate bodhisattvas with bodies capable of transforming others.

Feminist scholarship arguably has made the most important contributions to recent research on bodies, countering the problematic presumption of a generic body in the work of earlier scholars such as Foucault. In this book I draw especially on the work of the feminist philosopher Elizabeth Grosz. Rejecting a Cartesian body–mind dualism, Grosz asks us to reconceptualize human beings in such a way that we acknowledge the corporeal specificity of human beings—that is, the fact that human beings are (1) bodied, and (2) bodied in different kinds of ways.[20] The *Compendium of Training* is especially well suited for such a project, because it displays a fascination with the details of bodily differences. Bodies are marked in diverse ways in this text (as in Buddhist literature in general), including by one's realm of rebirth (*gati*)—that is, whether one is reborn as a god, human, demon (*asura*), animal, hungry ghost (*preta*), or hell being—as well as by physical beauty, health, longevity, absence or presence of physical or mental disability, sex, caste (*varṇa, jāti*), and family (*kula*). Although bodies are marked in different ways, one form of bodily difference is especially important in the *Compendium of Training,* namely, sexual difference. As we will see, the text primarily represents a male monastic perspective on the bodhisattva ideal. Thus I pay particular attention to the ways in which sexual difference affects the ability of bodhisattvas to use their bodies to transform living beings.

Third, the book is inspired by Charles Hallisey's research on "the ethics of care and responsibility" in Theravāda Buddhism.[21] Hallisey explores the critical role human relationships play in the formation of ethical persons. According to Hallisey, we do not become virtuous by ourselves but are made virtuous through relationships with others. Hallisey shifts the focus of inquiry in ethical projects from individual to community. In this book I am especially interested in how the *bodies* of ideal ethical persons such as bodhisattvas influence the ethical development of other living beings.

Literary Genre of the Text

The *Compendium of Training* employs the literary genre of the compendium to make its case for the importance of bodies to the bodhisattva ideal. The text consists of Śāntideva's generally brief comments in prose and verse along with copious quotations from diverse Buddhist texts variously classified as *sūtra, paripṛcchā, dhāraṇī, prātimokṣa, avadāna,* and *vimokṣa.* (It should be noted that although the *Compendium of Training* is a Mahāyāna Buddhist text, not all of its sources belong exclusively to the Mahāyāna tradition.) As a compendium, the text shows us, among other things, how Buddhist texts circulated in the past. Texts or portions thereof often circulated as part of compendia or anthologies. Readers did not necessarily have access to an entire text, as these are constituted in modern print editions, but rather had particular chapters, passages, or other smaller units of a text. Not only is the *Compendium of Training* itself an instantiation of this fact, but, as Bendall notes, it cites passages that were regularly quoted in other works and appear to have circulated as stock pieces.[22] The *Compendium of Training* thus reminds us that the boundaries of texts were much more fluid in medieval Indian Buddhist manuscript culture than they are in modern print culture.

The *Compendium of Training* has sometimes been dismissed by modern scholars precisely because it is a compendium. They dismiss the work because so much of it consists of quotations from other sources. For instance, one scholar characterizes it as "more of an encyclopedia of sources than a creation of original thinking."[23] Paul Harrison observes, "Right from the start [the *Compendium of Training*'s] general lack of originality and largely derivative nature have been taken as a matter of fact."[24] Harrison, however, has recently discovered that a significant number of verses in the final chapter of the text, heretofore attributed to other sources, were actually penned by Śāntideva himself. Harrison, who together with Jens-Uwe Hartmann is currently preparing a new English translation of the text, believes that this may be the case for other verse and prose passages as well.[25] Assessment of the full extent of Śāntideva's original contributions to the text will have to wait until Harrison and Hartmann complete their study and translation of the text. Nevertheless it is already apparent from Harrison's research that a greater portion of the text may be original to Śāntideva than was previously recognized by scholars.[26]

Regardless of how much of the text was written by Śāntideva himself, the text as a whole offers an original and compelling vision of the bodhisattva ideal. Maria Heim has drawn attention to the importance of compendia as a literary genre in South Asia. She cautions against the tendency of scholars to assume that compendia are merely "redundant reiterations of earlier material."[27] Rather, the very act of choosing which material to include in a compendium entails significant editorial interpretation.[28] Additionally, the *Compendium of Training* guides the reader's understanding of quoted passages by framing these with commentary. Anne M. Blackburn's study of eighteenth-century Sri Lankan Buddhist textual practices demonstrates the extent to which an author's commentary "orchestrat[es] his readers' encounter with the texts in ways that privileged his understanding of their significance."[29] Although I regret that this study of the *Compendium of Training* will not benefit from Harrison and Hartmann's research, it makes no difference to my overall argument which passages are original to Śāntideva and which he has drawn from other sources. The text *as a whole* represents his vision of the bodhisattva ideal. That vision is one in which bodies play critical roles in the ethical development of living beings.

The *Compendium of Training*'s summary of Buddhist teachings was meant to serve as a practical handbook or manual of bodhisattva—especially monastic bodhisattva—practice. Writing on South Asian Pāli Buddhist compendia (*saṅgaha*), Heim argues that these "handbooks" or "manuals" "often usurp the earlier canonical and more authoritative sources in their use as training material for monks up to the present day."[30] Similarly, Schopen observes that most monks in ancient and medieval India probably did not read the canonical monastic regulations (*vinaya*) because these were so lengthy. Instead they would have relied on summaries, manuals, and handbooks.[31] The *Compendium of Training* calls itself a bodhisattva *vinaya* and likely was intended to function in the manner outlined by Heim and Schopen.[32] Unfortunately, however, it is difficult to ascertain the actual extent or manner of the *Compendium of Training*'s use in medieval India. In the first place, as Jan Nattier has noted, most Buddhist scriptures are prescriptive rather than descriptive.[33] The *Compendium of Training* tells us how bodhisattvas should live, not necessarily how they actually lived. In the second place, we do not know how many Buddhists had access to this text in medieval India. Only one complete Sanskrit manuscript and a fragment of a second one, both from north India, have survived to the present day (see the next section, "Locating the Text in Time and Place"). Passages from the text are cited in the works of a number of other famous Indian monastic scholars such as Prajñākaramati and Atīśa (ca. tenth and eleventh centuries).[34] We also know from references to the text in writings of Tibetan scholars such as Tsong kha pa (1357–1419) that its influence extended well beyond north India.[35] Indeed the text continues to be studied by contemporary Tibetan religious teachers. For example, H. H. the Dalai Lama has given teachings on the text in recent years. Modern scholars of Buddhism regard Śāntideva as one of the most important Buddhist intellectuals of his day. Nevertheless, the extent to which the *Compendium of Training* was disseminated in medieval north Indian monasteries and the precise manner in which it might have been used in these monasteries remains unclear.

Locating the Text in Time and Place

Very little can be known with absolute certainty concerning the historical origins of this text and its manuscript. On the basis of Indian and Tibetan Buddhist traditions, the original composition of the *Compendium of Training* is attributed to Śāntideva, a monk and scholar believed to have lived between the seventh and eighth centuries C.E. According to tradition, Śāntideva, a proponent of Mahāyāna Buddhism, lived at Nālandā monastery in north India in the modern state of Bihar. Nālandā was known as a *mahāvihāra*, that is, a great monastery. *Mahāvihāras* were the premier educational institutions of their day.[36] They attracted students from as far away as China and Southeast Asia.[37] They taught diverse subjects, including grammar, rhetoric, prose and verse composition, logic, metaphysics, medicine, ritual and meditation, fine arts, astronomy, and mathematics.[38] Nālandā was one of the greatest of the *mahāvihāras*. The Chinese monk and scholar Xuanzang, who visited Nālandā in the seventh century during the reign of King Harṣa, tells us,

> The priests [i.e., monks], to the number of several thousands, are men of the highest ability and talent. Their distinction is very great at the present time, and there are many hundreds whose fame has rapidly spread through distant regions. Their conduct is pure and unblamable. They follow in sincerity the precepts of the moral law. The rules of this convent are severe, and all the priests are bound to observe them. The countries of India respect them and follow them. The day is not sufficient for asking and answering profound questions. From morning till night they engage in discussion; the old and the young mutually help one another. Those who cannot discuss questions out of the *Tripiṭaka* [Buddhist canon] are little esteemed and are obliged to hide themselves for shame. Learned men from different cities, on this account, who desire to acquire quickly a renown in discussion, come here in multitudes to settle their doubts, and then the streams (*of their wisdom*) spread far and wide. For this reason some persons usurp the name (*of Nālandā students*), and in going to and fro receive honour in consequence.[39]

The sole complete extant Sanskrit manuscript of the *Compendium of Training* dates from several centuries after the life of Śāntideva. Bendall, who edited the manuscript, initially dated it to the fourteenth to fifteenth century C.E. and subsequently to the thirteenth to fourteenth century C.E.[40] The manuscript is written in Old Bengali script.[41] It consists of 166 folios and was copied by two scribes. The second scribe took over for the first and chief scribe at the bottom of folio 122a (chapter 16 of the *Compendium of Training*). The first scribe resumed his work again at the top of folio 132a (chapter 17 of the *Compendium of Training*). The colophon, written in the hand of the first scribe, states that the manuscript was copied by a scholar (*paṇḍita*) named Vibhṛticandra, from the Jāgandala monastery.[42] The title *paṇḍita* indicates a person of considerable learning.[43] If this is a reference to the famous Indian Buddhist scholar-monk known as Vibhūticandra of the Jagaddala monastery, the manuscript must be dated to the late twelfth or early thirteenth century.[44] Vibhūticandra is famous for his transmission of Buddhist teachings from India and Nepal to Tibet in the early thirteenth century, a time when Indian Buddhist institutions were under attack by Turko-Afghan invaders.[45] He made three trips to Tibet, spending altogether at least fifteen years there.[46] He also lived for periods of time in Nepal, eventually serving as abbot of the Stham Bihar in Kathmandu.[47] Among the works that Vibhūticandra transmitted to Tibet is a commentary that he himself wrote on the *Bodhicaryāvatāra* (*Understanding the Way to Awakening*),[48] another work attributed to Śāntideva.[49] The commentary opens with a biography of Śāntideva.[50] Was this Vibhūticandra then also the scribe of the manuscript of the *Compendium of Training*? It is possible but far from definite. Regrettably, the evidence is inconclusive at this time.

The precise location of the Jagaddala monastery is also uncertain. D. D. Kosambi and V. V. Gokhale locate it in the northern region of ancient Bengal, called Varendrī or Varendra.[51] According to Susan L. Huntington, Varendra, also called Gauḍa, is "contiguous with Bihar and roughly corresponds with the modern districts of Malda and West Dinajpur in India, and the western portion of Dhaka (formerly Pabna) District and Rajshahi District (including former Rajshahi, Bogra, Dinajpur, and Rangpur districts) in Bangladesh. It lies north of the main branch of the Ganges known as the Padma River and west of the Brahmaputra River (called the Jamuna River in Bengal)."[52] Jagaddala monastery "enjoyed special royal patronage" under the reign of Rāmapāla (ca. 1087–1141), one of the last great rulers of the Pāla dynasty (eighth to twelfth centuries) in north India.[53] Like Nālandā, Jagaddala was one of the most important Buddhist monasteries in north India in its day.[54]

Rāhula Sāṅkṛityāyana discovered the very last folio of a *second* Sanskrit manuscript of the *Śikṣāsamuccaya* at the Sa skya monastery in Tibet. The folio is written in Māgadhī script and unfortunately contains only two lines.[55] The colophon dates the manuscript to the third regnal year of a king named Kumārapāla. This may suggest that the manuscript was copied in the mid-twelfth century. A Kumārapāla of Gujarat reigned from ca. 1143–1172.[56] A much lesser-known Kumārapāla of Bengal ruled very briefly at the end of the Pāla dynasty from ca. 1141–1143.[57]

The colophon of Bendall's Old Bengali manuscript and that of the only remaining folio of the Māgadhī manuscript do not specify an author. Scholars have instead relied upon long-standing Indian and Tibetan traditions of textual exegesis as well as hagiography in attributing authorship of this text to

Śāntideva. It is clear, however, that the author of the *Compendium of Training* had at his disposal a sizable corpus of texts from which to cite, suggesting composition at a major monastic center such as Nālandā.[58] The text bespeaks the high value placed on scholarship in medieval Indian Buddhism and also the fact that scholarship was supposed to inform religious practice. The *Compendium of Training* quotes extensively from other sources specifically in order to create a handbook of bodhisattva practice. If the scribe of the Old Bengali manuscript is indeed the famous Vibhūticandra of Jagaddala monastery, the transcription of this manuscript also reveals a commitment to preserving its vision of a bodhisattva's way of life precisely at a time when Buddhist monastic institutions were increasingly threatened in north India. Raids by a series of Turko-Afghan rulers, beginning in the very late tenth century with Mahmud of Ghazni and continuing into the thirteenth century, resulted in the destruction of Indian Buddhist monasteries, including Nālandā and Jagaddala, and the eventual decline of Buddhism in India. Buddhist monastics such as Vibhūticandra, who transmitted Buddhist texts to Nepal and Tibet, enabled works like the *Compendium of Training* to inform the nature of bodhisattva practice outside the borders of north India.

Sanskrit and Tibetan biographies sometimes credit Śāntideva with three works: the *Śikṣāsamuccaya* (*Compendium of Training*), the *Bodhicaryāvatāra* (*Understanding the Way to Awakening*), and the *Sūtrasamuccaya* (*Compendium of Scriptures*).[59] Already in medieval India, however, some Buddhist scholars attributed authorship of a text called the *Sūtrasamuccaya* (*Compendium of Scriptures*) to a scholar-monk named Nāgārjuna rather than to Śāntideva.[60] This has been the position of a number of modern scholars as well, although Ulrich Pagel has recently suggested that this position be reconsidered.[61] While Śāntideva is generally regarded by Buddhist tradition as well as by modern scholars as the author of both the *Compendium of Training* and *Understanding the Way to Awakening* (*Bodhicaryāvatāra*), it is impossible to determine at this point exactly what form these two texts may have taken at the moment they were penned by Śāntideva.[62] I therefore do not make comparisons on the assumption that the texts *as they have come down to us* represent a single author's intention or vision. The relationship between the extant recensions of these texts remains unclear, particularly in light of evidence that an earlier Tibetan recension of *Understanding the Way to Awakening*, preserved among the Dunhuang manuscripts, is shorter than the later Tibetan and extant Sanskrit recensions by some 210.5 verses.[63]

Comparison between the *Compendium of Training* and *Understanding the Way to Awakening* has been further complicated by the extent to which exegesis of *Understanding the Way to Awakening* has been dominated by

Prajñākaramati's late tenth-century commentary on this text. Prajñākaramati devotes roughly one-third of his commentary to a single chapter, the ninth chapter on wisdom.[64] This chapter presents a Madhyamaka philosophical interpretation of the nature of ultimate reality. (The Madhyamakas are a Mahāyāna Buddhist philosophical school to which Śāntideva is said to have adhered.) The chapter refutes the interpretations of other Buddhist and Hindu philosophical schools such as Cittamātra and Sāṃkhya. Because the *Compendium of Training* is attributed to Śāntideva, readers may assume that this text is also concerned with demonstrating the superiority of a Madhyamaka philosophical point of view. The *Compendium of Training*, however, does not engage in the kind of doctrinal debates found in chapter 9 of *Understanding the Way to Awakening*, and it should not be read as an exemplar of Madhyamaka thought. The text draws on a wide range of sources, most of which are Mahāyāna, but not specifically Madhyamaka. In order to discourage problematic comparisons between the *Compendium of Training* and *Understanding the Way to Awakening*, I refer to the *Compendium of Training* by title rather than by author. My hope is that readers will be encouraged to approach this text afresh with as few preconceptions as possible.

I do not take *Understanding the Way to Awakening* as the framework for my investigation of the *Compendium of Training* because of problems of transmission not yet settled and also because I wish to place the *Compendium of Training* on its own terms. The *Compendium of Training* has often been valued in the modern scholarly community because it preserves passages from Sanskrit texts that are no longer extant or because it is thought to preserve "better readings" of extant texts.[65] In such scholarship the *Compendium of Training* serves as a linguistic resource for the study of *other* texts. It is precisely because, until very recently, scholars have not studied the *Compendium of Training* as a text in its own right that they have overlooked, among other matters, its interest in bodhisattva bodies.[66] In this book I study the *Compendium of Training* as a text in its own right—one that offers a coherent vision of the bodhisattva ideal and one that highlights the roles bodies play in the ethical maturation of living beings.

Overview of Chapters

Chapter 2 outlines what the *Compendium of Training* calls the "vital points" of the bodhisattva discipline (*saṃvara*), demonstrating the centrality of body to the bodhisattva ideal. This includes analysis of the text's Sanskrit vocabulary for body as well as consideration of what the concept of body meant to a medieval Indian Buddhist audience. Chapter 3 examines the physically and morally transformative effects bodhisattva bodies have on other living beings, demonstrating that these bodies play a critical role in the "ripening," or ethical maturation, of living beings. Situating the *Compendium of Training* within broader patterns of ethical thought and practice in South Asia, chapter 4 explores the complex relationship between body and morality presumed by the physiomoral discourse. Chapter 5 turns its attention to the ascetic discourse. Side by side in the *Compendium of Training* we find both positive and negative statements about bodies. Chapter 5 investigates how even an apparently negative discourse on bodies serves the text's larger purpose of producing bodhisattvas with bodies that have transformative effects on others. Throughout the book there is attention to the gendered nature of the bodhisattva ideal in the *Compendium of Training*. The final chapter employs a feminist hermeneutics of recovery and suspicion in order to suggest how an early medieval Indian Buddhist discourse on bodies can offer intellectual resources to contemporary scholars and practitioners.

2

The Vital Points of the Bodhisattva Discipline

I must cast away this very body [*kāya*] in doing whatever needs to be done for all living beings. Just as the four great outer elements—the element of earth, the element of water, the element of fire, and the element of wind—turn into various forms of enjoyment for living beings in various ways, in various manners, with various objects, various necessities, and various enjoyments, in the same way I will make this body, which is an accumulation of the four great elements, something for the enjoyment of all living beings in various ways, in various manners, with various objects, various necessities, and various enjoyments, etc. Seeing it is subject to this aim, [the bodhisattva] observes bodily suffering, but is not exhausted by bodily suffering since he has regard for living beings.[1]

Contemporary theorists of body such as Elizabeth Grosz challenge scholars across academic disciplines to take seriously the fact that a human being is a "corporeal being."[2] Grosz rejects body–mind dualisms that locate subjectivity exclusively in mind. Instead she proposes a notion of "embodied subjectivity" or "psychical corporeality," redefining subjectivity as the product of a complex interplay between body and mind, in which both play equally important roles in defining who we are.[3] This study of the *Compendium of Training* is, in part, an attempt to work out the implications of Grosz's work for the field of Buddhist ethics. If we take seriously that human beings are corporeal beings, it becomes apparent that ethical development entails the cultivation of virtuous bodies as well as virtuous heartminds. Hence the prominent role of bodies in Buddhist ethical discourse.

The *Compendium of Training* indicates from the very outset that bodies are a central concern in this text. The text is a handbook or manual of bodhisattva practice. The *Compendium of Training* refers to bodhisattva practice as the "bodhisattva discipline," or bodhisattva *saṃvara. Saṃvara* literally means "restraint"; the bodhisattva *saṃvara* connotes the moral restraint or discipline that all bodhisattvas should observe as they proceed along the path to buddhahood. The *Compendium of Training* characterizes the bodhisattva discipline as either a supplement to, or a substitute for, the monastic discipline, or *prātimokṣa saṃvara.* Specifically, it argues that bodhisattvas cannot attain buddhahood by "merely" observing the monastic discipline. All bodhisattvas must observe the bodhisattva discipline if they are to achieve the "supreme perfect awakening" of buddhahood. The problem, according to the *Compendium of Training,* is that the bodhisattva discipline was outlined in great detail by the Buddha himself in numerous scriptures. Therefore, it can be difficult to grasp. Consequently, the *Compendium of Training* summarizes in its first chapter the "vital points" (*marma-sthāna*) of the bodhisattva discipline. This summary, delivered in a single verse, serves as the structural plan for the text as a whole. As we will see, the verse summary places body—more correctly, bodied being (*ātmabhāva*)—front and center in the bodhisattva discipline.[4]

Scholars have only recently given the verse summary of the vital points of the bodhisattva discipline the attention it deserves in analyses of the *Compendium of Training.* The verse summary is the fourth in a set of twenty-seven verses penned by Śāntideva in the *Compendium of Training.* Scholars have long argued that these twenty-seven verses, which also appear as a separate work in the Tibetan canon, constitute the structural core of the text.[5] Until very recently, however, scholars have not noticed that it is the verse summary in particular that provides the organizational and conceptual framework of the entire text.[6] As a result, they have also overlooked the importance of bodies in the text. In this chapter I investigate the centrality of bodies to the bodhisattva discipline by analyzing the significance of the verse summary in the text as a whole. My analysis includes an examination of the text's Sanskrit vocabulary for "body" and "bodied being," with attention to the differences and similarities between medieval Buddhist perspectives on bodies and those of contemporary theorists of body.

The Vital Points of the Bodhisattva Discipline

The verse summary of the vital points of the bodhisattva discipline reads as follows: "Giving away to all living beings one's bodied being [*ātmabhāva*], goods [*bhoga*], and merit [*śubha*] of the three times; protecting, purifying, and increasing these."[7] The verse summary tells us that bodhisattva practice focuses on three key issues: bodied being (*ātmabhāva*), goods (*bhoga*), and merit (*śubha, puṇya*). Bodied being (*ātmabhāva*) is a complex term and will be discussed in full below. For now, provisionally, it stands as a synonym for body. *Bhoga*, a term I will also discuss further, refers to the goods, or belongings, of a bodhisattva. Merit means good karma, which Buddhists believe one can dedicate to other living beings. The verse summary indicates that bodhisattvas are to give away, protect, purify, and increase their bodied beings, goods, and merit. The fact that bodhisattvas are asked to give away everything they have—bodied being, goods, and merit—is in keeping with the bodhisattva ideal of dedicating oneself to the welfare of others. The verse summary also informs us that bodhisattvas must protect, purify, and increase their bodied being, goods, and merit. Why? Because otherwise they will not have much of value to give away. The *Compendium of Training* devotes its first chapter to describing how to give away bodied being, goods, and merit, and then the rest of the text teaches bodhisattvas how to protect, purify, and increase these so that they will actually have something worthwhile to give away.

Śāntideva had a large and diverse corpus of Buddhist literature at his disposal, as is evident from the fact that he quotes from approximately one hundred different sources. He could have defined the vital points of the bodhisattva discipline in many different ways. He chose to define them as giving away, protecting, purifying, and increasing bodied being, goods, and merit. The *Compendium of Training* transforms a bewildering array of texts with various concerns and practices into a coherent and systematic program of training for bodhisattvas. Strikingly, this program places bodied being at the very center of bodhisattva practice. Of the three issues of paramount concern for bodhisattvas—bodied being, goods, and merit—bodied being receives by far the most attention in the *Compendium of Training*. Twelve of the nineteen chapters fall within the sections dedicated to bodied being; another two address bodied being together with goods and merit (see table 2.1). The *Compendium of Training* thus focuses most of its attention on teaching bodhisattvas how to give away, protect, purify, and increase bodied being. We will see that, in doing so, it underscores the transformative effects bodhisattva bodies have on others.

TABLE 2.1. The Vital Points of the Bodhisattva Discipline by Chapter

Chapter 1	giving away bodied being, goods, and merit
Chapter 2	protecting bodied being
Chapter 3	protecting bodied being
Chapter 4	protecting bodied being
Chapter 5	protecting bodied being
Chapter 6	protecting bodied being
Chapter 7	protecting goods and merit
Chapter 8	purifying bodied being
Chapter 9	purifying bodied being
Chapter 10	purifying bodied being
Chapter 11	purifying bodied being
Chapter 12	purifying bodied being
Chapter 13	purifying bodied being
Chapter 14	purifying bodied being
Chapter 15	purifying goods and merit
Chapter 16	increasing bodied being, goods, and merit
Chapter 17	increasing merit
Chapter 18	increasing merit
Chapter 19	increasing merit

Bodied Being

Before we go any further, we need to understand what the Sanskrit term *ātmabhāva*, or bodied being, means. The *Compendium of Training* reflects the existence of a diverse Sanskrit vocabulary for body. Most frequently it uses the Sanskrit terms *ātmabhāva, kāya,* and *śarīra* to designate body.[8] Since it quotes extensively from so many different sources, often its choice of vocabulary is dictated by its sources. Nevertheless, *ātmabhāva* is its term of choice for body. As we have seen, *ātmabhāva* is the word that occurs in the text's summary of the "vital points" of the bodhisattva discipline. The verse summary of these vital points is not a quotation from other sources; it was penned by Śāntideva himself. Throughout the *Compendium of Training* Śāntideva introduces and comments upon passages cited from other sources specifically in order to clarify how these exemplify the vital points of the bodhisattva discipline. Thus the term *ātmabhāva* comes up again and again in the text. We need to understand what *ātmabhāva* means if we are to understand the significance of bodies in bodhisattva training. Doing so entails a brief philological excursus which will demonstrate the close connection between the physical and moral dimensions of living beings.

Ātmabhāva, which I translate as "bodied being," has been variously translated as "frame," "self," "person,"[9] "Persöhnlichkeit/personality,"[10] "personal being,"[11] "own being,"[12] "individuality,"[13] "corporal individuality,"[14] "egoity,"[15] "one's whole person,"[16] and simply "body."[17] The term has a broad semantic range and may suggest different meanings in different contexts. The *Compendium of Training* and its sources emphasize the corporeality of *ātmabhāva*.[18] For instance, we are told that a person's *ātmabhāva* is composed of the four great elements (*mahābhūta*),[19] namely earth, water, fire, and wind. In other instances, when a bodhisattva gives his *ātmabhāva* to another being, that gift is explicitly defined in terms of bodily sacrifice—for example, giving away hands, feet, eyes, flesh, blood, marrow, great and small limbs, and head.[20] In one passage *ātmabhāva* designates that which endures torment in hell.[21] In other passages it designates a corpse.[22] Finally, *ātmabhāva* may be employed when describing the corporeal effects of merit, or good karma. Thus certain ritual acts result in rebirth with a golden-colored (*suvarṇa-varṇa*) *ātmabhāva*[23] or an incomparable (*asadṛśa*) *ātmabhāva* that is studded (*kavacita*) with the thirty-two marks (*lakṣaṇa*) of an exalted being called the great man (*mahāpuruṣa*).[24] In Buddhist literature the great man refers to a man who, by virtue of his store of merit, has the capacity to become either a buddha or a universal monarch (*cakravartin*) in his present lifetime. The thirty-two marks are a set of extraordinary physical features such as a golden complexion or the imprint of a wheel on the soles of one's feet.[25]

Although there is no doubt that the *Compendium of Training* uses the term *ātmabhāva* to designate a person's body, the text also suggests that *ātmabhāva* cannot be reduced to body alone. Instead the *Compendium of Training* uses the term to designate "one's whole person," that is, the entire complex of body, feelings, and thoughts.[26] For example, purifying *ātmabhāva* entails purifying *citta* (heartmind).[27] Additionally, the purification of *ātmabhāva* requires purification of the defilements (*kleśa*), defined as lust (*rāga*), anger (*dveṣa*), and delusion (*moha*).[28] If *ātmabhāva* designated a body totally distinct from a person's affective and cognitive processes, it would make no sense to describe its purification in terms of purifying heartmind or eradicating lust, anger, and delusion. Thus while *ātmabhāva* is often best translated as "body" in the *Compendium of Training*—for instance, in descriptions of bodily sacrifice or the corporeal effects of merit-making—the term has a broader semantic range. This is particularly the case when it occurs in the verse summary of the vital points of the bodhisattva discipline or in explanations of that discipline. Given the breadth of the term, there is no ideal translation of *ātmabhāva*. When "body" will not do, I translate the term as "bodied being," borrowing this felicitous phrase from Margaret R. Miles.[29]

The most important point of this philological analysis is that *ātmabhāva* is a term that resists translations or interpretations that assume any absolute separation between the physical and moral dimensions of living beings, since it includes the entire complex of body, feelings, and thoughts. In its broadest sense, *ātmabhāva* designates a bodied being, or what Elizabeth Grosz calls an embodied subject.[30] My own focus on body in this study is not intended to reinscribe a body–mind dualism; rather it is an effort to illumine the corporeal dimension of Buddhist ethical ideals, which has heretofore been largely overlooked in studies of Buddhist ethics.

Giving Away Bodied Being

We are now in a position to examine the vital points of the bodhisattva discipline in greater detail, focusing the analysis on bodied being. What does it mean to give away bodied being? Most literally, it means to sacrifice life and limb for other living beings. At the highest levels of the bodhisattva path, bodhisattvas engage in acts of bodily sacrifice for the benefit of others. The bodily sacrifice of bodhisattvas is a common theme in Buddhist literature. There are many gruesome narratives that praise bodhisattvas for giving away part or all of their bodies to other living beings.[31] The most famous ones are the *jātaka*, or birth stories, which describe the past lives of the historical Buddha Śākyamuni. For example, in one well-known story the future Buddha offers his body as food to a starving tigress. The *Compendium of Training* is thus not unusual in valorizing the bodily sacrifice of bodhisattvas. The text repeatedly asks them to imagine that their bodied beings are entirely at the disposal of other living beings. For example, in the following passage from chapter 1 of the text a bodhisattva's bodied being is likened to a medicinal plant intended for the consumption of living beings:

> Well-born son, just as a medicinal plant, when it is stripped of its roots, stripped of its stalk, branches, bark, or leaves, stripped of its flowers, fruits, or sap, does not imagine, "I am being stripped of my roots," *and so on until* "I am being stripped of my sap," but instead without imagining [this] at all, it eliminates the illnesses of living beings—whether they are lowly, average, or superior living beings—so too, well-born son, a bodhisattva mahāsattva should regard his bodied being [*ātmabhāva*], which is composed of the four great elements, as medicine, [thinking], "Let any living beings whatsoever take absolutely anything of mine for any purpose whatsoever—a hand for those wanting a hand, a foot for those wanting a foot," *as stated previously*.[32]

Is the *Compendium of Training* literally exhorting its readers to bodily sacrifice? No. It is important to recall that the bodhisattva path is a multilifetime path. Bodily sacrifice is the prerogative and duty of bodhisattvas who have traversed so far along the bodhisattva path that they possess virtues and powers beyond the range of ordinary beings. They have been bodhisattvas already for many, many lifetimes. They alone are capable of literal acts of bodily sacrifice. The *Compendium of Training* makes it absolutely clear that bodily sacrifice is not appropriate for other bodhisattvas, especially those it calls "beginner" (*ādikarmika*) bodhisattvas,[33] who likely comprise the intended audience of this text. Thus the *Compendium of Training* warns beginner bodhisattvas not to permit an "untimely enjoyment" (*akāla-paribhoga*) of their bodies, that is, not to give away part or all of their bodies before they have progressed sufficiently along the bodhisattva path. If bodhisattvas perform bodily sacrifice prematurely, it can have serious negative consequences for themselves as well as others. Overcome with physical pain, such a bodhisattva might actually be tempted to abandon the bodhisattva path altogether.[34] Those who abandon the bodhisattva path incur great sin, since they have reneged on their promise to liberate others from the suffering of saṃsāric existence. In doing so, they place themselves and others at risk of future pain.

Although beginner bodhisattvas are prohibited from performing acts of bodily sacrifice, they can still use their bodied beings to benefit others. One fascinating feature of the *Compendium of Training* is that it insists that bodhisattva bodies are meant for the enjoyment (*bhuj-*, *paribhuj-*, *upabhuj-*) of living beings. This is a theme that runs throughout the text. As the quotation at the start of this chapter indicates, bodhisattvas are told that they should turn their bodies into "something for the enjoyment of all living beings." Such enjoyment takes many different forms in the *Compendium of Training*, from that of animals enjoying (*paribhuj-*) the flesh of dead bodhisattvas, to that of humans experiencing pleasure (*prasāda*) at the sight of monastic bodhisattvas with impeccable etiquette and deportment. Bodhisattvas give their bodied beings to others in a variety of ways. They need not commit literal acts of bodily sacrifice in order to benefit others. Even beginner bodhisattvas can convey great benefit on others by mastering monastic etiquette and deportment, a point to which I return in the next two chapters of this book.

The *Compendium of Training* repeatedly instructs bodhisattvas to give enjoyment to living beings. We have already seen that one of the three foci of the bodhisattva discipline is goods, or *bhoga*. Bodhisattvas are to give away, protect, purify, and increase bodied being, goods, and merit. The word *bhoga*, which I translate as "goods," literally means "enjoyment." *Bhoga* can refer either to the act of enjoying something or to those items that are enjoyed. Generally, in the context of the verse summary of the bodhisattva discipline, *bhoga* refers to the material belongings of the bodhisattva, which are meant for the enjoyment of other living beings.[35] It is clear, however, that bodhisattvas themselves are goods intended for the enjoyment of living beings. The *Compendium of Training* weaves together the common Buddhist theme of the bodily sacrifice of bodhisattvas with its own theme of the enjoyment of bodhisattva bodies. Giving away bodied being entails giving enjoyment to others. Bodhisattva bodies thus convey both benefit and pleasure on living beings.

Why is there such an emphasis on the enjoyment of bodhisattva bodies in the *Compendium of Training*? An answer is suggested by the following passage, which brings to a close the first chapter of the text and its discussion of giving away bodied being, goods, and merit: "Therefore with bodied being, and so forth, as if with bait on a fish hook that has no enjoyment itself, [the bodhisattva] attracts others and carries them across [the ocean of saṃsāra]."[36] Bodhisattvas use everything they have to attract living beings to them and therefore to the Dharma. Unless bodhisattvas can attract living beings, they will not be able fully to liberate these beings from the suffering of saṃsāric existence. Attracting living beings is so important that bodhisattvas can even violate lay and monastic precepts to achieve their aim of turning living beings to the Dharma. For example, elsewhere in the text the *Compendium of Training* quotes from the *Ugraparipṛcchā*, which maintains that bodhisattvas can go so far as to offer alcoholic drink to a drunkard (*madyapa*) in spite of the fact that doing so violates the lay Buddhist precept to abstain from intoxicants. According to the source text itself, the reason is that bodhisattvas must cultivate the perfection of generosity (*dāna*), one of six perfections required to attain buddhahood. Bodhisattvas are thus duty-bound to fulfill the desires of all living beings even when that desire is for alcohol.[37] The *Compendium of Training*, however, adds another reason for offering alcoholic drink to a drunkard. If a bodhisattva were to refuse alcohol, he might generate hostility (*pratigha*) toward himself and thus would fail in his duty to attract living beings. If, on the other hand, a bodhisattva uses the gift of alcohol as an occasion to generate pleasure (*prasāda*) with regard to himself, then he is permitted to give alcohol to a drunkard.[38] We see here a striking illustration of the fact that the *Compendium of Training* is more than an "encyclopedia of sources";[39] the text uses its sources to create its own arguments, at times using a passage for somewhat different purposes than it served in the original source text. Here the *Ugraparipṛcchā* passage is pressed into the service of the *Compendium of Training*'s larger argument that a bodhisattva's highest duty is to attract living beings.

The duty to attract living beings is of such paramount importance that monastic bodhisattvas may even violate their vow of celibacy. For example, the

Compendium of Training includes an excerpt from a story in the *Upāyakauśalyasūtra* about a celibate Brahmin youth (*māṇavaka*) named Jyotis. Jyotis maintained celibacy for 42,000 years. One day a woman pleaded with him to marry her. Although Jyotis realizes he will pay a karmic price for breaking his vow of celibacy, he marries the woman. Quoting from another story in the *Upāyakauśalyasūtra*, the *Compendium of Training* concludes that bodhisattvas must be prepared to undergo torment in hell if it serves the purpose of generating even a single root of merit (*kuśalamūla*) in another living being.[40] The *Compendium of Training* turns again to the *Upālipariprcchā* to argue that of all the sins a bodhisattva might commit, sins associated with lust (*rāga*) are least harmful to the bodhisattva as long as they are committed in order to attract living beings to the Dharma. Specifically, the text compares sins associated with lust and sins associated with anger (*dveṣa*). Sins associated with lust are far less serious, because they are conducive to attracting living beings (*satva-saṃgraha*), whereas sins associated with anger are conducive to rejecting living beings (*satva-parityāga*).[41] According to the *Compendium of Training* and some of its sources, bodhisattvas who possesses "skillful means" (*upāya-kauśalya*) can use even sensual pleasures to productive ends. Skillful means entails having the right motivation for one's actions (i.e., the desire to attract others to the Dharma) and not being attached oneself to sensual pleasures. Bodhisattvas with skillful means can use any resources at their disposal to attract living beings. Significantly, the *Compendium of Training* regards a bodhisattva's bodied being as one of the most important means of attracting living beings. Such attraction, however, need not be sexual. There are many reasons why living beings are attracted to bodhisattvas. For instance, some may be attracted to the serenity manifest in a well-disciplined monastic's features, gestures, and movements. When bodhisattvas give away their bodied beings, they confer a variety of benefits and pleasures on others, from the mundane benefits of providing food for animals or a home to a destitute woman, to the supramundane benefit of attracting living beings to the Dharma.

Protecting Bodied Being

Cultivating bodied beings that can be enjoyed by others takes a good bit of work. Such bodied beings are the products of extensive Buddhist practice in previous as well as current lifetimes. Before bodhisattvas can give away their bodied beings, they need to protect, purify, and increase them, otherwise the gift will be of little use to anyone. The *Compendium of Training* devotes five full chapters to instructions on how to protect bodied being. Its rationale for devoting so much attention to this is that bodhisattvas cannot give away what they do not have. Unless bodhisattvas learn to protect bodied being, they will not have anything worth giving away. Thus the *Compendium of Training* states: "Bodied being, and so forth, are given for the enjoyment [*paribhoga*] of living beings. If unprotected, how will they be enjoyed? What kind of gift is it that is not enjoyed? Therefore, one should protect bodied being, and so forth, for the sake of the enjoyment [*upabhoga*] of living beings."[42] Thus the primary reason to protect bodied being is to make that bodied being available for the enjoyment of others.

How do bodhisattvas protect bodied being? They learn to avoid anything that might be harmful (*anartha*) to them. Sometimes harm takes the form of immediate physical danger. Thus, for example, the *Compendium of Training* provides mantras to protect one from the poisonous effects of snakebite.[43] More commonly, harm is defined as any being, activity, or attitude that might cause bodhisattvas to act improperly and thereby earn sin (*pāpa*). The karmic effects of sin can be experienced in one's immediate lifetime or in future lifetimes. Most often, sin results in a bad rebirth, such as rebirth in one of the many Buddhist hells, rebirth as an animal, or rebirth as a human being with significant physical or mental disabilities. Like other Buddhist texts, the *Compendium of Training* regards such rebirths as very painful. Additionally these rebirths make it difficult or even impossible for bodhisattvas to maintain the bodhisattva discipline. This situation has negative consequences not only for bodhisattvas but for the countless living beings these bodhisattvas had promised to liberate from the suffering of saṃsāric existence. Thus it is particularly important that bodhisattvas refrain from sin.

The list of beings, activities, and attitudes harmful to bodhisattvas is far too extensive to be replicated in full here. Chief among these are the path of the ten nonmeritorious actions (*daśākuśalakarmapatha*)—that is, killing, stealing, sexual misconduct, lying, slander, harsh speech, senseless talk, covetousness, malice, and false views. The *Compendium of Training* also warns bodhisattvas not to engage in any number of activities that would impede their own or others' progress on the bodhisattva path. For instance, bodhisattvas should not embrace non-Mahāyāna Buddhist teachings, they should not abandon their bodhisattva vow, they should not permit an "untimely enjoyment" of their bodies, and they should not associate with inappropriate companions, called ugly or sinful friends (*akalyāṇamitra, pāpamitra*).[44] Male bodhisattvas in particular are also strongly advised to eradicate sexual desire for women. Additionally, bodhisattvas should not discourage others from the bodhisattva path, for instance, by giving undue criticism or teaching them concepts too difficult to understand.

Avoiding harm is not always easy. Therefore the *Compendium of Training* recommends, among other strategies, that bodhisattvas keep company with teachers and mentors, called beautiful friends (*kalyāṇamitra*), and that they carefully study Mahāyāna scriptures. Both beautiful friends and Mahāyāna scriptures teach bodhisattvas how to avoid sin.

Purifying Bodied Being

When the *Compendium of Training* speaks of purifying bodied being, it means purifying bodied being of sin (*pāpa*) and defilements (*kleśa*).[45] Sin has already been defined as negative karma; defilements are negative characteristics, notably lust (*rāga*), anger (*dveṣa*), and delusion (*moha*), which cause a person to sin and which prevent him or her from attaining liberation.[46] Purity, sin, and defilements have both physical and moral connotations in the *Compendium of Training*. When bodhisattvas purify bodied being, they purify body as well as heartmind.

A full seven chapters of the *Compendium of Training* are devoted to instructions on how to purify bodhisattvas of sin and defilements. The *Compendium of Training* offers many techniques for purifying bodied being of sin and defilements, not all of which can be listed here. For example, bodhisattvas can perform rituals such as the confession ritual to expunge or mitigate the negative effects of any previously earned sin. Observance of monastic and bodhisattva disciplines helps bodhisattvas to cultivate meritorious actions (*kuśalakarma*) and to refrain from unmeritorious actions. Bodhisattvas also perform a wide range of meditations. For example, those afflicted with lust are instructed to meditate on the foulness of bodies (*aśubhabhāvanā*). Those afflicted with anger are instructed to meditate on lovingkindness (*maitrī*). Those afflicted with delusion are instructed to contemplate philosophical concepts such as dependent origination (*pratītyasamutpāda*).[47] Additionally, bodhisattvas can engage in ascetic practices such as living for periods of time in solitude in the wilderness. Finally, they must study Mahāyāna scriptures.

Increasing Bodied Being

The *Compendium of Training* opens its discussion of increasing bodied being, goods, and merit by remarking that a bodhisattva has but little to give to the many beings asking him or her for something. In order to satisfy their wishes, the bodhisattva will need to increase his or her bodied being, goods, and merit.[48] The *Compendium of Training* has far less to say about increasing bodied being than it does about protecting and purifying it. In brief, increasing bodied being entails increasing strength (*bala*) and the opposite of sloth (*anālasya*), namely, industriousness. Like purity, sin, and defilements, strength and industriousness have physical and moral connotations. A bodhisattva needs a certain amount of physical and moral stamina to traverse the bodhisattva path. The *Compendium of Training* suggests a variety of ways to increase bodied being. For instance, one can increase strength by never giving up the true Dharma, by humbling oneself before others, and by caring for living beings in a variety of ways. A bodhisattva can increase industriousness by increasing his or her degree of vigor (*vīrya*). Vigor is an important bodhisattva virtue. It is one of the six perfections a bodhisattva must cultivate in order to attain buddhahood. Increasing bodied being, like protecting and purifying bodied being, enables a bodhisattva to turn his or her body into "something for the enjoyment of all living beings."

The *Compendium of Training* devotes most of its discussion of increasing bodied being, goods, and merit to the increase of merit. Significantly, however, body remains a central concern in the text's discussion of merit. Specifically, the *Compendium of Training* emphasizes the positive physical effects of earning merit. For example, the text quotes at length from the *Avalokanasūtra*, which describes the fabulous kinds of bodies one will achieve in future rebirths as a result of performing merit-making rituals.[49] Such bodies include the golden colored bodies studded with the thirty-two marks of the great man, discussed above. Additionally, the *Compendium of Training* prescribes for the increase of merit a form of meditation called recollection of the three jewels, that is, Buddha, Dharma, and Saṅgha. This meditation also places body front and center. Specifically, the recollection of the Buddha entails bringing to mind his physical as well as moral perfections. To that end, the *Compendium of Training* quotes at length from the *Rāṣṭrapālasūtra*, which extols the physical beauty of the Buddha.[50] Finally, it quotes from the same text in describing what recollecting the saṅgha, or monastic community, entails. Here too body is a key concern because bodhisattvas are taught to imagine themselves as capable of assuming limitless different physical forms in order to meet the diverse needs of living beings. This passage reflects a widespread Mahāyāna Buddhist belief that as bodhisattvas progress toward buddhahood they become capable of manifesting bodies of magical transformation (*nirmāṇakāya*). I will return to this idea in the next chapter. For now I wish simply to emphasize that even in those portions of the *Compendium of Training* that are not directly focused on the topic of bodied being, body remains a central concern. The

Compendium of Training's concept of the Mahāyāna bodhisattva ideal foregrounds the central role bodies play in the bodhisattva discipline.

What Are Bodies?

We have already seen that bodied being (*ātmabhāva*) has a broad semantic range, designating at times primarily a physical body and at other times the larger complex of body, feelings, and thoughts. But what does body itself mean? More precisely, what did it mean to a medieval Indian Buddhist audience? We cannot assume that medieval Indian Buddhists conceptualized bodies in exactly the same ways that we do today. Although there are marked similarities, there are also important differences.

To begin, the *Compendium of Training*'s discourse on bodies includes reference not only to what we commonly think of as biological features such as complexion or health, but also to forms of bodily "inscription" such as dress, postures, and movements. For instance, the bodies of monastic bodhisattvas are marked as such by a range of features, including shaven head, robes, begging bowl, and decorous gait. Grosz's observation that bodies are constituted *as particular types of bodies* by a combination of genetic and environmental factors is pertinent to the *Compendium of Training*.[51] Grosz draws attention to the ways in which features such as dress, hair style, various forms of adornment, gait, and posture render bodies culturally meaningful.[52] Significantly, as Grosz would argue, monastic dress and deportment are not simply added to monastic bodies but constitute these bodies as monastic bodies in the first place.[53] Thus the concept of body includes a broad range of physical features, not limited to biology.

Bodies are also inherently "pliable,"[54] that is, subject to transformation, because bodies are largely the products of our own actions. In the first place, bodies are the products of an individual's karma. Karma dictates the kind of body we get in any given lifetime—whether we are male or female, healthy or sick, beautiful or ugly, and so forth. Additionally, bodies are shaped by the bodhisattva discipline. For instance, monastic bodhisattvas observe extensive rules governing etiquette and deportment. It has become commonplace for scholars to remark that bodies are "socially constructed." They mean thereby that bodies take determinate form under the influence of social norms. For instance, ideals of masculinity and femininity produce male and female bodies that conform to these ideals. Modern theories about the socially constructed nature of bodies would be quite foreign to a medieval Buddhist audience (as to other medieval audiences around the world). But the belief that human beings can shape their own bodily forms by engaging in particular kinds of practices is fundamental to the *Compendium of Training*. The text invites its readers to undertake its program of training specifically in order to transform their bodied beings into "something for the enjoyment of all living beings." Thus, bodhisattvas are literally "materialized," to borrow a term from Judith Butler, through the bodhisattva discipline.[55]

The materialization of bodhisattvas is a process that occurs not just in one lifetime, but over the course of countless lifetimes. The bodhisattva discipline sets in motion a physical and moral transformation that continues far into the future until one attains buddhahood. Thus medieval Indian Buddhists assumed a much broader temporal range for the construction of determinate types of bodies than that generally assumed in contemporary body theory. It is not coincidental that of all the words for "body," *ātmabhāva* (bodied being)—the term of choice in the *Compendium of Training*—has the broadest temporal range of any body vocabulary in this text. *Ātmabhāva* is regularly employed in the plural to refer to bodied beings throughout the cycle of rebirth. When the *Compendium of Training*'s sources want to refer to a bodied being over the course of multiple lifetimes, they tend to use a plural form of *ātmabhāva* rather than of another Sanskrit word for body.[56] The *Compendium of Training* and its sources remind us in their very choice of vocabulary that the materialization of bodhisattvas is a multilifetime project.

Implicit in the pliable nature of bodies is the fact that bodies are constantly changing. They are, as some contemporary theorists of body have remarked, process rather than stasis.[57] The most radical changes occur from one rebirth to the next, but even in the course of one lifetime bodies undergo enormous change, including those changes wrought by observance of the bodhisattva discipline. It is important to note that bodies change not only over time, but also according to circumstance. For instance, junior monks must engage in physical displays of respect such as bowing when in the presence of senior monks. A monk might be junior in one relationship and senior in another. His body language will change accordingly.

The whole point of constructing bodhisattva bodies is to create bodies that can be given away to others. As we have seen, bodhisattva bodies are meant for the enjoyment of living beings. Such enjoyment confers on living beings mundane as well as supramundane benefits and pleasures. The *Compendium of Training* emphasizes the profoundly transformative effects bodhisattva bodies have on other living beings. For example, the text describes at length an encounter between a student and his teacher. Both are bodhisattvas, but each is at a very different stage of development. The teacher, a highly realized, or advanced, bodhisattva, is called a "beautiful friend" (*kalyāṇamitra*). Beautiful friends are quite common in Buddhist literature. The term can refer to any person "who is well prepared with the proper qualities to teach, suggest, point out, encourage, assist, and give guidance for getting started on the Path of Buddhist training."[58] Beautiful friends are a very particular kind of friend; they are one's moral superiors and therefore function as teachers and mentors. What happens when the student, named Sudhana, meets his beautiful friend, a monastic bodhisattva named Sāradhvaja?

> Then noble Sudhana touched his head to the feet of the monk, Sāradhvaja, circumambulated him many hundreds of thousands of times, looked at the monk, Sāradhvaja, prostrated, looking again and again, all the while prostrating, bowing, bowing down, bearing him in mind, thinking about him, meditating on him, soaking him in, making an inspired utterance, exclaiming in admiration, looking at his virtues, penetrating them, not being frightened of them, recollecting them, making them firm in his mind, not giving them up, mentally approaching them, binding them fast to himself, attaining the bodhisattva vow, yearning for his sight, grasping the distinctive characteristic of his voice *and so on until* he departed from his presence.[59]

Sudhana responds powerfully to the physical presence of his beautiful friend. He looks at him again and again, performs physical gestures of respect, focuses all of his attention on his beautiful friend, and yearns for his sight. The same passage records another profoundly transformative encounter between Sudhana and a different beautiful friend. We are told that "beholding the omniscience come to his beautiful friend," Sudhana departs from his presence, weeping with tears running down his face.[60] Omniscience is visible in the very features of the beautiful friend's body. It is something that Sudhana can literally see. The description of both of these encounters draws attention to the importance of the beautiful friend's physical presence and appearance, as does the very term "beautiful friend" itself. The Sanskrit word *mitra* means friend. *Kalyāṇa* means both beautiful and good. Thus beautiful friends are at once beautiful and good. Virtue takes specific bodily form; virtue is beautiful. Sudhana's beautiful friends have cultivated virtuous bodies as well as virtuous heartminds. The *Compendium of Training* emphasizes again and again that bodhisattvas use both their bodies and their heartminds to transform living beings in positive ways.

The encounters between Sudhana and his beautiful friends demonstrate not only that bodhisattva bodies have transformative effects on living beings, but that these effects are themselves physical as well as affective and cognitive.

The *Compendium of Training* includes these descriptions of encounters with beautiful friends specifically in order to describe for its audience the proper attitude of intense (*tīvra*) respect (*gaurava*) and affection (*prema*) that students should display toward their beautiful friends.[61] Sudhana literally materializes these virtues when he performs physical gestures of respect and affection, notably, gazing at his beautiful friend, circumbulating him, and bowing and prostrating before him. Respect and affection are physical as well as affective and cognitive qualities; they register in body as well as heartmind. This fact leads me to an important point: when living beings "enjoy" bodhisattva bodies, they are changed in physical as well as moral ways. We might therefore say that bodies in this text are both individually and communally constructed—in other words, they are materialized through an individual's own efforts as well as through transformative encounters with other bodhisattvas. The *Compendium of Training* pushes contemporary body theory beyond the limits of an individualistic perspective, since its primary interest in body is in the kinds of physical and moral effects bodhisattva bodies have on others. The *Compendium of Training* places body and bodied being at the center of the bodhisattva discipline because bodhisattvas use their bodies as much as their heartminds to benefit others.

The Corporeal Specificity of the Bodhisattva Ideal

A key point of contemporary body theory is that there is no such thing as a generic body. Following Miles, I avoid the expression "the body," because this implies a generic body.[62] As Miles argues, "While 'bodyness,' the condition of being body, is a universal trait of humanness, bodies are invariably gendered. They are also young or old, healthy or ill; they are socially located, along with other factors that loudly and intimately affect the experience of body."[63] Consequently feminist theorists of body such as Grosz have insisted that scholarship take into account the corporeal specificity of human beings. In other words, scholars need to take account not only of the fact that human beings are bodied, but also that they are bodied in different kinds of ways. Grosz's attention to the corporeal specificity of human beings raises for me the question of the corporeal specificity of Buddhist ethical ideals, notably, the bodhisattva ideal. What kinds of bodhisattva bodies does the *Compendium of Training* seek to produce? What kinds of bodies count as virtuous bodies? What kinds of bodies have positive transformative effects on other living beings?

In order to answer these questions, we need to begin by considering the intended audience of the *Compendium of Training*. This bodhisattva training manual was written primarily for a male monastic audience and, as Paul J. Griffiths observes, especially those in the early stages of their training.[64] The *Compendium of Training* urges bodhisattvas to renounce in every lifetime and, given the extensive references to the dangers women pose to men, it appears to have a male renunciant in mind.[65] On the surface, however, it appears as if the text was meant for a broader audience. Throughout the *Compendium of Training* there are periodic references to householder (*gṛhin*) bodhisattvas, suggesting that laity as well as monastics are encouraged to undertake bodhisattva training. Additionally, we are told that "even women" can pursue the discipline of a bodhisattva. It is important to note, however, that the *Compendium of Training*'s bodhisattva discipline is not intended for *all* householders or *all* women; it is intended for *exceptional* householders and *exceptional* women. Householders (always addressed in the masculine form) should embrace the ideals of a renunciant, eradicating sexual desire even for their own wives.[66] These are not ordinary householders. They fall somewhere in between the categories of ordinary householder and monastic. They are best characterized as an asceticized laity.[67] Similarly the women invited to observe the bodhisattva discipline are not ordinary women. The *Compendium of Training* specifies that these women must have weak defilements and their heartminds must long for awakening.[68] In spite of the fact that exceptional householders and women can observe the bodhisattva discipline, the *Compendium of Training* still envisions ideal bodhisattvas as monastic men. Thus it comes, perhaps, as no surprise that the kinds of bodies that have positive transformative effects on other living beings are almost exclusively male bodies in the *Compendium of Training*. In the next chapter I explore in greater detail the physically and morally transformative effects of bodhisattva bodies and, in doing so, continue to pay attention to the corporeal specificity of the bodhisattva ideal in the *Compendium of Training*.

3

Ripening Living Beings

Blessed One, a bodhisattva should behave in such a way that merely upon seeing him beings are pleased. Why? Blessed One, a bodhisattva has no other duty than attracting living beings. Blessed One, this very ripening of living beings is a bodhisattva's recitation of the Dharma.[1]

The Compendium of Training's focus on bodhisattva bodies reflects a larger Mahāyāna Buddhist interest in this topic. Bodhisattvas are frequently depicted in Mahāyāna literature as beings who use their bodies to liberate others from the various kinds of suffering inherent in saṃsāric existence. For example, it is a common Mahāyāna belief that as bodhisattvas progress along the path to buddhahood, they gain the ability to create bodies of magical transformation (*nirmāṇakāya*). Highly advanced bodhisattvas can manifest an infinite variety of such bodies in order to meet the needs and wishes of other living beings. These bodhisattvas are able to create bodies of magical transformation, in part, because of the supernatural powers (*ṛddhi*) they acquire from mastering advanced states of meditation.[2] The Mahāyāna Buddhist concept of the body of magical transformation is thus related to the Mainstream (also known as Śrāvakayāna, sometimes misleadingly referred to as Hīnayāna) Buddhist concept of the mind-made body (*manomāyakāya*).[3] Some Mainstream Buddhist texts provide instructions to meditators on how to manipulate their physical appearance.[4] It is generally accepted in Buddhist traditions and more broadly in South Asian traditions that supernatural powers are a by-product of advanced states of meditation.[5]

In Mahāyāna Buddhism the concept of the body of magical transformation is linked to the bodhisattva ideal of liberating others from diverse kinds of suffering. Specifically, bodhisattvas use their bodies of magical transformation to provide living beings with a vast array of mundane as well as supramundane benefits and pleasures. Bodies of magical transformation are thus expressions of a bodhisattva's compassion for living beings. Bodhisattvas are depicted in Mahāyāna literature as "wonder-workers" skillfully manipulating reality for the benefit of others.[6] The ability of bodhisattvas to manipulate reality at will derives not only from their supernatural powers but also from the nature of reality itself. According to Mahāyāna Buddhism, all phenomena are empty (*śūnya*), or devoid, of any intrinsic existence (*svabhāva*). Mahāyāna Buddhists mean thereby that all phenomena lack permanence as well as independence. Everything in the universe, including ourselves, is constantly changing in relationship to everything else. As William R. LaFleur puts it,

> Buddhists do not so much deny the reality of the things we experience as they deny their permanence. They insist that all the particulars we know—including the ones that presently respond when our individual names are called—are bound, sooner or later, to succumb to the law of impermanence (*anitya*); every "thing" in existence is really a changing constellation of other "things" and is, even while we observe it, already undergoing a reconstellation into something else.[7]

Reality is thus quite fluid. For this reason it is often likened to a dream or a magical illusion. The image of the bodhisattva as compassionate wonder-worker fuses together the Mahāyāna doctrine of emptiness with a broader belief in the supernatural powers of highly skilled religious practitioners. As David L. McMahan argues,

> If everything lacks inherent existence and has no fixed identity, then the buddhas and bodhisattvas, realizing this, can create any appearance appropriate for the spiritual level of any sentient being. The lack of inherent existence, fused with the image of bodhisattva as dharmic thaumaturge, implies a basic malleability of the world, such that the adept can control appearances so that they all become skillful means (*upāya*) to lead others to awakening.[8]

Bodhisattvas can use their vast powers to manipulate reality because reality is inherently malleable. Ultimately, bodies of magical transformation are no more or less real than anything else since everything—whether magically created or not—is empty of intrinsic existence. Most important, these bodies have significant positive effects on living beings. Bodhisattvas manifest bodies of magical transformation specifically in order to help others. The concept of the body of magical transformation thus reveals an extraordinary degree of self-consciousness within Mahāyāna traditions about the ways in which bodhisattvas use their bodies to benefit others.

Although the *Compendium of Training* rarely employs the vocabulary of "body of magical transformation," this concept is implicit in the text, especially in two extended excerpts from the *Vimalakīrtinirdeśa* and the *Ratnolkādhāraṇī*. Both appear in chapter 18 of the *Compendium of Training*, which is dedicated to teaching bodhisattvas how to increase their merit. One way to increase one's merit is to perform a meditation called the recollection of the three jewels—that is, recollection of the Buddha, Dharma, and Saṅgha. The recollection of the saṅgha, or monastic community, entails bringing to mind a bodhisattva's ability to "display infinite physical forms (*rūpa*) in all of the ten directions."[9] These physical forms need not be human or even anthropomorphic. Bodhisattvas manifest whatever physical forms are most suited to the needs and wishes of living beings. For example, in order to teach living beings that everything is impermanent, bodhisattvas manifest the appearance of someone who is old, sick, or dead, offering in this guise an "iconic preaching" about the emptiness of all phenomena.[10] Bodhisattvas assume whatever forms are most likely to attract living beings. For instance, they appear as prostitutes, using the "hook of lust" to lead men to the Dharma.[11] In a time of disease, they assume the form of medicine; in a time of famine, they assume the form of food and water. Having satisfied the immediate needs and wishes of living beings, they preach the Dharma to them.[12] Thus the bodies of these bodhisattvas literally become wish-fulfilling jewels (*cintāmaṇi*), offering both mundane and supramundane benefits and pleasures to countless living beings.[13]

Chapter 18 of the *Compendium of Training* is filled with fantastic descriptions of bodhisattvas manifesting an astonishing array of physical forms for the benefit of living beings. Their ability to do so is linked to the supernatural powers acquired from the mastering of advanced states of meditation.[14] In one of the most fantastic of these descriptions bodhisattvas enter into meditation (*samādhi*) and thereby gain the ability to emit rays of light from every pore of their bodies. These rays touch living beings and transform them for the better. For instance, when living beings are touched by the ray of light called the "light-making ray," they are impelled to worship the Buddha with offerings of lights and consequently eventually become buddhas themselves.[15] Other rays of light generate pleasure among living beings in the three jewels, knowledge about the true nature of reality; some eliminate the defilements (*kleśa*) of lust, anger, and delusion; some result in visions of innumerable buddhas; and some produce states of fearlessness and health.[16] When touched by these rays, the blind see, the deaf hear, the insane regain their senses; foul smells are transformed into the finest perfumes, and poisons into the finest tastes (*rasa*).[17]

Bodhisattvas clearly use their bodies to liberate living beings from diverse kinds of suffering. They manifest countless physical forms in order to attract living beings, satisfy their immediate desires, and lead them to the Dharma. The positive effects of bodhisattva bodies, however, do not stop here. Bodhisattva bodies have profoundly transformative effects on living beings. Thus, as we have just seen, living beings who are touched by rays of light emanating from bodhisattva bodies are changed in a variety of ways. For example, some gain knowledge, some are freed of their defilements, and some acquire the ability to see or hear. Strikingly, the transformative effects of these rays of light affect bodies as well as heartminds; they change living beings in physical and moral ways. The *Compendium of Training* and its sources depict *all* living beings—not just bodhisattvas—as bodied beings.[18] Thus the *Compendium of Training* is as interested in the physical effects that bodhisattva bodies have on living beings as it is in the moral effects of such bodies.

In this chapter I investigate how bodhisattvas use their bodies to transform other living beings in both physical and moral ways. In doing so, I pay attention to a common Buddhist metaphor used to describe the impact bodhisattvas have on living beings. Bodhisattvas are said to "ripen" (*paripac-*) living beings. In Buddhist literature, "ripening" is a metaphor for ethical and spiritual maturation. Although bodhisattvas can ripen living beings in a variety of ways, the *Compendium of Training* is especially interested in how they do so with their bodies.[19] It teaches bodhisattvas how to cultivate, in present and future lifetimes, bodies that are capable of transforming living beings in physical and moral ways.

Bodhisattva Vows and Bodies

As was noted above, chapter 18 of the *Compendium of Training* attributes the ability of bodhisattvas to produce bodies that ripen others to the supernatural powers acquired from mastering advanced states of meditation. Elsewhere in the text we learn that bodhisattvas also gain this ability by making particular kinds of vows. This is the case in chapter 8, which is dedicated to teaching bodhisattvas how to purify their bodied beings. The chapter depicts bodhisattvas making different kinds of vows in order to cultivate bodies in present and future lifetimes that have physically and morally transformative effects on other living beings. The chapter opens with the rather startling claim that purified bodhisattva bodies are good to eat. We are told, "The enjoyment [*bhoga*] of a purified [*śodhita*] body [*ātmabhāva*] will be healthy for bodied beings [*dehin*], just like well-prepared, boiled rice without husk-powder."[20] This enigmatic statement is explained by the following example: Animals who eat the dead body of a bodhisattva lying in a cemetery are reborn as gods in heaven and eventually attain *parinirvāṇa*, or final liberation. Why? Because the bodhisattva had made a previous vow (*pūrva-praṇidhāna*) that those who should enjoy, or eat (*paribhuj-*), his flesh (*māṃsa*) be reborn in heaven and eventually attain *parinirvāṇa*:

> There too, in the great cemeteries that are found in great cities, filled as they are with many hundreds of thousands of living creatures, the bodhisattva mahāsattva displays a great [*mahānta*] body [*ātmabhāva*], which is dead and whose time has come. There those beings who are born as animals eat his flesh according to their needs, and at the completion of their life spans when they die and their time comes, they are reborn in a good realm, among the gods in heaven. This alone is the cause for them [of that heavenly rebirth and all other good rebirths] until they attain *parinirvāṇa*. That is to say, it is by virtue of the purity of that same bodhisattva's previous vow [*pūrva-praṇidhāna-pariśuddhi*]. [Thus] the intention is fulfilled, the aspiration is fulfilled, the vow is fulfilled of that moral person who had for a very long time made the following vow, "For those who eat my flesh when I die and my time has come, may that alone be for them the cause of rebirth in heaven, and eventually *parinirvāṇa*."[21]

According to traditional Buddhist cosmology, the transition from animal to god represents a change of both physical and moral status, because it takes more merit to be reborn as a god than as an animal. When animals eat the dead body of the bodhisattva, they are changed in physical as well as moral ways; eventually they are fully transformed in the experience of *parinirvāṇa*.

This passage is immediately followed by another which similarly suggests that bodhisattvas make vows to produce bodies that have a physically and morally transformative effect on others. The second passage describes a bodhisattva who conveys benefit on beings "even when they see him . . . even when they hear him, even when they touch him."[22] The bodhisattva is likened to a medicine girl (*bhaiṣajya-dārikā*) created from a collection of medicinal plants by the legendary Buddhist physician Jīvaka. When sick men have sex with the medicine girl, they are cured of their illnesses. So too when living beings who are inflamed with the defilements of lust, anger, and delusion touch the bodhisattva's body (*kāya*), they are cured of the pain of the defilements. Again we are told that this effect is due to the "excellent purity of that same bodhisattva's previous vow [*pūrva-praṇidhāna-supariśuddhatva*]." The passage reads in full:

> One who is constituted by the dharma body [*dharmakāya-prabhāvita*] benefits living beings even when they see him. He benefits living beings even when they hear him, even when they touch him. Śāntamati, [this is just like] the king of physicians, Jīvaka, who collected all medicines and created the form [*rūpa*] of a girl, made of the collection of medicinal plants, who was pleasing, good-looking, well made, well put together, and well turned out. She comes, she goes, stands, sits, and lies down. Sick persons who come there—great-souled kings, or royal ministers, or merchants, householders, ministers, and fort rulers—are united sexually [*saṃyojayati*][23] by the king of physicians, Jīvaka, with the medicine girl. Immediately following their sexual union [*saṃyoga*], all the illnesses of those who had been afflicted are subdued [*prasrabhyante*] and they become healthy, happy, and balanced [*nirvikāra*].[24] Śāntamati, see if the knowledge of the king of physicians, Jīvaka, concerning curing worldly illness is found among other physicians. So too, Śāntamati, as many living beings as there are—women, men, boys, and girls—who are inflamed with lust, anger, and delusion, who touch the body [*kāya*] of a bodhisattva who is constituted by the dharma body, immediately upon their touch all their defilements [*kleśa*] are subdued [*prasrabhyante*] and they recognize that their bodies are no longer afire [*vigata-saṃtāpaṃ ca kāyaṃ saṃjānanti*]. That is to say, it is by virtue of the excellent purity of that same bodhisattva's previous vow [*pūrva-praṇidhāna-suparisuddhatva*]. This is the reason a bodied being [*ātmabhāva*] should be purified [*śodhya*].[25]

This passage presents us with a number of interpretive challenges. Foremost among these is the vocabulary for body. Three terms are employed to designate various kinds of bodies in this passage: *kāya*, *ātmabhāva*, and *dharmakāya*. The living beings who touch the bodhisattva possess a *kāya*, an ordinary physical body that serves as the locus of the defilements. Their *kāyas*, or bodies, are literally on fire with lust, anger, and delusion prior to the moment when they touch the bodhisattva. The bodhisattva possesses a broader range of bodies, namely, a *kāya*, *ātmabhāva*, and *dharmakāya*. What do these terms mean and exactly what are living beings touching when they touch the bodhisattva's body? When living beings touch the body of the bodhisattva, they touch his *kāya*, suggesting that they touch a physical body similar in some way to their own. At the end of the passage, however, bodhisattvas are instructed to purify their *ātmabhāvas*. Why must they purify their *ātmabhāvas* if the passage describes living beings touching a bodhisattva's *kāya*? As we saw in the previous chapter, *ātmabhāva* has the broadest semantic range of all body vocabulary, designating not just the physical body, but the entire complex of body, feelings, and thoughts. Thus I translate the term as "bodied being." It is not enough for bodhisattvas to purify only their physical bodies; they must also purify their feelings and thoughts if their physical bodies are to be transformative for other living beings. Therefore bodhisattvas must purify their *ātmabhāvas*.

But what are we to make of the fact that living beings touch the physical body of a bodhisattva "who is constituted by the dharma body"? What is a dharma body, or *dharmakāya*? The concept of the dharma body has a long and complex history in Buddhist traditions.[26] Usually it refers to the body of a buddha, but sometimes, as in this passage, it may refer to the body of a very advanced bodhisattva.[27] These highly realized beings possess not only a physical body, generally called a form body (*rūpakāya*), but also a different kind of body called a dharma body. There is no one single definition of the dharma body. Sometimes the term designates the body of the Dharma, that is, the body, or collection, of Buddhist teachings; sometimes it designates the body, or collection, of qualities, called *dharmas*, which all buddhas possess. Thus the bodhisattva in this passage might be constituted by the body of Buddhist teachings, which, if followed, lead to buddhahood, or he might be constituted by the body of qualities, the full possession of which would also make him a buddha.[28]

There is, however, another definition of dharma body that we need to consider. The concept of the dharma body receives particular attention in the doctrine of the three bodies (*trikāya*) of a buddha, associated with the Yogācāra philosophical branch of Mahāyāna Buddhism. According to the three-body doctrine, all buddhas have three "aspects," called bodies.[29] These are the dharma body, the enjoyment body (*saṃbhogakāya*), and the body of magical transformation (*nirmāṇakāya*). In this schema, the dharma body takes on a new meaning. The dharma body designates "the transcendent aspect of the buddha which fully embodies all the characteristics of enlightenment and is identified with emptiness, the ultimate nature of the universe."[30] Ontologically, the dharma body is equated with ultimate reality itself; epistemologically, it is equated with the "intrinsically radiant consciousness of a Buddha"[31] that perceives reality as it is. Thus the bodhisattva in this passage might also be constituted by the "intrinsically radiant consciousness" of an awakened being. According to the three-body doctrine, the dharma body is a formless, eternal, and unchanging body. The other two kinds of bodies—the enjoyment body and the body of magical transformation—are defined as manifestations of this ultimately formless, eternal, and unchanging reality. The enjoyment body is a glorified body visible to advanced bodhisattvas in Buddhist paradises called pure lands. The body of magical transformation is frequently defined as an ordinary human body, but buddhas, like bodhisattvas, can manifest an infinite variety of bodies of magical transformation to meet the needs of diverse living beings. The three-body doctrine underwent significant refinement and elaboration at the hands of philosophers in both the Yogācāra and later Madhyamaka philosophical branches of Mahāyāna Buddhism. The *Compendium of Training*, however, never discusses the three-body doctrine, nor does it offer its own definition of the dharma body. It is thus impossible to know precisely what the term means in this passage.[32]

Unfortunately, it is also impossible to know exactly what the living beings are touching. They clearly touch some kind of a physical body. The passage attributes the transformative power of this body to both a specific vow and a more general purification of bodied being. (We will see shortly that vows themselves are a means of purifying bodied being.) The precise relationship between the physical body and the dharma body remains unclear, as does the exact nature of the physical body. Is the physical body a manifestation of an ultimately formless, eternal, and unchanging reality, as would be suggested by the three-body theory? The text does not say. Its lack of clarity on this matter is itself telling. The *Compendium of Training* is simply less interested in defining the nature of the bodhisattva's body than it is in describing the transformative effects it has on living beings. We may not know exactly what kind of body he has, but we do know what it does. It transforms living beings in physical and moral ways. Specifically, it alleviates them of the torment of the defilements. It is no accident that the defilements are likened in this passage to a disease. Lust, anger, and delusion are rooted in body as much as in heartmind. Hence liberation from the defilements is described as an experience of one's body no longer being on fire.

Chapter 8 offers yet another example of a bodhisattva who makes a vow to render his body capable of transforming living beings in physical and moral ways. In this case, the living beings are women. The bodhisattva, appropriately named Pleasure-maker (Priyaṃkara), makes a vow (*praṇidhi*) that should a woman gaze at him with lust (*rāga*), she will be reborn as a man and perhaps even a male god.

> Because of Priyaṃkara's vow, a woman who looks at him again and again with a lustful mind abandons her existence as a woman and becomes a man—such a noble being.
>
> See, Ānanda, the virtues [of lust] are such that they cause some living beings to go to hell, but, having given rise to lust for the heroes [i.e., bodhisattvas], they cause others to go to heaven and indeed a state of masculinity.[33]

The first verse of this passage indicates that women who lust after Priyaṃkara are transformed into men. The second verse suggests that they are transformed into male gods.[34] Both transformations represent a change in physical as well as moral status since, according to traditional Buddhist cosmology, it takes more merit to be reborn as a man than as a woman; similarly, it takes more merit to be reborn as a god than as a human being.[35] Surprisingly, women achieve such positive rebirths because they give rise to the defilement of lust. Ordinarily lust results in negative rebirths. The *Compendium of Training* displays a decidedly monastic attitude toward sex. It encourages bodhisattvas to renounce householder life and even encourages male householders to refrain from sex with their own wives.[36] More broadly, the *Compendium of Training* condemns the entire arena of "foul, disgusting, and stinking sensual pleasures," since these commonly result in sin.[37] Nevertheless, when women lust after Priyaṃkara, they achieve excellent rebirths. When the object of lust is a bodhisattva, lust results in merit instead of sin. Thus the *Compendium of Training* concludes its discussion of this passage by proclaiming that even the defilements (*kleśa*) bring happiness when their object is a bodhisattva.[38]

We saw in the last chapter that the *Compendium of Training* enjoins its bodhisattvas to turn their bodies into "something for the enjoyment of all living beings."[39] This is precisely what Priyaṃkara and the deceased bodhisattva do when they offer their bodies as objects of female sexual desire or as food for animals. There are several reasons why bodhisattvas are enjoined to turn their bodies into "something for the enjoyment of all living beings." First, bodhisattvas have promised to liberate living beings from diverse kinds of suffering. Thus they use their bodies to satisfy the immediate needs and wishes of others. Second, by satisfying these immediate needs and wishes, bodhisattvas gain an opportunity to attract living beings to the Dharma. Attracting living beings to the Dharma is so important that bodhisattvas may even enter into the arena of the "foul, disgusting, and stinking sensual pleasures" to do so. Thus, as we saw in the previous chapter, bodhisattvas may offer alcohol and sex to living beings, provided that these bodhisattvas possess the skillful means (*upāya*) to use sensual pleasures to benefit others without themselves becoming addicted to them.

Chapter 8 of the *Compendium of Training* suggests that there is yet another reason why bodhisattvas should turn their bodies into "something for the enjoyment of all living beings." Such enjoyment is itself profoundly transformative. When animals "enjoy" the deceased bodhisattva's body, they become gods; when women "enjoy" Priyaṃkara's body, they become men and possibly male gods. Enjoyment is no trivial matter in the *Compendium of Training*. When living beings enjoy bodhisattva bodies, they are changed for the better in physical as well as moral ways. Thus the enjoyment of bodhisattva bodies serves to ripen living beings. Although the *Compendium of Training* regards the arena of sensual pleasures as inherently dangerous, such pleasures are physically and morally transformative when the object of pleasure is a bodhisattva. Indeed such pleasures may even be liberative, as in the case of animals who eventually attain *parinirvāṇa* after "enjoying" a bodhisattva's corpse.[40]

Chapter 8 of the *Compendium of Training* highlights the transformative effects of various kinds of encounters with bodhisattva bodies, from eating bodhisattva bodies, to touching bodhisattva bodies, to lusting after bodhisattva bodies. Some of these encounters highlight the positive value the *Compendium of Training* places on "enjoying" the bodies; all of them highlight the role specific vows play in rendering bodhisattva bodies transformative. Recently the relationship between bodhisattva vows and bodies has received scholarly attention. Paul Williams argues that bodhisattva bodies function in Mahāyāna traditions as a "medium for fulfilling the bodhisattva vow" to become a buddha in order to liberate others from suffering.[41] When Williams speaks of "the bodhisattva vow," he is referring to the *bodhicitta*. *Bodhicitta* is a generic, or universal, bodhisattva vow that all bodhisattvas make. This vow motivates bodhisattvas to place their bodies in the service of other living beings in diverse kinds of ways. According to Williams, their bodies become, in Sartrean terms, a "Being-for-others."[42] They are the physical expressions of a bodhisattva's compassionate commitment to helping other living beings. The *Compendium of Training* clearly bears out Williams's point, since one of its key concerns is teaching bodhisattvas how to use their bodies to benefit others.[43] The *Compendium of Training*, however, also offers another insight into the relationship between bodhisattva vows and bodies. Bodhisattva bodies not only are a *medium* for fulfilling the generic bodhisattva vow; they are also the *products* of other more particular and individualized vows. As we have seen, bodhisattvas make specific kinds of vows to produce bodies that have specific kinds of physical and moral effects on other living beings. Vow-making is thus one of a range of bodhisattva practices prescribed by the *Compendium of Training* to produce bodhisattvas with bodies capable of ripening others.

Buddhist confidence in the efficacy of vows reflects both general South Asian views on the power of certain linguistic utterances to affect reality, as well as Buddhist belief that as bodhisattvas progress toward buddhahood they attain, among other qualities, supernormal powers and vast amounts of merit which they can use to make their vows a reality. The *Compendium of Training* is aware of different classes of bodhisattvas. There are superhuman bodhisattvas such as Mañjuśrī, Avalokiteśvara, and Ākāśagarbha, who are commonly referred to as "celestial bodhisattvas" in secondary literature on Buddhism. In addition to these superhuman bodhisattvas, there are also ordinary human bodhisattvas such as those who comprise the audience for this text. Although the kinds of vows discussed so far may pertain especially to superhuman bodhisattvas, the *Compendium of Training* closes chapter 8 with a discussion of *bodhicitta*, which is the generic bodhisattva vow that all bodhisattvas, whether human or superhuman, make.

Generating *bodhicitta* is presented in the *Compendium of Training* as one of the most powerful means of purifying bodied being, particularly of sin. The text uses a variety of metaphors to describe the purificatory effects of *bodhicitta*. *Bodhicitta*, also called the aspiration for omniscience (*sarvajñatācitta*), is likened to the fire that destroys the world at the end of an eon (*kalpa-uddāha-agni*) because it burns up all bad deeds; to a region under the earth called Pātāla because it makes an end of all unmeritorous things (perhaps in the sense of swallowing up or consuming them); to a lamp because it dispels the blinding darkness of the obstructions of bad karma and defilements; to the wish-fulfilling jewel on the crowns of Nāga kings, or serpent deities, because it protects one from unfortunate rebirths; and to mercury (*rasajāta*).[44] The reference to mercury is a reference to alchemy. We are told that just as mercury transforms base metals into gold, so too the "mercury" of the aspiration for omniscience (i.e., *bodhicitta*) transforms the "base metals" of the obstructions of bad karma and defilements into the "gold" of omniscience. The passage reads in full:

> Well-born son, just as there is a mercury called "having the appearance of *hāṭaka* gold,"[45] one measure of which turns one thousand measures of metal into gold, but the measure [of mercury] cannot be overcome by one thousand measures of metal, nor turned into metal; so too a single drop of the mercury of the arising of the aspiration for omniscience, which is accompanied by the transformation of the roots of merit and by knowledge, having overcome the

> metals of the obstructions of all karma and defilements, turns all dharmas into the color [i.e., gold] of omniscience [*sarvajñatā-varṇa*]. But the drop of the mercury of the arising of the aspiration for omniscience cannot be defiled or overcome by the metals of all karma and defilements.[46]

Unlike the other passages discussed so far, this passage does not tell us the effects this particular vow has on other living beings. Instead it tells us the effects the vow has on bodhisattvas themselves. It purifies a bodhisattva's bodied being of sin.[47] *Bodhicitta* is presented as the final and perhaps most powerful practice prescribed in chapter 8 for purifying bodied being. The alchemical metaphor is particularly apt for describing the purificatory effects of the vow, since alchemists in medieval India were not just interested in producing gold; they also sought to produce immortal bodies by ingesting refined mercury. As David Gordon White argues, the ingested mercury "takes over the body into which it enters, transforming human tissue into alchemical diamond or gold."[48] *Bodhicitta* purifies body as well as heartmind; it changes bodhisattvas in physical as well as moral ways.

Bodhicitta is an example of what Foucault calls "technologies of the self." Foucault defines technologies of the self as disciplinary practices individuals self-consciously adopt in order to transform themselves into ideal ethical subjects. For example, he investigates how elite men of Greek and Greco-Roman cultures adopted health regimens, physical exercises, "the carefully measured satisfaction of needs," and forms of introspection such as meditation, reading, and writing in order to achieve self-mastery, especially in the arena of pleasure.[49] Of particular relevance to this study of the *Compendium of Training* is the fact that Foucault illumines the corporeal as well as psychological effects of technologies of the self. These disciplinary practices affect bodies as much as they do heartminds. For instance, Foucault demonstrates that Greek and Latin writers of the first two centuries of the common era characterized moderation in diet, exercise, and sex as good for body and soul.[50] *Bodhicitta* is a technology of the self in the Foucauldian sense of the term. This vow is a disciplinary practice Buddhist practitioners self-consciously adopt in order to transform themselves into ideal ethical subjects, namely, bodhisattvas. In doing so, they purify not only their heartminds, but also their bodies.

The passage on *bodhicitta* clarifies that vows serve to purify bodied being. The earlier passages clarify that a purified bodied being has physically and morally transformative effects on other living beings. Scholars of Buddhism are quite familiar with the role bodhisattva vows play in the creation of pure lands, or Buddhist paradises. The evidence from the *Compendium of Training* indicates that bodhisattva vows play an equally important role in the creation of pure bodied beings. Further, just as living beings are physically and morally altered by rebirth in a pure land,[51] so too living beings are physically and morally altered when they encounter purified bodied beings. Although the *Compendium of Training* is but one text, the very fact that it draws upon approximately one hundred Buddhist sources suggests that its interest in the transformative power of bodhisattva bodies is not without precedent in Buddhist literature. Indeed, similar stories of bodhisattvas making vows to create bodies that have positive physical and moral effects on living beings can be found in other Buddhist texts. Paul Demiéville cites from a number of *sūtras*, or scriptures, which describe bodhisattvas making vows that should beings hear, touch, see, smell, or eat them, they will be healed of illnesses or defilements.[52] For example, according to the *Upāsakaśīlasūtra*,

> In a previous existence the Buddha, suffering from hunger, uttered a vow thanks to which he obtained the body of a great fish; and with his body he fed starved sentient beings.... In another lifetime when he was ill he uttered a vow to receive a body [like] a "tree of medicine"; all those who were ill—in seeing him, in smelling him or in touching him, or in consuming his skin, his blood, his flesh, his bone, or his marrow—were healed of all illness.[53]

The *Mahāparinirvāṇasūtra* likewise contains examples of bodhisattvas making vows to produce bodies that transform others:

> Just as the king of medicinal trees heals all the sick who may take the root, trunk, branches, leaves, flowers, fruits, or bark, so the bodhisattva frames the following vow: May anyone who hears my voice, touches my body, or imbibes my blood, flesh, bone, or marrow be healed of all illnesses! When sentient beings eat my flesh, may they be unable to give rise to any bad idea, as though they were eating the flesh of their own child![54]

Similarly, the *Bodhisattvapiṭakasūtra* also enjoins bodhisattvas to make vows that produce bodies capable of benefiting others:

> The bodhisattvas, the great heroes, should conceive of all sentient beings as patients, ceaselessly burned and tormented by the three fiery passions of greed, hatred, and confusion. They should apply this ointment-panacea [*agada*] of the good doctrine to them.... They should by the strength of their vow obtain a body that will be a good medicine to heal sentient beings of that threefold illness.

The passage goes on to recount a story of a past life of the Buddha in which he transformed himself into a body which, when dismembered and eaten, cured living beings of illness.[55] Finally, Demiéville also cites the story of Jīvaka and the medicinal girl, which is quoted in the *Compendium of Training*, adding that there is a similar story about a medicinal man. Jīvaka creates a beautiful young man out of medicinal herbs. We are told that

> in contemplating him, in "singing and playing" with him, in examining his beautiful appearance, the patients of Jīvaka obtain healing, pacification, and absence of desire; in the same way, the bodhisattvas, the great heroes, actualize bodies in order to procure love and pleasure for sentient beings—men or women—whom the three passions torment to excess: thus they calm their desires and guide them to calm meditation and to discipline.[56]

The *Compendium of Training* is not an isolated example of the capacity of bodhisattva bodies, fashioned by vows, to ripen others. By drawing such marked attention to the transformative power of bodhisattva bodies, the *Compendium of Training* illumines a concern that has a broader currency in Mahāyāna literature.

Ripening Living Beings

"Ripening" (*paripac-*) is a common Buddhist metaphor for ethical and spiritual maturation. Thus much of Mahāyāna Buddhist literature, including the *Compendium of Training*, describes the transformative effects that bodhisattvas have on others as the "ripening" of living beings. This study of the *Compendium of Training* demonstrates that bodies as much as heartminds are involved in the ripening of living beings. Bodhisattvas use their bodies to ripen living beings; when they do so, living beings are changed in physical as well as moral ways. In the remainder of this chapter I explore some of the implications the metaphor of ripening has for understanding medieval Indian Buddhist ethics.

The term *paripac-*, which I translate as "ripening," has a broad semantic range, including to "ripen," "mature," "perfect," "cook," "bake," "burn," "roast," and "digest." I translate the term as "ripening" because of a preference for agricultural metaphors in Buddhist literature. For example, Buddhists commonly speak of the "ripening" of karma, of "planting" roots of merit or demerit; they characterize the monastic community as a "field" of merit; they speak of the "seed" of *bodhicitta*, and the "seeding" of consciousness with good and bad karma.[57] "Ripening," however, is not the most literal translation of *paripac-*. The most literal translation is "to cook fully." The term consists of the prefix *pari* plus the verb *pac-*. This verb itself means "to cook." The prefix *pari*, which most literally means "round" or "round about," indicates an encircling motion and thus conveys a sense of completion.[58] "To cook fully" means "to cook to completion" or "to cook to perfection." There is, in fact, at least one passage in the *Compendium of Training* that invokes the imagery of cooking instead of ripening, indicating that some Buddhist writers were cognizant of the full semantic range of the term. Therefore sometimes bodhisattvas appear to cook living beings rather than to ripen them. This is hardly surprising, since the imagery of ripening is so closely related to the imagery of cooking in South Asia. Ripening is regarded as a particular kind of cooking. Specifically, the sun cooks the earth, thereby bringing seeds to fruition.[59] The metaphor of ripening is thus a variation on the much broader metaphor of cooking.

The broader metaphor of cooking has wide currency in South Asia. As White observes, the metaphor of cooking emerges from Vedic religion and is used to describe "such transformative processes as sacrifice, cremation, digestion, aging, and the yogic austerities."[60] For example, Charles Malamoud has drawn attention to the centrality of the metaphor of cooking in the Vedic sacrifice. The Vedic sacrifice is a ritual reenactment of the primal sacrifice that gave rise to the world. Brahmins who perform this sacrifice are said to "cook the world" (*lokapakti*). Such cooking signifies the ritual renewal of the world through sacrifice.[61] Bodies are also "cooked" in South Asian traditions. For instance, when religious practitioners engage in yogic austerities, they cook themselves, generating enormous amounts of *tapas*, or ascetic heat. Malamoud, among others, has argued that this process represents an "internalization" of the Vedic sacrifice.[62] A different kind of "internalization" of the Vedic sacrifice underlies the Indian Āyurvedic conception of digestion, according to which food is cooked over a series of seven internal digestive fires. Thus White comments, "As in Vedic sacrifice, so in yoga and Āyurveda: the body is to be 'cooked to a turn' [*paripakvā*]," that is, cooked to perfection.[63]

The *Compendium of Training* invokes the imagery of cooking rather than ripening at one point in the text through recourse to a subtle pun. It contrasts the experience of being fully cooked (*paripac-*) by bodhisattvas with the experience of being just plain cooked (*pac-*) by the fires of hell. The former action cooks living beings to perfection, whereas the latter action roasts them in hell. The *Compendium of Training* makes its point by quoting from another text, the *Dharmasaṃgītisūtra*. I have already quoted a portion of this passage at the beginning of this chapter. I give it here in full, substituting "cooking" for "ripening."

> This then is the duty of the bodhisattva, namely, attracting living beings. As it has been clarified in the *Holy Dharmasaṃgītisūtra* by the holy Priyadarśana Bodhisattva: "Blessed One, a bodhisattva should behave in such a way that merely upon seeing him beings are pleased [*prasad-*]. Why? Blessed One, a bodhisattva has no other duty than attracting living beings. Blessed One, this very cooking of living beings [*satva-paripāka*][64] is a bodhisattva's recitation of the Dharma." But what is the fault in not doing so? The world, having despised the nascent Jina [i.e., bodhisattva] as unwelcome like a fire hidden by ash, is cooked [*pac-*] in hell, and so forth.[65]

The *Compendium of Training* suggests through a subtle pun on the verb "to cook" that if bodhisattvas fail to attract and consequently fully cook living beings, these living beings will be cooked in the fires of hell. The nascent Jina himself is likened to a fire hidden by ash. As Paul Harrison explains, living beings do not realize that he is a bodhisattva. Like a fire hidden by ash, the bodhisattva's identity remains hidden to living beings. Hence they reject him. From a Mahāyāna Buddhist perspective, rejecting a bodhisattva constitutes a grave sin. Living beings who reject bodhisattvas may burn in the fires of hell. Thus when bodhisattvas fail to attract and cook living beings, they risk consigning these beings to rebirth in hell. As Harrison puts it, "like a fire that seems to be out, [the bodhisattva] can burn those who do not take him seriously."[66]

Rebirth in hell has physical and moral consequences for living beings. Physically, they suffer horrific torment. Morally, they have little or no opportunity to earn merit. Bodhisattvas have the capacity to transform living beings physically and morally for the better; if they fail to do so, living beings are transformed physically and morally for the worse. Since the Sanskrit term *paripac-* has such a broad semantic range, Buddhists can imagine the physical and moral maturation of living beings as a process of either ripening or cooking. The imagery of ripening suggests a process of bringing seeds to fruition. In South Asia the imagery of cooking frequently suggests a process of perfecting or refining. For example, brahmins perfect the world when they perform the Vedic sacrifice, yogins perfect themselves when they engage in yogic austerities, and the internal digestive fires perfect, or refine, food.[67]

Like the other passages discussed so far, the above passage emphasizes the important role bodhisattva bodies play in the ripening/cooking of living beings. The passage maintains that a bodhisattva must conduct himself in such a way that "merely upon seeing him beings are pleased." The context for this passage is a discussion of etiquette and deportment. Let us recall that the

Compendium of Training calls itself a bodhisattva *vinaya*.[68] Like all *vinayas*, or monastic regulations, this text devotes significant attention to etiquette and deportment, especially for monastics. Its instructions concern a wide range of matters, including posture (*īryāpatha*);[69] tone of voice and proper speech;[70] the importance of maintaining a very pleasing countenance (*suprasanna-mukha*);[71] prohibitions against disgusting acts such as discharging urine, excrement, phlegm, or pus in inappropriate places;[72] and regulations concerning eating and begging food.[73] The reason the *Compendium of Training* cares so much about etiquette and deportment is precisely that bodhisattvas have the power to ripen living beings with their bodies; they can do so by cultivating the serene, graceful, and decorous features, gestures, and movements of well-disciplined monastics. If bodhisattvas please and attract living beings by mastering proper etiquette and deportment, they will ripen these living beings. The text warns, however, that if they fail to please and attract living beings, they may cause these beings to roast in hell. Thus it is imperative that they learn how to conduct themselves in such a manner that they please and attract rather than displease and repel.

The above passage enables us to connect the fantastic stories we have encountered about living beings eating, touching, and lusting after bodhisattva bodies, as well as the fantastic descriptions of bodhisattvas manifesting an infinite variety of physical forms, with the more mundane reality of day-to-day monastic life. Bodhisattvas do not need to possess superhuman powers in order to ripen living beings. Even those with ordinary human powers can do so by conducting themselves in such a way that the mere sight of them "pleases" living beings. I will say more about the physical and moral consequences of being "pleased" (*prasad-*) by the sight of well-disciplined monastic bodhisattvas in the next chapter. For now, I simply wish to make the point that the *Compendium of Training* assumes that *all* bodhisattvas, whether human or superhuman, can use their bodies to ripen others. Bodhisattvas take a variety of vows—including monastic vows—all of which serve to render their bodies transformative for others.[74]

Buddhist Technologies of the Self

Foucault's research on the technologies of the self illumines the physical effects of a wide range of disciplinary practices. As a result, his work informs and supports this study of the *Compendium of Training*, which argues that Buddhist ethical discourse knows no absolute separation between the physical and moral dimensions of living beings. Buddhist technologies of the self, like those of Greek and Greco-Roman cultures, blur the boundaries between body and morality. The Buddhist technologies of the self prescribed by the *Compendium of Training,* however, also blur other boundaries and, in doing so, suggest ways to nuance Foucault's research on the technologies of the self and, more broadly, his understanding of ethical self-cultivation. Specifically, the other boundaries that the *Compendium of Training* blurs are those between self and other, and between ethical agents and ethical "patients."[75]

The *Compendium of Training* blurs the boundaries between self and other because in Mahāyāna Buddhism *self*-transformation is always in the service of the transformation of *others.* Bodhisattvas undertake disciplinary practices such as vow-making in order to produce bodies capable of transforming other living beings. The quintessential bodhisattva act is thus defined as ripening *others.* The ethical formation of self and other are fully interconnected processes in the *Compendium of Training.* The text also blurs the distinction between ethical agents and ethical patients, because the metaphor of ripening living beings implies both an agent and a patient: one who ripens and one who is ripened. Additionally, the roles of agent and patient are not mutually exclusive. According to the *Compendium of Training,* the ideal community for ethical cultivation is the monastic community; thus it suggests that this is the arena within which living beings are most likely to ripen others and be ripened by others. It conceives of monastic communities as places of communal ripening. The intervention of other bodhisattvas—whether those with superhuman powers or one's very human monastic companions—is vital to a monastic bodhisattva's ethical development. Bodhisattvas help each other take shape as such by ripening each other. In these communities bodhisattvas are simultaneously ethical agents and ethical patients. Significantly, the *Compendium of Training* even provides to bodhisattvas who are on solitary retreat in the wilderness instructions on how to receive visitors, both human and divine. Furthermore, these solitary practitioners are reminded that they are never really alone. A whole host of divine beings and buddhas are constantly watching. Even when they are on solitary retreat, ethical maturation occurs in the context of various kinds of relationships.[76] Although Foucault notes that the formation of ethical subjects entails "the interplay of the care of the self and the help of the other," his primary focus remains the "ethical work" one performs on oneself.[77] The *Compendium of Training,* on the other hand, is more interested in the ways in which individuals shape each other into ideal ethical subjects—that is, into bodhisattvas. The ethical subject of the *Compendium of Training* is not a discrete and autonomous individual, as is so often the case in modern Western ethical discourse; rather this ethical subject takes form within and by means of a broader community—he or she is simultaneously ethical agent and ethical patient.

Charles Hallisey's research on "the ethics of care and responsibility" in Theravāda Buddhism draws attention to the critical role that relationships play in the formation of ethical persons.[78] His work has inspired scholars of Buddhist ethics such as Karen Derris to explore the varieties of ways in which ethical subjectivity emerges within the context of community. Derris's work is particularly pertinent to this study, because she investigates the ethical development of bodhisattvas, specifically the ethical development of *the* Bodhisattva, that is, the future Buddha. She focuses her investigation on a Thai Theravāda narrative text called the *Sotaṭṭhakīmahānidāna*, which narrates the entirety of the Bodhisattva's multilifetime career, from the moment he first forms the aspiration to become a buddha to his final lifetime, when he achieves his aim.[79] Derris argues that the Bodhisattva, or Bodhisatta in the Pāli language of this text, achieves his aim only with the help of other living beings. She thus argues against "the monotone vision" in Theravāda scholarship of bodhisattas as exclusively the benefactors of others. According to Derris, not only are bodhisattas the benefactors of others; "they are the beneficiaries of care and the recipients of aid as well."[80] The living beings who aid the Bodhisatta are both extraordinary and ordinary beings. Buddhas, other bodhisattas, gods, humans, and even animals all contribute to the Bodhisatta's progress along the path to buddhahood. Surprisingly, even living beings whose level of ethical and spiritual development is far less than that of the Bodhisatta have something important to contribute to his progress. All of the living beings in this Theravāda narrative, including the Bodhisatta himself, "are constantly shifting between the roles of benefactor and beneficiary."[81] At times the Bodhisatta benefits others; at times these others benefit him. Derris thus reveals a "shifting hierarchy" of ethical actors in Theravāda narrative literature in which even "beings with superior ethical virtues can be dependent on the care of others."[82]

Derris's concept of a shifting hierarchy of ethical actors provides a useful way of thinking about the mutual ripening of living beings in the *Compendium of Training*. Bodhisattvas at all stages of the path learn to see themselves as both the benefactors and beneficiaries of others. On the one hand, bodhisattvas cultivate a sense of responsibility for others, having dedicated themselves to the alleviation of all suffering. On the other hand, they cultivate what Hallisey calls a "grateful openness to others,"[83] recognizing that they are also dependent upon others for their own ethical development. The *Compendium of Training* demonstrates that benefits, whether given or received, often come via the medium of bodies. Bodhisattvas use their bodies to ripen others, and when they ripen living beings these beings are changed in physical and moral ways. This is as much the case for superhuman bodhisattvas whose flesh can turn animals into gods as it is for ordinary bodhisattvas whose impeccable etiquette and deportment attracts and pleases others. The *Compendium of Training* thus offers us a complex picture of ethical self-cultivation in which the boundaries between body and morality, self and other, and ethical agents and ethical patients are blurred.

The Gendering of the Bodhisattva Ideal in the *Compendium of Training*

What kinds of bodies ripen other living beings? At first glance it would appear that an infinite variety of bodies ripen others, since bodhisattvas assume countless different forms in accordance with the needs and wishes of diverse living beings. Chapter 18's recollection of the saṅgha envisions bodhisattvas as male, female, young, old, healthy, sick, and associated with a wide range of social classes and professions. Elsewhere in the text, however, the focus is almost exclusively on male bodhisattva bodies. For example, chapter 8 contains no accounts of transformative encounters with female bodhisattva bodies, although, as we have seen, there are several accounts of such encounters with male bodhisattva bodies. The privileging of male bodhisattva bodies reflects the male monastic orientation of the *Compendium of Training*. This orientation is also reflected in the fact that the one extended discussion of a female bodhisattva in the text characterizes her as dangerous because her physical beauty generates lust in men. We meet this female bodhisattva, called Candrottarā, in an extended quotation from the *Candrottarādārikāparipṛcchā*. Candrottarā is a highly advanced bodhisattva with some supernatural powers. When we meet her, she has just risen up into the air in order to escape a crowd that had been chasing her. The crowd appears to consist of men enamored by her beauty.[84] Candrottarā is indeed extremely beautiful. Her body (*kāya*) is described as pleasing (*manojña*) and, like a buddha's body, it is golden in color (*suvarṇavarṇa*).[85] Additionally a fine fragrance (*atigandha*) emanates from all her pores.[86] We will see in the next chapter that physical beauty of form and scent are both markers of virtuous bodies. The *Compendium of Training* explicitly states that Candrottarā's beauty is the result of the merit she has earned from practicing generosity (*dāna*) and self-restraint (*dama*), especially sexual restraint.[87] Regardless of the fact that Candrottarā's beauty is a karmic marker of her virtue and regardless of the fact that she is an advanced bodhisattva, her presence has a deleterious effect on men. She is forced to deliver a sermon on the dangers of lust. She begins by reminding her audience that she may well have been their mother in a past life; similarly, she may have been their enemy.

She then goes on to warn of the horrific karmic consequences of lust, which include rebirth in hell, as hungry ghosts, as animals, as demons (*kumbhāṇḍas, yakṣas, asuras,* and *piśācas*); those reborn as humans will be one-eyed, lame, dumb (*vijihvaka*), ugly, blind from birth, deaf, or mentally disabled (*visaṃjña*); those reborn as animals will be dogs, swine, camels, donkeys, monkeys, elephants, horses, cows, tigers, moths, or flies.[88]

Unlike women who experience positive karmic benefits from lusting after the male bodhisattva Priyaṃkara, men who lust after the female bodhisattva Candrottarā suffer terribly negative consequences. Lust for a male bodhisattva produces positive karmic results, whereas lust for a female bodhisattva produces negative karmic results. The *Compendium of Training* includes no accounts of female bodhisattvas making vows to render their bodies transformative for others. Instead, the text repeatedly warns men to stay away from women. The Candrottarā episode appears in the midst of the text's most flagrantly misogynist passages—passages that urge lay and monastic male bodhisattvas to eradicate their lust for women. I return to these passages in chapter 5 of this book. For now I wish to make the point that the male monastic orientation of the *Compendium of Training* codes all women, even advanced bodhisattvas such as Candrottarā, as dangerous for men. Thus the bodies that ripen others in this text are almost exclusively male bodies.

The *Compendium of Training* is by far not the only example of Sanskrit Mahāyāna literature written from a male and sometimes sexist point of view.[89] Nevertheless, there *are* accounts in some of this literature of women who, like the male bodhisattvas of the *Compendium of Training,* use their bodies to ripen other living beings. For example, the *Gaṇḍavyūha,* a text cited on a number of occasions in the *Compendium of Training,* presents several female beautiful friends (*kalyāṇamitra*), or teachers. One of these, called Vasumitrā, uses her physical beauty to attract and transform male living beings. Vasumitrā explains, "To gods, in accord with their inclinations and interests, I appear in the form of a goddess of surpassing splendor and perfection; and to all other types of beings I accordingly appear in the form of a female of their species, of surpassing splendor and perfection. And all who come to me with minds full of passion, I teach them so that they become free of passion."[90] Some are freed of passion simply by seeing her, others by talking with her, holding her hand, staying with her, gazing at her, embracing her, or kissing her.[91] Sanskrit Mahāyāna literature also contains accounts of female figures who challenge the sexist assumption that female sex is inferior to male sex. One famous example occurs in the *Vimalakīrtinirdeśa,* a text also cited in the *Compendium of Training.* Śāriputra, a monastic disciple of the Buddha, is so impressed by the wisdom of a goddess that he inquires why she has not yet transformed herself into a man, as would befit a living being of her advanced ethical and spiritual development. The goddess teaches Śāriputra that sexual differences have no ultimate significance, and therefore it makes no difference whether one is male or female.[92] The *Candrottarādārikāparipṛcchā* itself expresses a similar sentiment. In a section of the text not quoted in the *Compendium of Training*, Candrottarā argues that notions of male and female have no ultimate reality. Nevertheless, once Candrottarā receives a prediction of buddhahood, she magically transforms herself into a man.[93] The *Candrottarādārikāparipṛcchā* delivers a decidedly mixed message about women—one, however, that is not nearly as uniformly negative as the one delivered by the *Compendium of Training*. The *Compendium of Training* includes only a small excerpt from the *Candrottarādārikāparipṛcchā* and does not include any references to Vasumitrā or the goddess. We, of course, do not know whether Śāntideva had at his disposal the complete texts of the *Candrottarādārikāparipṛcchā*, the *Gaṇḍavyūha*, and the *Vimalakīrtinirdeśa*, at least as they have come down to us. We do know, however, that some Mahāyāna writers were able to imagine women playing transformative roles in the lives of others. We also know that Mahāyāna Buddhists engaged in worship of various female divinities, who, according to Miranda Shaw, "receive substantial attention in Mahāyāna literature, practice, and iconography."[94] Jacob N. Kinnard observes that images of a female wisdom deity called Prajñāpāramitā "have been discovered at virtually all of the monastic sites in northeastern India."[95] In other words, they have been discovered in Śāntideva's very own milieu, although most, if not all, of the images likely date from a slightly later period of time. Thus the absence of positive female images in the *Compendium of Training* reflects not an overall absence of positive female images in Mahāyāna Buddhist literature and art, but rather the particular perspectives of this text.

The bodhisattva ideal is a universal ideal, accessible in theory to all living beings. The *Compendium of Training* acknowledges the universality of this ideal when it admits that even women can observe its bodhisattva discipline.[96] The bodhisattva ideal is, however, also an embodied ideal. The *Compendium of Training*'s bodhisattva discipline is as dedicated to the cultivation of virtuous bodies as it is to the cultivation of virtuous heartminds, since bodhisattvas use both their bodies and their heartminds to ripen other living beings. Throughout the text, the *Compendium of Training* foregrounds the central roles that bodies play in the ethical development of self and other. There is, of course, no such thing as a generic body, and therefore ethical ideals, like that of the bodhisattva, are embodied in particular kinds of ways. Although there is no theoretical limit to the kinds of physical forms bodhisattvas can assume, the form privileged in the *Compendium of Training* is male. There is thus a tension between the universality of the bodhisattva ideal and the limited ways in which this ideal is embodied in the *Compendium of Training*. This study of the *Compendium of Training*, which places body rather than heartmind at the center of ethical inquiry, illumines not only the centrality of body to the bodhisattva ideal, but also the corporeal specificity of that ideal as it is envisioned in this text.

The next chapter situates the *Compendium of Training* within a broader physiomoral discourse evident in Buddhist literature that associates morality with body. The *Compendium of Training*'s discussion of the physically and morally transformative power of bodhisattva bodies is itself a creative appropriation of this larger physiomoral discourse. Although sexual difference is a particular concern of the *Compendium of Training*, sexual difference is not the only marker of the relative moral worth of bodies. This text, like other Buddhist texts, is cognizant of a much wider range of physical features, including, beauty, health, and comportment, which affect the ethical development of both self and other. The next chapter thus turns its attention to the complex relationship between body and morality in the *Compendium of Training* and Buddhist literature more broadly.

4

Virtuous Bodies

A Physiomoral Discourse on Bodies

Therefore with bodied being, and so forth, as if with bait on a fish hook that has no enjoyment itself, [the bodhisattva] attracts others and carries them across [the ocean of saṃsāra].[1]

There is a story told in the monastic regulations (*vinaya*) of the Mūlasarvāstivāda, a Mainstream Buddhist school, about a monk named Devadatta.[2] Devadatta was a cousin and rival of the historical Buddha Śākyamuni. In this cycle of stories Devadatta attempts at different points to take over either the leadership of the monastic community or the Śākyan kingdom. The former act would make him a buddha and the latter a king. Periodically, Devadatta appeals to his supporter, King Ajātaśatru, for aid in taking over the monastic community. King Ajātaśatru rules primarily because under Devadatta's bad influence he had his own father, King Bimbisāra, thrown into prison, where he died of hunger. Therefore, on one occasion Devadatta tells the king, "I established you in kingship; establish me too in buddhahood."[3] The king refuses. This refusal comes, perhaps, as no surprise, since the immoral Devadatta hardly seems a likely candidate for buddhahood. But the king does not object to Devadatta's conduct. He objects to Devadatta's appearance. King Ajātaśatru refuses to grant Devadatta's request because Devadatta does not *look* like a buddha. Specifically, he does not have a buddha's golden-colored body (*suvarṇa-varṇa kāya*).[4] Undaunted, Devadatta visits a goldsmith and has himself gilt in gold. The story ends with Devadatta screaming in pain, no closer to buddhahood than before.[5] In another version of this story in the same monastic regulations, King Ajātaśatru refuses to establish Devadatta in buddhahood because Devadatta does not have the sign of a wheel on the soles of his feet, as is the case with buddhas. With remarkable perseverance, Devadatta commissions a blacksmith to brand his feet with the sign of a wheel, but once again he gets nothing for his efforts but severe pain.[6] Unfortunately for Devadatta, a buddha's looks are hard to fake. A buddha's body is a visible marker of his moral character. His golden complexion and the sign of a wheel on the soles of his feet are two of the thirty-two marks (*lakṣaṇa*) that adorn all buddhas. The thirty-two marks, about which I will say more below, are the karmic effects of many eons spent as a bodhisattva cultivating the requisite virtues of a buddha. Thus a buddha's physical qualities, no less than his affective and cognitive qualities, indicate his status as a buddha.

These stories about Devadatta display an assumption implicit in much of Buddhist literature that body and morality are closely connected.[7] Bodies are rarely morally neutral in Buddhist literature. This is the case not just for extraordinary beings such as buddhas or highly realized bodhisattvas, but for all living beings, good and bad. Thus Buddhist literature is replete with living beings who literally stink with sin, are disfigured by vices, and, conversely, are perfumed or adorned with merit and virtues. The close relationship between body and morality in Buddhist ethical discourse reflects broader patterns of thought and practice in South Asia. Scholars such as E. Valentine Daniel, Ronald Inden, Ralph W. Nicholas, and McKim Marriott have demonstrated that body and morality are closely connected in South Asian traditions more broadly.[8] Speaking of Hindus in Bengal, Inden and Nicholas state that there is "no absolute separation between natural and moral orders or material and spiritual orders."[9] For example, the Hindu life cycle rituals (*saṃskāra*) refine or perfect a person physically and morally. They are "outward and visible symbols of a stage of refinement or perfection (always further perfectible) that is both outer and inner, both visible and invisible."[10] Jain tradition reveals a similar relationship between body and morality. For instance, the Jain scholar Hemacandra (1089–1172) describes the bodies of Jain ascetics as made beautiful by their practice of asceticism.[11] Although it is beyond the scope of this study to analyze the different ways in which the relationship between body and morality is articulated (and sometimes also contested) in South Asian traditions, it is important to realize that Buddhists were not alone in South Asia in positing such a close relationship.

Buddhist traditions contain more than one kind of discourse on bodies. I call the body discourse that associates morality with body a "physiomoral discourse." In the next chapter I will examine a very different kind of body discourse, namely, an ascetic discourse. On the surface, the physiomoral discourse is a "positive" discourse on bodies, since it ascribes to bodies important roles in the ethical development of self and other. On the surface, the ascetic discourse is a "negative" discourse on bodies, since it dismisses bodies as impermanent, foul, and without any intrinsic or lasting worth. The truth is much more complicated, as we will see in the next chapter. The goal of this chapter is to situate the *Compendium of Training*'s perspectives on body within the larger context of a physiomoral discourse in South Asian Buddhist materials. Doing this entails examining the precise nature of the relationship between body and morality. We will see that this relationship is quite complex. On the one hand, bodies are cast as the *effects* of morality. Through the workings of karma, the body a person has in any given lifetime is the effect of his or her past deeds. On the other hand, bodies are also cast as the *very conditions* for morality. The kind of body a person has can actually enable or disable particular kinds of moral agency. Most strikingly, as we have already seen in this book, certain kinds of bodies such as those of bodhisattvas have positive effects on the ethical development of *others*. Buddhist traditions thus offer different perspectives on the relationship between body and morality. It is important to note that these perspectives are not mutually exclusive. I treat them separately for heuristic purposes only. In actuality the *Compendium of Training*, like other Buddhist texts, is often able to suggest multiple perspectives simultaneously.

Bodies as the Effects of Morality

The Devadatta story construes bodies as the effects of morality. Specifically, the story portrays the Buddha's body, which is adorned with the thirty-two marks of a great man (*mahāpuruṣa*), as the karmic effect of his past deeds. The concept of the great man, which is pre-Buddhist in origin, refers in Buddhist traditions to two extraordinary beings: a buddha and a world-conquering king (*cakravartin*).[12] Both are adorned with the thirty-two auspicious marks of a great man. Both appear only rarely in the world.[13] Both disseminate the Dharma. The Buddha does so by teaching the Dharma. The world-conquering king does so by ruling in accordance with the Dharma. Anyone familiar with the life story of the Buddha knows that at his birth learned men skilled in the art of prognostication were asked to predict the destiny of the infant Buddha on the basis of his physical appearance. Seeing the thirty-two marks, some predicted that he would become either a buddha or a world-conquering king. Others, most notably the sage Asita, predicted that he definitely would become a buddha.[14]

In both cases the thirty-two marks function as signs predictive of the infant Buddha's future destiny. Apparently that destiny is not obvious to everyone. Only men skilled in prognostication are capable of interpreting the thirty-two marks.[15] There are, however, other stories about encounters between the adult Buddha and future disciples in which the significance of the thirty-two marks is obvious even to ordinary people.[16] In these stories, the thirty-two marks function no longer as predictors of a future destiny, but rather as proof that this destiny has been fulfilled. Specifically, they serve as proof that Śākyamuni is a buddha. James R. Egge, who provides this comparative analysis, argues that in such instances the marks "produce immediate recognition of a buddha's greatness and elicit devotion to that buddha."[17] The Buddha's "physical splendor" thus serves as evidence of his "transcendent nature."[18] Egge, focusing on the Pāli literature of the Theravāda tradition, demonstrates that Buddhist narratives offer different interpretations of the significance of the thirty-two marks. Sometimes they indicate the Buddha's status as a great man with two possible futures before him. Sometimes they indicate his status as a buddha. In the Devadatta story, they signify buddhahood. King Ajātaśatru cannot declare Devadatta a buddha, because he does not look like a buddha. The thirty-two marks of a buddha are the karmic effect of countless lifetimes spent cultivating the qualities of a buddha.

A complete list of the thirty-two marks appears in a number of Sanskrit and Pāli works. The following list, translated by Paul J. Griffiths, comes from a Mahāyāna text called the *Bodhisattvabhūmi*:

> 1) A great person has firmly placed feet and walks evenly upon the ground. 2) Upon the soles of his feet there are thousand-spoked wheels with hubs and rims, complete in every aspect. 3) The great person has long fingers. 4) He has broad heels. 5) His hands and feet are soft and delicate. 6) His hands and feet are weblike. 7) His ankles are hidden. 8) His legs are like those of an antelope. 9) His body does not bend. 10) His penis is sheathed. 11) He is round, like a banyan tree. 12) He has a halo extending as far as his arms can reach. 13) His body hairs point upward. 14) His body hairs are separate; each separate hair grows in its own pore and is blue, curled, and turned to the right. 15) His skin is golden. 16) His skin is smooth; because of the smoothness, dust and dirt do not stick to his body. 17) His body has seven protuberances: two on his hands, two on his feet, two on his shoulders, and one on his neck. 18) The front of his body is like a lion. 19) His torso is well-rounded. 20) He has no hollow between his shoulders. 21) He is straight and tall. 22) He has forty

> even teeth. 23) His teeth have no spaces [between them]. 24) His teeth are very white. 25) His jaw is like a lion's. 26) His tongue is long and thin; because of the length of this tongue, when he sticks it out he covers his entire face up to the edge of his hair. 27) He has obtained an excellent sense of taste. 28) His voice is like Brahma's: it speaks as delightfully as a Kalaviṅka bird's. 29) His voice is like the sound of a magical drum. 30) His eyes are intensely blue, and his eyelashes are like a cow's. 31) His head is like a turban. 32) The hair growing between his eyebrows is white, soft, and turned to the right.[19]

Various lists of the thirty-two marks may differ in order and phraseology.[20] Additionally, the precise meaning of some of the marks has been debated by Buddhists, as is evidenced by commentaries in the Theravāda tradition.[21] The extent to which the thirty-two marks are represented in Buddhist iconography varies, but some of the most common ones are the imprint of the wheel on the soles of the feet or the palms of the hands, the webbed fingers, the turbanlike protuberance atop the head (*uṣṇīṣa*), and the tuft of hair growing between the eyebrows (*ūrṇā*).[22] The thirty-two marks are variously construed in Buddhist texts as the karmic effect of the cultivation of the six or ten perfections (*pāramitā*), the accumulation of merit (*puṇya-saṃbhāra*), or the performance of specific sets of deeds.[23] Frequently the thirty-two "major" marks of a great man are paired with a secondary set of eighty "minor" marks (*anuvyañjana*), which are largely physical in nature and, like the thirty-two marks, are also the karmic effect of past deeds.[24]

The *Compendium of Training* provides numerous examples of the widespread Buddhist fascination with the physical body of the Buddha. John S. Strong has argued that Buddhists have always been as interested in the "rupalogical" dimension of the Buddha as they have been in his "dharmalogical" dimension. In others words, both the physical body of the Buddha and his teachings matter to Buddhists.[25] In an extended quotation from the *Rāṣṭrapālasūtra*, the *Compendium of Training* praises the physical body of the Buddha, focusing particular attention on the thirty-two major and eighty minor marks. The passage praises the Buddha for the beauty of his golden-colored skin; the softness of his hair and nails; the magnificence of his turbanlike head; the brilliance of the tuft of hair between his eyebrows; the beauty of his lotuslike eyes; the length, shape, and hue of his tongue; the whiteness and evenness of his teeth; the shape of his calves; and the majesty of his gait.[26] We are told,

> Blessed One, your body [*kāya*] is covered with the marks [of a great man], your delicate skin resembles the color of gold. The world is

> never sated by gazing at your beautiful form [*rūpa*], you who bear an incomparably beautiful form.[27]

This passage celebrates the physical beauty of the Buddha, citing a number of the major and minor marks, including the golden-colored body. The passage also indicates that his physical qualities are inextricably linked to his affective and cognitive qualities, which are also celebrated in the same passage. For instance, when praising the lotuslike eyes of the Buddha, the verse also reminds us that these eyes gaze upon the world with compassion. When extolling the length, shape, and hue of the Buddha's tongue, the verse also proclaims the sweetness of his voice as he preaches the Dharma. His perfect teeth and smile are associated with his ability to discipline the world and also with the sweetness and truthfulness of his speech. His calves and gait are associated with a downcast gaze that is itself evidence of self-discipline. The passage describes a common meditation called the "recollection of the Buddha" (*buddhānusmṛti*). Recollecting the Buddha thus entails bringing to mind the full complex of his physical, affective, and cognitive qualities, all of which mark him as a buddha. For our purposes, the most important point is that the Buddha's body, no less than his heartmind, is the karmic effect of countless lifetimes of virtuous deeds.

Buddhas are no different from other living beings when it comes to the relationship between body and morality. All bodies, not just those of extraordinary beings, are the karmic effect of past deeds. According to Buddhism, the kind of body one has in any given lifetime is the direct result of one's karma. Good karma, or merit, produces superior bodies, and bad karma, or sin, produces inferior bodies. Additionally, these bodies, which are the effects of *past* deeds, often figure in Buddhist traditions as markers of *present* moral character. The Buddha's physical beauty is a sign of both past and present virtue; the same is often the case for the bodies of other living beings. For example, Steven Kemper provides the following insightful commentary on popular assumptions about the connection between body and morality in contemporary Sri Lanka:

> The most attractive monks, ones with reputations for great virtue or learning, are said to be *pin pāṭa*. Literally, they have the "color" or "look" of merit. They have accumulated such great amounts of merit that, like mastery over the self, their virtue shows itself in their appearance. Lay people are drawn to such monks because to be *pin pāṭa* is to be *saumya* (moonlike and, hence, beautiful). Certain physical traits are associated with being *pin pāṭa*. For a man to be so, he must be heavily set, if not slightly obese, his face must be smooth and full,

and his skin tone must be vital and light brown in color. In a word, he must look "healthy."[28]

Kemper notes that although Sri Lankans believe it is possible to have the "look of merit" without being virtuous in one's present life, most often it is assumed that good looks bespeak good character.[29]

Buddhist texts such as the *Compendium of Training* associate a wide range of bodily features with morality. These include one's realm of rebirth (*gati*)—that is, whether one is reborn as a god, human, demon (*asura*), animal, hungry ghost (*preta*), or hell being—beauty (including beauty of physical form, voice, and bodily scent), health, longevity, the absence or presence of physical or mental disability, sex, caste (*varṇa, jāti*), and family (*kula*). Recall that bodies are constituted *as particular types of bodies* by a combination of genetic (i.e., biological) and environmental factors. Thus the way a person dresses or carries himself or herself may also serve as a marker of moral character. The *Compendium of Training* devotes attention to features such as monastic dress, posture, and movement.

The close relationship between body and morality in Buddhist traditions means that we can speak of "virtuous bodies" and their opposite. Clearly the Buddha has the most virtuous body of all, but there are a range of virtuous bodies in Buddhist literature. What are the features of a virtuous body? To begin, a virtuous body is the body of a god or a human being. Demons (*asuras*) occupy a more ambiguous position in Buddhist literature. Sometimes they are grouped together with gods and, as such, represent a good rebirth; other times they are assigned a separate realm of rebirth, which can represent a good or bad rebirth, according to one's source. The *Compendium of Training* explicitly defines rebirth as an *asura* as the result of immoral deeds, and it groups *asuras* together with various other undesirable demonic rebirths, notably, *kumbhāṇḍas, yakṣas*, and *piśācas*.[30] Rebirth as an animal, hungry ghost, or hell being is unambiguously bad. Such rebirths are painful; more important, they afford little or no opportunity to engage in Buddhist practice whereby one might earn merit and improve one's karmic condition. Although divine rebirths are good rebirths, human rebirths are the best of all, because only humans can become buddhas, which is the end goal of bodhisattva practice. It is thought that gods simply have too much fun to give liberation much thought. Humans, on the other hand, experience the right mixture of suffering and happiness. Suffering motivates humans to seek liberation, but at the same time humans do not suffer so much that they become incapable of engaging in Buddhist practice.

Virtuous bodies are also marked by beauty of physical form, voice, and bodily scent, as well as health, longevity, and the absence of physical or mental disability.[31] For example, the *Compendium of Training* promises great karmic rewards for worshipping the Buddha, and among these are a good complexion (*varṇavant*), perfect looks (*rūpa-saṃpanna*), stamina (*sthāma*), strength (*bala*), a pleasing voice (*manojña-ghoṣa*), and protection from physical disability and illness.[32] The female bodhisattva Candrottarā, discussed in the previous chapter, possesses beauty of both physical form and bodily scent. Concerning the latter, a beautiful scent (*atigandha*) emanates from all her pores.[33] Conversely, the *Compendium of Training* warns that anyone who commits the sin of eating meat will stink (*durgandha*) in his or her next life.[34]

Buddhist literature often reflects a widespread belief that it takes more merit to be reborn as a man than as a woman. The *Compendium of Training* is no exception, routinely portraying female rebirth as unfortunate.[35] The *Compendium of Training* prescribes various rituals for women so that they can earn the merit to be reborn as men. For instance, it is recommended that they hear or preserve the names of various buddhas or bodhisattvas.[36] Bodhisattvas are also instructed to ritually dedicate their merit to women so that these women can be reborn as men.[37] The fact that female rebirth is less desirable than male rebirth does not mean that women never possess virtuous bodies. Candrottarā is clearly a case in point. Sex is but one of many physical features that mark virtuous bodies. Nevertheless, the *Compendium of Training* seems to accept the general view that male rebirth is a marker of superior virtue.

Sex is a complicated matter in the *Compendium of Training,* because South Asian religious and medical literature recognizes the existence of more than two sexes. There are non-normatively sexed persons, classified as neither male nor female, who exhibit a wide range of sexual practices, sexual dysfunctions, and anomalous anatomies. Terms for such persons vary. They may be called *ubhatovyañjana, paṇḍaka, ṣaṇḍa/ka, ṣaṇḍha/ka, ṣāṇḍya,* and *napuṃsaka.*[38] The precise meaning of each of these terms is often unclear. They designate a wide variety of perceived "sexual abberations."[39] According to Michael J. Sweet and Leonard Zwilling, non-normatively sexed persons include "individuals whom we might view as gay men, lesbians, bisexuals, and transvestites; the impotent; those with sexual dysfunctions other than impotence; those with sexual paraphilias or unconventional sexual behavior; and the sexually anomalous, anatomically or physiologically (for example, hermaphrodites)."[40] The fact that we find references to "female *paṇḍakas*" indicates that there can be both male and female *paṇḍakas,* who in various ways deviate from normative notions of maleness and/or femaleness.[41] Although some modern scholars have argued that the various terms for non-normative sex may serve, in part, as code words for homosexuality, Janet Gyatso cautions against such interpretations, arguing that in Buddhist literature non-normative sex has at least as much to do with "abnormal physical condition" as with "sexual practice."[42] In the *Compendium of Training* non-normatively sexed persons are called *ṣaṇḍaka, paṇḍaka, strīpaṇḍaka,* and *napuṃsaka.*[43] The *Compendium of Training* regards these sexes as bad rebirths. Such rebirths are explicitly characterized as the karmic effects of past sin. *Ṣaṇḍakas, paṇḍakas, strīpaṇḍakas,* and *napuṃsakas* do not have virtuous bodies in the *Compendium of Training* and its sources.

Virtuous bodies are also marked by social location, such as rebirth into wealthy families, royal families, and high castes. For example, the *Compendium of Training* prohibits eating meat, warning that those who do so will experience terrible rebirths, including rebirth in very low castes, namely, the *caṇḍāla, pukkasa,* and *ḍomba* castes.[44] Those who refrain from eating meat will experience excellent rebirths, including rebirth in the high caste of *brāhmaṇas* (priests), in families of yogins (i.e., dedicated religious practitioners), and as wise and wealthy persons.[45] Among the many positive karmic consequences of worshipping the Buddha are rebirth into the prosperous (*sphīta*) and wealthy (*āḍhya*) families of merchants (*śreṣṭhin*) and rebirth as a world-conquering king.[46] Many modern interpreters of Buddhism regard the historical Buddha as an egalitarian social reformer; they often point to passages in which the Buddha appears to repudiate the caste system. For instance, in the Pāli *Dhammapada,* the Buddha declares that one becomes a *brāhmaṇa* not by birth but only by practicing the Dharma.[47] Scholars have argued, however, that although the Buddha was critical of caste, he was not a social reformer. His efforts were directed at encouraging men and women to leave society for the monastic life rather than at reforming society itself.[48] Although passages such as those in the *Dhammapada* have inspired modern Buddhists to fight various forms of social hierarchy, including the caste system in India, premodern Buddhist literature indicates that social hierarchy was generally an accepted part of Buddhist life. This is evident in the fact that social location is frequently a physiomoral marker of worth.

Finally, various forms of bodily inscription such as dress, posture, and movement also serve as physiomoral markers of worth. This point is of particular relevance for consideration of monastic bodhisattva bodies, which are most obviously constituted as such by shaven head, monastic robes, and the absence of conventional forms of adornment such as jewelry. Additionally, monastic regulations place great emphasis on training in etiquette and deportment. The manner in which monastics dress or carry themselves is widely regarded to reflect a monastic's moral character. The virtuous bodies of monastic bodhisattvas display serene, graceful, and decorous features, postures, and movements.

The physiomoral discourse foregrounds the fact of bodily differences. The *Compendium of Training,* like other Buddhist texts, is filled with descriptions of bodies, virtuous and otherwise. These bodies are enormously diverse. For instance, they are not just male or female; they are also *ṣaṇḍaka, paṇḍaka, strīpaṇḍaka,* and *napuṃsaka.* Similarly, even the various realms of rebirth which produce gods, humans, demons, animals, and hell beings are further subdivided so that there is great diversity within each category. The focus on bodily differences is particularly pronounced in passages that predict the karmic consequences of actions. Recall from the previous chapter the karmic consequences of male lust for women: rebirth in hell, as hungry ghosts, as animals, as a variety of demons (*kumbhāṇḍas, yakṣas, asuras,* and *piśācas*); those reborn as humans will be one-eyed, lame, dumb (*vijihvaka*), ugly, blind from birth, deaf, or mentally disabled (*visaṃjña*); those reborn as animals will be dogs, swine, camels, donkeys, monkeys, elephants, horses, cows, tigers, moths, or flies.[49] Another equally negative list of the karmic consequences of sin includes the possibility of being reborn in every lifetime as either blind from birth, stupid (*jaḍa*), dumb (*ajihvaka*), an outcaste (*caṇḍāla*), a *ṣaṇḍaka* or *paṇḍaka,* a perpetual servant (*nityadāsa*), a woman, a dog, a swine, an ass, a camel, or a venomous snake.[50] Such detailed lists of the karmic consequences of good and bad deeds are quite common in Buddhist literature. Consequently, this literature presents us with an extraordinary range of bodies. Buddhist texts do not simply predict that good and bad deeds will produce generically good and bad rebirths. Instead they specify in precise detail the variety of body one can expect in the future. These bodies, construed as the effects of morality, serve as markers of both past and present moral character.

Bodies as the Conditions for Morality

Not only are bodies the effects of morality, they are also the conditions for particular kinds of moral agency. Let us return to the example of the Buddha. On the one hand, the Buddha's body, adorned with the thirty-two marks of a great man, is the karmic effect of lifetimes of virtuous deeds. On the other hand, he would have never become a buddha in the first place if he had not materialized the right kind of body at critical moments in his multilifetime career as a bodhisattva. For example, it is commonly assumed in Mainstream Buddhist traditions that bodhisattvas must attain male sex before they can become buddhas. Hence Theravāda Buddhist literature stipulates that bodhisattvas (Pāli: bodhisattas) cannot receive a prediction of future buddhahood until they meet eight conditions, one of which is male sex.[51] According to Mainstream Buddhist traditions, male sex is a critical condition for the attainment of buddhahood. Mahāyāna Buddhists debated whether male sex was a requisite condition for buddhahood. Consequently, their literature offers mixed and frequently ambiguous opinions on this issue.[52]

As bodhisattvas progress along the path to buddhahood their bodies are characterized as both the effects of past deeds and the conditions for continued progress toward buddhahood. According to Theravāda tradition, once bodhisattvas receive a prediction of future buddhahood, they are no longer subject to a set of eighteen unfavorable rebirths. These eighteen "impossible states" (*abhabbaṭṭhāna*) are largely physical in nature and include being born blind (*jaccandha*), deaf (*jaccabadhira*), insane (*ummataka*), deaf and dumb (*eḷamūga*), crippled (*pīṭhasappi*), with changeable sex (*liṅgaṃ parivattati*),[53] and as a leper (*kuṭṭhī*). A variant list of eighteen impossible states includes female rebirth as well as rebirth with non-normative sex (*ubhatobyañjanā, paṇḍakā*).[54] Most of the eighteen impossible states were traditionally characterized in Buddhist texts as hindrances to religious practice. Thus rebirth in one of these states would have made further progress toward buddhahood difficult, if not impossible. A similar assumption that bodhisattva bodies are both the effects of past deeds and the conditions for continued progress toward buddhahood is reflected in another Mainstream Buddhist text, the *Abhidharmakośabhāṣya*. According to this influential fourth- or fifth-century Indian scholastic text, a bodhisattva first receives the name "bodhisattva" when he begins to "cultivate actions which produce the [thirty-two] marks."[55] Long before the attainment of the thirty-two marks of a great man, however, bodhisattvas reap the karmic fruits of their actions by manifesting a variety of physical as well as affective and cognitive qualities, which are deemed critical to their progress toward buddhahood. We are told that once a bodhisattva begins to "cultivate actions which produce the [thirty-two] marks," he consistently attains favorable rebirths. Specifically, he attains good realms of rebirth (*sugati*), namely, human and divine; he is born into noble families (*kulaja*), namely, the wealthy families of *kṣatriyas* (royalty), *brāhmaṇas* (priests), and *gṛhapatis* (eminent householders);[56] he possesses all the organs (*avyakṣa*); he is male (*puṃs*) and never female or non-normatively sexed (*ṣaṇḍha*, etc.); he remembers his past lives (*jāti-smara*); and he does not desist (*anivṛt*), that is, he never turns back from the path to buddhahood.[57] Significantly, these qualities not only are the effects of good karma, they become, in turn, the conditions for further good karma and progress along the bodhisattva path. Good realms of rebirth, privileged families, the absence of mental or physical disability, male sex, along with the ability to remember past lives and steadfast commitment to the bodhisattva path, are all critical conditions for making further progress.

In Buddhist traditions bodies, as much as heartminds, can enable or disable particular kinds of moral agency. This is the case not only with bodhisattvas, but also with living beings more broadly. One very important example is that of monastics. Just as it takes a certain kind of body to become a buddha, it also takes a certain kind of body to become a monastic, since monastic regulations prohibit some individuals from ordination. These include those who "commit major crimes like murder, as well as those who lack permission from their parents or other masters, or who are fugitives from the law."[58] Additionally, certain physical criteria must be met. Candidates must be human and without any perceived physical deficiencies. Among those deemed physically deficient are "dwarfs, those missing a limb, the blind, the deaf, those with boils, or leprosy" and the non-normatively sexed.[59] Monastic regulations prohibit individuals with a range of physical and mental limitations from receiving ordination. The extent to which such prohibitions are enforced today varies. It is up to the ordination masters who perform the ceremony to determine whether or not a candidate is qualified. Ideally, decisions are based on pragmatic concerns rather than prejudice. Ordination masters must ascertain whether or not candidates are capable of handling the responsibilities of monastic life and whether or not their physical or mental condition would create an undue burden on their monastic communities.[60]

The very ability of all Buddhists—whether lay or monastic—to maintain any Buddhist moral discipline (*saṃvara*) is dependent in part on the nature of their bodies. According to the *Abhidharmakośabhāṣya*, only humans and gods are capable of maintaining the various moral disciplines enjoined upon living beings in different realms of the cosmos, including the lay and monastic vows followed by human beings (*prātimokṣa saṃvara*).[61] Living beings in all other realms of rebirth, referred to as the realms of painful rebirth (*apāyika*), cannot maintain any of these moral disciplines. Additionally, certain human beings are incapable of maintaining any of these moral disciplines. These are non-normatively sexed humans (called *ṣaṇḍha*, *paṇḍaka*, and *ubhayavyañjana*) and humans born in a continent to the north of the known world called Uttarakuru.[62] Paradoxically, these unfortunate beings are incapable of both *maintaining* and *breaking* these moral disciplines. They are altogether devoid of moral agency, whether for good or ill, when it comes to Buddhist moral disciplines. Why? They have the wrong kind of body. We are told: "Moreover, the very body [*āśraya*] of *ṣaṇḍhas*, *paṇḍakas*, *ubhayavyañjanas*, those living in Uttarakuru, and beings in painful realms of rebirth [*apāyika*] is similar to soil saturated with salt; where there is such a body, neither discipline [*saṃvara*] nor undiscipline [*asaṃvara*] grows, just as grain and weeds [do not grow] in great measure in a field saturated with salt."[63] Other Buddhist texts display a similarly negative assessment of the capacities of non-normatively sexed persons, in particular, to engage in Buddhist practice. Gyatso observes that monastic regulations may even prohibit such persons from making donations to begging monks; one Mahāyāna *sūtra* goes so far as to prohibit bodhisattvas from preaching to non-normatively sexed persons; and some texts claim that such persons are incapable of meditation.[64]

The *Compendium of Training* reflects a widespread Buddhist view that bodies not only are the effects of morality but also are the conditions for particular kinds of moral agency. Let us return to the text's prohibition on eating meat. The consequences are dire: Meat-eaters will be cooked (*pac-*) in the fires of terrible hells.[65] Additionally, they will be reborn into families of beasts of prey (literally, "eaters of raw flesh," *kravyāda*) or into the low-caste families of *caṇḍālas, pukkasas,* and *ḍombas;* they will be reborn with a foul smell (*durgandha*), despised (*kutsanīya*), insane (*unmatta*), or without shame (*nirlajja*); and they will be born of flesh-eating demonesses (*ḍākinī*), bears (*ṛkṣa*), and cats.[66] Significantly, these unfortunate rebirths are not just bad in their own right; they also create the conditions for further unfortunate rebirths. Born into families of beasts of prey, one has little choice but to eat raw flesh; the same can be said of those born of flesh-eating demonesses, bears, and cats; similarly those born into low castes are less likely to be prohibited from eating meat than those in high castes. Additionally, those who face social rejection, are insane, or are without shame will have a harder time earning merit than those with more favorable rebirths. Conversely, those who refrain from eating meat achieve rebirths conducive to earning merit. The *Compendium of Training* promises that vegetarians will be reborn into families of *brāhmaṇas* and yogins and that they will be wise and wealthy in their future rebirths.[67] Born into the families of *brāhamaṇas* and yogins, they are likely to remain vegetarian; born with wisdom and wealth, they are likely to continue to engage in acts of merit. It is important to note that wealth is regarded positively in Buddhist cultures because it affords one an opportunity to earn merit by making offerings to the monastic community. Hence when the *Compendium of Training* also promises that acts of worship will produce rebirths in the prosperous and wealthy families of merchants, as we saw above, it then predicts that such persons will become lords of generosity (*dānapati*).[68] Bodies, as much as heartminds, incline living beings to virtue or vice.

Bodies as the Conditions for the Ethical Transformation of Others

Buddhist texts frequently make reference to the transformative power the valorized bodies of buddhas, bodhisattvas, arhats, and monastics have on others. There is a story in the *Sinhala Thūpavaṃsa* about King Aśoka, the paradigmatic

Buddhist king who reigned in the third century B.C.E. in India.[69] This thirteenth-century Sri Lankan Sinhala Buddhist text of the Theravāda tradition recounts King Aśoka's conversion to Buddhism. According to the *Sinhala Thūpavaṃsa,* King Aśoka converted after seeing a young novice monk named Nigrōdha, who had attained nirvāṇa and was thus an arhat.[70] The text underscores the impeccable nature of Nigrōdha's deportment. His movements were graceful, his sense faculties were restrained, he walked with eyes downcast, he was properly dressed, and his mind appeared tranquil. Nigrōdha is described as possessed of "manifest virtue" (*pasak guṇa*).[71] His appearance caused a great stir as he entered the royal city. The very sight of him prompted all the people on the road to express their admiration for the Buddha's teaching and monastic community, since they had produced such a fine monk. Nigrōdha's appearance and deportment contrasted favorably with that of other religious figures who came to the king's palace for alms. For instance, these "heretics" seated themselves however they pleased, without any regard for distinctions between young and old. They ate, sat, and stood in an erratic fashion, causing the king to reflect, "There is no trace of virtue in the minds of mendicants like this."[72] Nigrōdha's physical appearance and deportment inspires King Aśoka and his retinue to convert to Buddhism. The king subsequently became a zealous patron of Buddhist institutions, supporting 60,000 monks and establishing 84,000 monasteries and relic shrines.[73]

The attractive features, postures, and movements of monastics figure prominently in a number of conversion narratives, a point Strong has also noted with reference to the *Catuṣpariṣatsūtra.*[74] According to this *sūtra,* the two chief disciples of Śākyamuni Buddha, Śāriputra and Maudgalyāyana, are first attracted to Buddhism when they see the physical effects Buddhist practice has on others. Śāriputra requests that the monk, Aśvajit, instruct him in the Dharma upon observing that Aśvajit's "way of moving and looking about, of wearing his robes and holding his bowl, was strikingly serene."[75] Some time later Maudgalyāyana requests a physically transformed Śāriputra to instruct him in the Dharma, asking, "Venerable One, your senses are serene, your face is at peace, and the complexion of your skin utterly pure. Did you reach the deathless state?"[76] These stories demonstrate that one of the reasons Buddhists place so much emphasis on bodies is that certain kinds of bodies, such as those of well-disciplined monastics, have positive moral effects on other living beings. Thus there are countless stories in Buddhist literature that describe the transformative effects of seeing buddhas, bodhisattvas, arhats, and monastics.

The *Compendium of Training* reflects a larger Buddhist interest in the beneficial effects certain kinds of bodies have on other living beings. It incorporates a physiomoral discourse on bodies into its own vision of the bodhisattva ideal, teaching bodhisattvas to cultivate virtuous bodies precisely because such bodies benefit other living beings. There are different kinds of bodhisattvas and thus different kinds of bodhisattva bodies. Here I focus largely on monastic bodhisattva bodies because these are especially important to the *Compendium of Training*, which advocates the renunciant bodhisattva lifestyle.

Critical to the formation of monastic bodies is training in etiquette and deportment. The serene, graceful, and decorous features, gestures, and movements of well-disciplined monastics do not necessarily come naturally or easily. The "spotless performance"[77] of monastics, to borrow a phrase from Steven Collins, is the product of careful training. Thus monastic regulations supply detailed instructions on etiquette and deportment (e.g., the *śaikṣa dharmas*). Witness, for instance, the numerous rules on etiquette and deportment in the Mahāsāṃghika and Mūlasarvāstivāda monastic regulations. I list but a few from the Mūlasarvāstivāda *Prātimokṣa*:

> We will not put on the robe raised too high. . . . We will not put on the robe too low. . . . We will go amongst the houses well restrained . . . [with the body] well covered . . . with little noise . . . looking at the ground. . . . We will not go amongst the houses jumping . . . with arms akimbo . . . shaking the body . . . shaking the head. . . . We will not sit down on a seat amidst the houses pulling up the feet . . . stretching out the feet . . . exposing the genitals. . . . We will not eat alms food in overly large mouthfuls. . . . We will not open the mouth when the morsel has not arrived. . . . We will not utter inarticulate speech with a morsel in the mouth. . . . We will not eat alms food stuffing the cheeks . . . making a smacking noise with the tongue.[78]

Unlike buddhas, who, as Griffiths argues, do not need to guard against breaches of etiquette, because they spontaneously do what is right,[79] monastics require careful and constant instruction in even the most basic rules of etiquette. Monastic regulations assume an imperfect monk or nun and make rules accordingly. We saw in the previous chapter that the *Compendium of Training* is no exception to this thoroughgoing realism, providing instructions on a wide range of matters of etiquette and deportment such as posture, tone of voice, and eating. Bodhisattvas are instructed to conduct themselves in such a manner that the mere site of them pleases (*prasad-*), attracts (*āvṛj-*), and ripens (*paripac-*) others.

The *Compendium of Training* is particularly insistent that bodhisattvas conduct themselves in such a manner that they generate pleasure (*prasāda*) rather than displeasure (*aprasāda*) in others.[80] *Prasāda* (Pāli: *pasāda*) is a highly prized emotion in Buddhism. I have translated the term as "pleasure," but this translation cannot do justice to its full range of meanings, which include pleasure, joy, satisfaction, clarity, brightness, purity, serenity, calmness, and faith.[81] Kevin Trainor argues that *prasāda* "cannot be reduced to either a quality of emotion or an intellectual state," but instead "embraces both cognitive and affective dimensions of consciousness."[82] It connotes "a calming and a clearing of consciousness, combined with a quality of joy or elation."[83] *Prasāda* is a complex cognitive and affective experience that "includes elements of joy, serenity, and confidence in the Buddha" or other object of Buddhist faith.[84] Trainor cites the research of Edith Ludowyk-Gyömröi, who maintains that *prasāda* "unites deep feeling, intellectual appreciation and satisfaction, clarification of thought and attraction towards the teacher."[85] The latter point is particularly significant for this study. Ludowyk-Gyömröi reminds us that *prasāda* is in part an expression of "aesthetic pleasure."[86] In Buddhist literature it is frequently the response living beings have to the sight of buddhas, bodhisattvas, arhats, or monastics. These beings, who, like Nigrōdha, are possessed of "manifest virtue," engender in others deep feelings of pleasure, joy, serenity, and confidence.

Andy Rotman has recently argued that certain objects such as buddhas, arhats, and *stūpas*, or shrines, are portrayed in Sanskrit Buddhist narrative literature as "agents of *prasāda*" (*prāsādika*). These objects exert an "overriding power" on individuals.[87] When individuals see an agent of *prasāda*, this emotion automatically arises in them.[88] The *Compendium of Training* represents a systematic attempt to transform monastics into "agents of *prasāda*" so that the sight of them will automatically engender pleasure in living beings. The ability of monastics to generate pleasure in others is critical to the ethical development of living beings. Buddhist literature commonly characterizes *prasāda* as an ethically transformative experience. For example, both Rotman and Trainor observe that in Sanskrit and Pāli literature, an experience of *prasāda* often manifests in a desire to perform ritual acts of worship (*pūjā*) or gift-giving (*dāna*).[89] These ritual acts earn individuals merit, thus procuring for them good rebirths. Performance of ritual acts also cultivates a karmic disposition to repeat such acts in the future. Thus even a single experience of *prasāda* can set in motion many lifetimes of virtuous deeds. This point is evident in the *Sinhala Thūpavaṃsa* account of King Aśoka's conversion. It is described as an experience of serene joy, or *prasāda* (Sinhala: *pähäda*).[90] The immediate cause of *prasāda* was the sight of the monk, Nigrōdha, particularly his impeccable deportment.[91] As a result of seeing Nigrōdha and experiencing *prasāda*, Aśoka became a lifelong patron of Buddhism.[92]

The *Compendium of Training* is fully aware of the ethically transformative nature of an experience of *prasāda*. It goes so far as to promise incalculable amounts of merit to anyone who feels *prasāda* in the presence of a bodhisattva committed to Mahāyāna Buddhism.[93] Merit, of course, manifests in physical as well as affective and cognitive ways; it produces virtuous bodies and virtuous heartminds. Thus encounters with the virtuous bodies of bodhisattvas materializes, in turn, other virtuous bodied beings. Bodies are, in the end, not just conditions for one's own ethical development but also conditions for the ethical development of others. The *Compendium of Training*'s focus on producing bodhisattvas with bodies capable of ripening others is part and parcel of a broader discourse in Buddhism on the physically and morally transformative effects of encounters with the bodies of valorized beings such as buddhas, bodhisattvas, arhats, and monastics.

What Are Virtues?

The close relationship between body and morality raises the question: What are virtues? Are these best described as affective and cognitive aspects of a person's psyche, or can virtues also be described as features, postures, and movements of a person's body? This study of the *Compendium of Training* suggests that virtues have both physical and moral dimensions. They are as evident in bodies as in heartminds.[94]

There are many virtues extolled in the *Compendium of Training*. Virtues are, as Lee Yearley, argues, "a group of related and relatively well-defined qualities that most individuals in a group think reflect admirable characteristics," although "the exact boundaries of the category always will be a matter of dispute."[95] There is no exact or exclusive equivalent in Sanskrit to the Greek *aretē* or Latin *virtus*, which we translate into English as "virtue." Instead Buddhist Sanskrit texts such as the *Compendium of Training* make use of quite a number of different terms, each with slightly different connotations, referring to qualities (*guṇa, dharma*), physical characteristics or attributes (*lakṣaṇa*), merit (*puṇya*), and morality (*śīla*). The *Compendium of Training* seeks to cultivate a broad range of virtues in bodhisattvas. Often these are codified in lists, such as the perfections (*pāramitā*), the moral precepts (*śikṣāpada*), and the path of the ten meritorious deeds (*daśakuśalakarmapatha*); we also find discussions of numerous particular virtues, including generosity (*dāna*), compassion (*karuṇā*), benevolence (*maitrī*), faith (*śraddhā*), respect (*ādara, gaurava*), humility (*nirmāna*), mindfulness (*smṛti*), awareness (*saṃprajanya*), wisdom (*prajñā*), celibacy (*brahmacarya*), fear (*bhaya*), and shame (*lajjā*), to name but a few that appear in the text.[96]

Although an exhaustive analysis of these virtues is beyond the scope of this study, attention to even a few will serve to demonstrate that virtues have a marked physical, as well as affective and cognitive, dimension. Let us begin with two virtues that are commonly paired in Buddhist traditions: mindfulness (*smṛti*) and awareness (*saṃprajanya*). These virtues are defined in a variety of ways in the *Compendium of Training*. Broadly speaking, they consist of careful and sustained attention to one's actions of body, speech, and heartmind, along with a similar attention to the consequences of these actions. The *Compendium of Training*, like so many Buddhist texts, assumes that all actions originate in heartmind. Good feelings and thoughts give rise to good actions; bad feelings and thoughts give rise to bad actions. Thus the *Compendium of Training* argues that heartmind is the actual locus of virtue (*guṇa*) and vice (*doṣa*).[97] One of the primary purposes of cultivating mindfulness and awareness is to focus attention on the condition of heartmind in order to direct it away from vice and toward virtue. Accordingly, the *Compendium of Training* concludes in the midst of its discussion of mindfulness and awareness that bodhisattva training consists solely in the preparation of heartmind (*citta-parikarma*).[98]

On the surface, these remarks might suggest that virtues are primarily affective and cognitive dimensions of persons. After all, heartmind is the locus of these. But interestingly, the text's discussion of mindfulness and awareness occurs at the outset of chapter 6, the same chapter that focuses on monastic etiquette and deportment. Immediately following the statement that bodhisattva training consists solely in the preparation of heartmind, we learn that the person who has mindfulness and awareness generates pleasure (*prasāda*) in others.[99] Here begin the instructions on etiquette and deportment. Mindfulness and awareness manifest in the serene, graceful, and decorous features, gestures, and movements of well-disciplined monastics. They are, among other things, a way of walking, talking, or eating. By cultivating mindfulness and awareness, bodhisattvas produce disciplined bodies as well as disciplined heartminds, turning both into instruments of the ethical transformation of self and other.

The *Compendium of Training*'s discussion of mindfulness and awareness blurs the distinction between body and morality, indicating that certain bodily features, postures, and movements constitute virtues in and of themselves. This is the case for other virtues as well. For instance, chapter 2 of the text admonishes bodhisattvas to cultivate affection (*prema*) and intense (*tīvra*) respect (*gaurava*) for their beautiful friends (*kalyāṇamitra*), that is, their teachers. The exemplar of such affection and intense respect is a bodhisattva named Sudhana, who was mentioned in chapter 2 of this book. What are the virtues of affection and intense respect? Clearly, these refer to particular affective and cognitive states. But they also refer to particular physical states.

Sudhana's affection and intense respect require that he engage in physical acts of worship and respect such as bowing, prostrating, and circumambulating his beautiful friend. These physical acts, no less than his feelings and thoughts, make Sudhana an exemplar of the virtues of affection and intense respect. The story of Sudhana also raises questions about how to define the virtue of wisdom. As we saw in chapter 2, there is a physical dimension to omniscience. We are told that "beholding the omniscience come to his beautiful friend," Sudhana departs from his presence, weeping with tears running down his face.[100] Omniscience is visible in the very features of the beautiful friend's body. Other virtues, such as generosity, humility, and celibacy, also clearly have a physical dimension. The gift par excellence is the gift of one's own body; humility manifests in gestures of respect; celibacy is a physical as well as moral state. In various ways we see a marked physical dimension to virtues.

The *Compendium of Training* makes no absolute distinction between the physical and moral dimensions of living beings. This is not to say that there is always a perfect isomorphism between body and morality in the *Compendium of Training*, or in Buddhist literature in general. There are a few passages in the *Compendium of Training* that reveal a disjunction between body and morality. For instance, one passage describes an immoral monk who nevertheless is still called a beautiful friend because his monastic appearance and comportment have a positive ethical effect on others. We are told that even the sight of this immoral monk inspires living beings to virtuous deeds and helps them attain a good rebirth.[101] Strong has also discussed the figure of Upagupta, who appears in Buddhist Sanskrit literature as a "Buddha without the marks" (*alakṣaṇaka-buddha*), that is, a buddha without the thirty-two major and eighty minor marks of a great man.[102] Significantly, disjunctions between body and morality often require comment in Buddhist literature, a fact suggesting that this literature assumes that a conjunction of the two is more commonly the norm. The *Compendium of Training* is thus obligated to explain why an immoral monk should still be treated with respect. In doing so, it insists that what matters here is body, not morality. Bodies play such an important role in the ethical transformation of other living beings that even the body of an immoral monk is valued.

Buddhist texts such as the *Compendium of Training* display a pervasive assumption that body and morality are interrelated. It is, however, all too easy to overlook the presence of a physiomoral discourse in Buddhist literature.[103] Such discourse frequently operates at the level of an implicit assumption rather than an explicit discourse in Buddhist texts. The Devadatta story is a case in point. The story makes sense only if readers understand that the

Buddha's body is the karmic effect of past moral deeds. Nowhere, however, does the story contain any explicit discourse on the relationship between body and morality. As is often the case in narrative literature, the relationship is assumed but never explicitly articulated. Similarly, the *Sinhala Thūpavaṃsa* assumes, but never explicitly articulates, a close relationship between body and morality when it contrasts the appearance and deportment of the heretics with that of the arhat Nigrōdha. The close link between body and morality in Buddhist literature becomes apparent only if one pays careful attention to narrative details such as the physical descriptions of good and bad characters or the ways in which living beings respond to these characters.

Another reason that it is easy to overlook the physiomoral discourse is the fact that there *are* explicit discourses on both ethics and body in Buddhism that suggest, at least on initial reading, that Buddhists were not very interested in bodies. For example, as was discussed in chapter 1 of this book, the emphasis on intention (*cetanā*), or "moral psychology,"[104] in Buddhist traditions has contributed to the scholarly privileging of heartmind at the expense of body in studies of Buddhist ethics. Additionally, body comes explicitly into focus in an ascetic discourse that represents all bodies—even those of buddhas—as impermanent, foul, and without intrinsic and eternal essence. The ascetic discourse on bodies has led some scholars to assume that Buddhists ascribed little value to bodies, a point I dispute in the next chapter. Finally, there is a scholastic discourse in Pāli Abhidhamma literature that defines *rūpa*—a word variously translated as "body," "corporeality," "matter," and "form"—as morally indeterminate (Pāli: *avyākata*).[105] This might suggest that bodies themselves are morally neutral and thus not connected to morality. Yet the Abhidhamma discourse on *rūpa* is framed by narrative elements that indicate that the Buddha's physical state is inextricably related to his moral state. For example, the *Atthasālinī* informs us that after the Buddha contemplated the last of the seven Abhidhamma texts, his body was physically transformed. Multicolored rays shot out of his body, lighting up the universe. Additionally: "But the blood of the Lord of the world became clear as he contemplated such an exquisite and subtle Dhamma. His material form [*vatthu-rūpa*] became clear. His complexion became clear."[106] The Buddha's physical transformation is clearly linked to his moral and spiritual transformation, a phenomenon suggesting that even the Pāli Abhidhamma literature displays aspects of a physiomoral discourse on bodies.

Finally, the physiomoral discourse may also be easy to overlook because until recently modern Western ethicists have tended to ground their moral theories in notions of reason, logic, or will, emphasizing mind at the expense of both bodies and emotions. In the last few decades, however, there has been an explosion of research on bodies across academic disciplines, leading to a widespread reevaluation of such modern Western intellectual prejudices. The *Compendium of Training*, which foregrounds the roles bodies play in bodhisattva practice, offers us an opportunity to rethink how we conceptualize the field of ethics in general, and Buddhist ethics in particular. The text, which assumes body and morality are closely related, seeks to produce both virtuous bodies and virtuous heartminds. And just as virtuous heartminds have an ethically beneficial effect on others, so too do virtuous bodies. In this text bodhisattva bodies become, in the end, virtues in and of themselves, because bodhisattvas use their bodies to change other living beings for the better.

The next chapter examines the ascetic discourse on bodies. Physiomoral and ascetic discourses on bodies co-exist in this text. The former ascribes to bodies an important role in the ethical development of self and other, and the latter seemingly dismisses bodies altogether. The challenge of the next chapter is to understand how and why the *Compendium of Training* draws on diverse kinds of body discourse in its efforts to cultivate bodhisattvas with bodies that ripen others.

5

Foul Bodies

An Ascetic Discourse on Bodies

Since life is unstable and outside one's control like an illusion or a dream, the fools who cling to this thoroughly putrid body commit terribly violent deeds, overcome by delusion. When these idiots die they end up in horrific hells.[1]

Blessed One, your body [*kāya*] is covered with the marks [of a great man], your delicate skin resembles the color of gold. The world is never sated by gazing at your beautiful form [*rūpa*], you who bear an incomparably beautiful form.[2]

Side by side in the *Compendium of Training* we find both negative and positive statements about bodies. The two quotations at the start of this chapter are a case in point. The first quotation characterizes bodies as putrid and warns that attachment to such bodies will lead to immoral deeds and bad rebirths. The second quotation characterizes the Buddha's body as irresistibly beautiful and offers no warnings about attachment. Indeed, as we will see, attachment to the Buddha's body can have profoundly positive effects. How do we make sense of these very different perspectives on bodies? In order to answer this question, we will need to examine the relationship between two distinct kinds of body discourse in the *Compendium of Training*: the ascetic and physiomoral discourses. According to the ascetic discourse, all bodies—even that of the Buddha—are impermanent, foul, and without any intrinsic or eternal essence. According to the physiomoral discourse, some bodies—such as that of the Buddha—have beneficial effects on others. The presence of seemingly contradictory body discourses in a single text is not uncommon in Buddhist literature. In order to place the *Compendium of Training* in a broader context, I begin with a well-known story in the Theravāda Buddhist Pāli canon.

A monk named Vakkali was a disciple of the historical Buddha.[3] Vakkali is gravely ill and therefore sends for the Buddha. When the Buddha asks Vakkali what he wants, Vakkali says, "For a long time, lord, I have been longing to set eyes on the Blessed One, but I had not strength enough in this body to come to see the Blessed One."[4] The Buddha reprimands him, saying, "Enough, Vakkali! What good is the sight of this putrid body [*pūti-kāya*] to you? The one, Vakkali, who sees the Dhamma [i.e., Buddhist teachings] sees me; the one who sees me sees the Dhamma."[5] The Buddha then delivers a very brief sermon on impermanence. He reminds Vakkali that all living beings are nothing but a collection of five impermanent aggregates (Pāli: *khandha*, Sanskrit: *skandha*)—body, feelings, perceptions, habitual mental dispositions, and consciousness. Hence all living beings are destined for death and decay. The Buddha closes by informing Vakkali that whoever understands the impermanence of the five aggregates will attain nirvāṇa. Vakkali never recovers from his illness. Consequently he resolves to attain nirvāṇa and, having done so, to commit suicide. Vakkali sends word to the Buddha that he understands the impermanence of the five aggregates and thus no longer harbors any attachments. He stabs himself with a knife, dies, and is fully liberated (*parinibbuto*) from this world.[6]

The Vakkali story seems to suggest that the Buddha's body is not worthy of attention because, like all bodies, it is foul and impermanent. Trainor has reminded scholars, however, that there is more than one version of the Vakkali story. In another version, we get a very different perspective on the Buddha's body.[7] In this version Vakkali sees the Buddha enter the city to receive alms, is immediately struck by the Buddha's physical beauty (*sarīra-sampatti*), and decides to become a monk so that he can dwell in the presence of that beauty. The Buddha, however, scolds Vakkali for spending so much time looking at him, saying, "Vakkali, what good is the sight of this putrid body [*pūti-kāya*] to you? The one, Vakkali, who sees the Dhamma sees me."[8] As in the first version of the story, Vakkali is told to shift his attention from the Buddha to the Dhamma, that is, from the teacher to the teaching. In fact in this version, the Buddha is so concerned over Vakkali's misplaced attention that he insists on a period of separation between the two of them. For the duration of the rainy season retreat, the two are to dwell in separate monastic establishments. Before they part, the Buddha teaches Vakkali about the impermanence of the five aggregates. Shortly thereafter Vakkali resolves to commit suicide, but for very different reasons than in the first version of this story. He wishes to do so because he cannot bear to live apart from the Buddha. As he is about to leap off a cliff to his death, the omniscient Buddha miraculously projects an image of himself in front of Vakkali, causing him intense joy and delight (*balava-pīti-pāmojja*). The Buddha stretches out his hand and says,

> Come, Vakkali! fear not, as you look upon the Tathāgata [i.e., the Buddha].
> I will lift you up, even as one extricates an elephant that has sunk in the mire.[9]

Vakkali leaps into the air so that he is face to face with the image of the Buddha. At that moment he suppresses his strong emotions and attains nirvāṇa. He thereby gains supernormal powers and, instead of crashing to his death, lands safely on the ground and lives to serve as an exemplar of faith for the monastic community.

Both versions of the Vakkali story tell us that the Buddha's body, like all bodies, is foul and impermanent, but the second version also tells us something else. It tells us that the sight of the Buddha's body is potentially salvific. Although Vakkali is admonished to focus on the Dhamma instead of on the Buddha, a vision of the Buddha accomplishes what the Dhamma did not: it liberates Vakkali. In the end, it is a vision of the beauty, rather than foulness and impermanence, of the Buddha's body that liberates Vakkali.[10]

The Vakkali story presents us with different body discourses. Most obviously, we find an ascetic discourse, which characterizes all bodies, no matter how virtuous, as impermanent, foul, and without any intrinsic and eternal essence. From an ascetic perspective, even the Buddha's body is putrid. Less obviously, we find a physiomoral discourse, which posits a close relationship between body and morality. From a physiomoral perspective, the Buddha's body is the most virtuous body of all and thus has profoundly transformative effects on other living beings. Whereas the first version offers only an ascetic perspective, the second version offers both ascetic and physiomoral perspectives. The second version tells us that the Buddha's body is foul and impermanent; it also tells us that Vakkali is liberated by the sight of this same body. Strikingly, even a single text may display more than one kind of body discourse.

To date, the ascetic discourse on bodies has received far more scholarly attention than the physiomoral discourse. This emphasis is due, in part, to the fact that the ascetic discourse is often the more obvious body discourse in Buddhist literature. The Vakkali story tells us point-blank that the Buddha's body is foul and impermanent. It would be hard to overlook the ascetic discourse in this story. It is, however, possible to overlook the physiomoral discourse, because it is never explicitly articulated. Nowhere are we told that body and morality are interrelated, that the Buddha's body is thus the material effect and visible marker of his buddhahood, and that therefore his body has transformative effects on those that see him. These facts become evident only when we pay careful attention to the narrative details of the story. Thus scholars are more likely to note the story's explicitly negative statements about the Buddha's body than they are to note its implicitly positive statements about that same body.[11]

Readers of Buddhist literature have sometimes assumed that the presence of an ascetic discourse therein indicates that Buddhists had little regard for bodies. This assumption is problematic for a number of reasons. First, there is more than one kind of body discourse in Buddhist literature. Second, an ascetic discourse on bodies hardly bespeaks a lack of interest in bodies. To the contrary, it demonstrates that Buddhists were extremely preoccupied with bodies. Scholars of diverse religious traditions have argued in recent years that ascetics were far more interested in bodies than scholars had heretofore recognized.[12] For example, Caroline Walker Bynum has studied the fasting practices of female saints in medieval Christian Europe. Some of these saints refused to eat anything other than the eucharist. Bynum disproves the common assumption that extreme forms of fasting represent a repudiation of body. To the contrary, medieval female saints fasted because they wanted to experience the full "possibilities of the flesh."[13] By fasting, these women identified with the suffering of Christ. By eating Christ's body in the form of the eucharist, they transformed their own bodies into his suffering body:

> Because Jesus had fed the faithful not merely as servant and waiter, preparer and multiplier of loaves and fishes, but as the very bread and wine itself, *to eat* was a powerful verb. It meant to consume, to assimilate, to become God. To eat God in the eucharist was a kind of audacious deification, a becoming of the flesh that, in its agony, fed and saved the world.[14]

Thus Bynum argues that medieval female saints "were not rebelling against or torturing their flesh out of guilt over its capabilities so much as using the possibilities of its full sensual and affective range to soar ever closer to God."[15]

Ascetic practices are powerful technologies of the self whose aim is the transformation of bodied being. Bodies function in ascetic practice as both the means and objects of transformation. Medieval Christian female saints used their bodies to transform both body and soul in the hopes of transforming others in turn. Similarly, the *Compendium of Training* enjoins a range of practices on its bodhisattvas in order to produce bodied beings capable of transforming others. The *Compendium of Training*'s ascetic discourse on bodies consists in large part of meditations and philosophical reflections on the unsatisfactory nature of bodies. Bodhisattvas are instructed to meditate and reflect that bodies are foul, impermanent, and without intrinsic and eternal essence. According to the *Compendium of Training*, bodhisattvas ideally should do so in the solitude of a wilderness retreat.[16] The *Compendium of Training*, however, also makes provision for such practice in more urban monastic settings, arguing that one should live as if one were in the solitude of the wilderness wherever one is.[17] The purpose of these meditations and philosophical reflections is the elimination of desire for sensual pleasures (*kāma*) and the eradication of the defilements of lust (*rāga*), anger (*dveṣa*), and delusion (*moha*), which give rise to various kinds of desires in the first place. Given the male monastic orientation of the *Compendium of Training*, it should come as no surprise that male sexual desire for women receives particular attention. Of all desires, male lust for women is most frequently the target of attack. Thus a key aim of the ascetic discourse on bodies is the production of celibate male monastics.

Celibacy is a physical and moral condition. The text's ascetic discourse does not represent a repudiation of bodies. Instead its prescribed meditations and philosophical reflections on the unsatisfactory nature of bodies are Buddhist technologies of the self that, like vow-making, are intended to produce bodhisattvas with virtuous bodies as well as virtuous heartminds. The central goal of this chapter is to demonstrate that, in spite of their differences, the ascetic and physiomoral discourses on bodies share the same end: producing bodhisattvas with bodies capable of ripening others. These are the bodies of well-disciplined monastics whose very features, postures, and movements instantiate for others their moral achievement. Eventually, if these bodhisattvas reach the end of their path, they too will materialize the most virtuous body of all, namely, that of a buddha. We saw in the last chapter that the physiomoral discourse on bodies is ubiquitous in Buddhist literature. This is likewise the case for the ascetic discourse. Thus this chapter also affords an opportunity to reevaluate the significance of the ascetic discourse in Buddhist literature more broadly by challenging the common assumption that it bespeaks a Buddhist repudiation of bodies.

Ascetic Discourse on Bodies

The ascetic discourse on bodies attempts to weaken attachment to sensual pleasures such as sex by teaching bodhisattvas to experience their bodies, and sometimes especially the bodies of women, as impermanent, foul, and without intrinsic and eternal essence. Before we can examine the text's meditations and philosophical reflections on bodies, we need to understand why the ascetic discourse characterizes the desire for sensual pleasures as being so problematic. Sensual pleasures are dangerous because they bind living beings to saṃsāra, or the cycle of rebirth, which is characterized as endless suffering. Additionally, sensual pleasures are especially dangerous because desire for self-gratification can cloud moral judgment and lead to sinful deeds with terrible karmic consequences, making saṃsāric existence even worse than it might otherwise be. For bodhisattvas, attachment to sensual pleasures is even more problematic, because the desire for self-gratification can conflict with their vow to dedicate all their lifetimes to the well-being of others. Bodhisattvas must be able to put the needs and wishes of others ahead of their own. Thus bodhisattvas engage in ascetic meditations and reflections on bodies in order to render themselves better able to care for others.

Ascetic meditations and philosophical reflections on bodies take many different forms. Let me begin with those that focus on the impermanence of bodies and bodied beings. One of the most basic teachings of Buddhism is that everything, including bodied being, is by nature impermanent. Consequently, attachment to oneself or any other person, object, or experience is destined to cause suffering, since none of these will last forever. Critical to the attainment of liberation is the experiential realization of the impermanence of all phenomena and the attendant cultivation of detachment from these. The *Compendium of Training* regards attachment to one's own bodied being as the strongest of attachments. It attempts to weaken self-attachment and the accompanying desire for self-gratification by repeatedly reminding bodhisattvas of the impermanence of their bodied beings. In one striking passage quoted from another source, the text addresses a lay Buddhist king. The king is warned to contemplate his impermanence because no amount of wealth or power will prevent the inevitable pain, death, and decay of his bodied being. He must reflect as follows: Although his bodied being (*ātmabhāva*) has long been fed with the choicest of foods, at death his bodied being will be overcome with hunger and thirst. Although he is dressed in the finest of garments, at death they will be soaked and stained with sweat. Although his bodied being has been bathed and scented with the best of perfumes, at death this bodied being will quickly start to stink. Even though he is entertained by women skilled in music, at death he will experience nothing but suffering. Once comfortably and safely housed, at death his bodied being will lie in a cemetery filled with animals and corpses. Left there by loved ones, it will be eaten by crows, vultures, dogs, jackals, and the like. Battered by the elements, his bones will scatter and rot.[18]

Another meditational technique for combating attachment to self-gratification is meditation on the foulness of bodies (*aśubhabhāvanā*). Let us recall that in the Vakkali story the Buddha characterizes his body and, by extension, all bodies as both putrid and impermanent. He offers a similarly negative evaluation of bodies in this passage quoted in the *Compendium of Training*:

> Surely this body [*kāya*] poses great danger [*bahvādīnava*]. It is a frame of bones, bound together by sinews, smeared with flesh, covered up by the dermis, encased in the epidermis, full of breaches and holes, swarming with a mass of worms, harmful to living beings, and a dwelling for the defilements and karma. Various illnesses arise in this body [*kāya*], namely, eye disease, ear disease *and so on until* piles, boils, and fistulas.... There are bodily aches and bodily pains. The body [*kāya*] ages, falls apart, grows crooked, becomes bald, gray, and full of wrinkles. The sense faculties mature and decay. The components of a bodied being [*saṃskāras*] grow old and worn out. *And so on until* you must not cater in this way to this leaky, oozing, disgusting body [*kāya*].... Monk, why are you restless for sensual pleasures? Who seduces you? How have you become obsessed, infatuated, attached, and fallen into attachment? When I have attained final liberation [*parinirvāṇa*] and the true Dharma has disappeared, you, having pursued sensual pleasures, will fall into a disastrous rebirth [*vinipāta*]. When will you free yourself from old age and death? Enough, monk! Keep your mind off of sensual pleasures. This is not the time for pursuing sensual pleasures. This is the time for pursuing the Dharma.[19]

Meditation on the foulness of bodies often entails, as it does in this passage, contemplation of the various disgusting features that comprise bodies. The point is to learn to see bodies as both foul and impermanent, with particular emphasis placed on their foulness. Frequently practitioners contemplate a standardized list of thirty-one or thirty-two repulsive body parts, but the length of lists can vary.[20] For instance, at one point the *Compendium of Training* provides the following abbreviated list of repulsive body parts: head hairs, body hairs, nails, teeth, bones, skin, flesh, marrow, sinews, fat, grease, synovia, liver, urine, excrement, stomach, blood, phlegm, bile, pus, snot, and brain.[21] Meditation on the foulness of bodies may also involve contemplating corpses in varying stages of decay. A bodhisattva must reflect, while he observes a corpse, that his own body has the same nature as that of the corpse and will suffer the same fate.[22]

The *Compendium of Training* reflects a widespread belief that meditation on the foulness of bodies is especially useful for eradicating the defilement of lust. Living beings can, of course, lust after a range of sensual pleasures, but meditation on the foulness of bodies is specifically intended for eradicating sexual desire. Given the *Compendium of Training*'s male heterosexual orientation, it tends to define lust narrowly as male sexual desire for women. Thus it declares that women, represented in idealized form as a figure called the *janapada-kalyāṇī*, or most beautiful woman in the country, are the primary cause of lust.[23] Although all bodies, including one's own, are appropriate subjects for a meditation on the foulness of bodies, Liz Wilson demonstrates that South Asian monks often meditated on the foulness of women's bodies in particular.[24] By learning how to see women's bodies as nothing but a collection of repulsive body parts, "what attracts is easily resolved into what repels."[25] One passage in the *Compendium of Training* mocks men who lust after women, likening them to flies speeding toward an open wound, donkeys chasing after dirt, and dogs searching for meat in a slaughterhouse.[26] Such men are attracted to women like crows to carrion, and worms to a pile of excrement.[27] After a graphic description of the foulness of bodies, the passage concludes as follows: "The buddhas say that women stink like excrement. Therefore a base man maintains contact with base women. He, who grabs a bag of excrement, enters the dwelling of a fool. He earns fruit [i.e., karma] in accordance with his actions."[28]

If such statements are deeply shocking to a modern audience, we should bear in mind that they were also shocking to a medieval audience. That, in fact, is the point of such statements. They were intended to evoke strong feelings of shock, agitation, and fear, known in Sanskrit as *saṃvega*. *Saṃvega* arises when the truth of Buddhist teachings finally hits home and becomes personally relevant. In the context of an ascetic discourse on bodies, it is the moment when a person realizes, perhaps for the first time, the truly unsatisfactory nature of bodied being. Wilson thus aptly characterizes *saṃvega* as an "aha experience" which enables a person to see the world "through the eyes of a renouncer."[29] The *Compendium of Training* uses meditations on the foulness of bodies to shock bodhisattvas out of their attachment to sensual pleasures, especially sex. Male bodhisattvas have the option of meditating upon the foulness of their own bodies or the foulness of women's bodies. No provision is made in the *Compendium of Training*, however, for female bodhisattvas to meditate on the foulness of men's bodies. Such meditations are rare in Buddhist literature, although not unknown.[30]

The *Compendium of Training* goes to great lengths to undermine the conventional view that women's bodies are desirable. It characterizes women as disgusting, dangerous, and the source of all men's suffering. This is particularly the case in chapter 4 of the text, which contains the most flagrantly misogynist passages of the entire book, including the one just quoted above. For instance, that chapter quotes at length from the *Saddharmasmṛtyupasthāna*, which describes the hellish torments awaiting men who engage in sexual misconduct, the exact nature of which is left unspecified except that it involves women. Men who engage in sexual misconduct with women are reborn in hells inhabited by women with flaming bodies made of iron and diamonds. Consumed with lust, the men chase after the women. The women eat them alive or crush them to death, whereupon the men spring back to life and the whole cycle repeats over and over.[31] Of particular note is the way in which the quoted passage blames women for male sexual misconduct. The passage states at the outset that these female hell beings are actually nothing but the products of male karma. Thus initially we are led to believe that the men are responsible for their own suffering. Yet at the end of the passage, this point is seemingly forgotten when the passage proclaims,

> Women are in every way the root cause of bad realms of rebirth and the destruction of wealth. So how could men who are controlled by women be happy? . . . *And so on until*: Women are the epitome of all destruction here in this world and in the next. Therefore women should be avoided if one desires happiness for oneself.[32]

Women, in fact, are so dangerous that even lay bodhisattvas are counseled to regard their own wives as foul (*aśubha*), reflecting that they are suitable companions for sex (*rati-krīḍā*), but not for the life to come; for food and drink, but not for experiencing the ripening of karma; they are good companions in times of happiness, but not in times of suffering. Wives should be regarded as obstacles to morality, meditation, and wisdom—indeed as thieves, murderers (*badhaka*), and guardians of hell.[33]

Alan Sponberg rightly characterizes such passages as examples of "ascetic misogyny," since they lay all the blame for sexual desire on women.[34] Buddhists were not alone in South Asia in portraying women as uniformly dangerous to male celibacy. Patrick Olivelle has observed a "deep-seated fear and hatred of women, a veritable gynephobia" in some of the Hindu Upaniṣads.[35] The *Compendium of Training* displays a fairly widespread male ascetic fear of women. It prescribes a variety of meditations and philosophical reflections on bodies to eliminate the desire for sensual pleasures and to eradicate the defilements. Of all pleasures and defilements, however, sexual desire for women receives the greatest degree of attention, indicating that a key concern of the ascetic discourse is producing celibate male monastics.

Countering the False Belief That Bodied Being Possesses an Intrinsic and Eternal Essence

Along with learning to regard bodies as impermanent and foul, bodhisattvas must also learn to regard bodies as devoid of any intrinsic and eternal essence such as an eternal self or soul (*ātman*). Such contemplation entails a more sophisticated level of philosophical reflection on the impermanence of bodied being. Contrary to many religious teachers of his day, the historical Buddha denied the existence of an eternal self or soul (*ātman*). He did so because the concept of an eternal self or soul implies in South Asian religious and philosophical traditions the "idea of a self as separate from the process of phenomenal experience."[36] A classic example of the belief in an eternal self or soul occurs in the Hindu *Bhagavadgītā*. The god Krishna urges the warrior Arjuna to fight even though circumstances have pitted him against his own relatives, teachers, and friends. Arjuna hesitates to fight because he does not wish to cause harm to those dear to him. Krishna teaches Arjuna that all living beings possess an intrinsic and eternal essence called a self or soul (*ātman*). That self or soul can never be harmed or in any way affected by the phenomenal world. It remains untouched and unchanged by any events we might experience:

> Weapons do not cut it,
> fire does not burn it,
> waters do not wet it,
> wind does not wither it.
>
> It cannot be cut or burned;
> it cannot be wet or withered;
> it is enduring, all-pervasive,
> fixed, immovable, and timeless.[37]

The self or soul is eternal precisely because it never changes. The Buddha, however, dismissed the idea that living beings possess an unchanging, intrinsic, and eternal essence. Whether we examine body, feelings, or thoughts, nothing remains the same from one moment to the next. What then accounts for reincarnation? Buddhists have answered this question in different ways. One normative answer in India was that consciousness transmigrates. Consciousness, however, is not the same as an eternal self or soul, because consciousness is always changing in response to experience, including the ripening of karma. Buddhists thus posit a continuity of being from life to life without positing the existence of an eternal self or soul.[38]

Buddhists have articulated their rejection of a belief in an intrinsic and eternal essence in a variety of ways, employing a diverse and complex technical vocabulary to do so. For instance, Buddhists might say that bodied beings are "empty" (*śūnya*) of self or soul (*ātman*), essence (*sāra*), and intrinsic nature (*svabhāva*). Or they might simply use a form of philosophical shorthand and refer to the emptiness of persons (*pudgala-śūnyatā*).[39] The correct way to view bodied being is as empty of any intrinsic and eternal essence such as an eternal self or soul. Most people, however, have an incorrect view of bodied being. They ascribe to it some form of intrinsic and eternal essence. The technical term for an incorrect view of bodied being is *satkāyadṛṣṭi*, which literally means "[false] belief in a real body." In this context, "real" designates that which is intrinsic and eternal; "body" designates not just the physical body, but the entirety of bodied being.[40] A false belief in a real body thus refers to the false belief that bodied being possesses an intrinsic and eternal essence.

Why is it important that bodhisattvas reject this false belief? They must do so because an incorrect view of bodied being can lead to self-centered and immoral conduct. Thus complex philosophical arguments have ethical implications. William R. LaFleur writes,

> Classical Buddhist doctrine goes on to say that among all the things we crave, perhaps the most important is the perpetuation and permanence of something each of us calls his or her own "self." Each cherishes this above all, wanting to believe that some part of us, perhaps a soul or some other kind of invisible and interior stuff, will endure even after our body dies and begins to decay. . . . According to Buddhism, it is this notion, a false one at bottom, that leads to the egotism, self-centeredness, and rapacious behavior that makes life on our planet so hazardous and difficult so much of the time.[41]

The self that living beings seek to gratify is ultimately a fiction.[42] In the words of Todd T. Lewis, there is no "intrinsic, unchanging entity at the core of a person."[43] Instead a person, or bodied being, is comprised of various material, affective, and cognitive elements, all of which are impermanent and constantly changing. Lewis observes that "the spiritual purpose of breaking down any apparently unchanging locus of individuality is to demonstrate that there is 'no thing' to be attached to or to direct one's desire toward. Attached to things, addicted to themselves, and in denial about their mortality, human beings misconstrue reality and bind themselves to suffering and inevitable rebirth in *samsara*."[44] Likewise, when bodhisattvas realize at an experiential level that their bodied beings possess no intrinsic and eternal essence, they become less attached to self-gratification. According to the *Compendium of Training*, this realization enables bodhisattvas to eradicate in themselves the defilements of lust, anger, and delusion which give rise to all self-centered action. Thus the text observes that just as "all the branches and leaves of a tree wither when its root has been cut out," so too the defilements are subdued (*upaśam-*) when "the [false] belief in a real body" is subdued.[45]

LaFleur aptly remarks that attachment to a notion of an intrinsic and eternal essence is probably "our deepest, most pernicious attachment."[46] How then does the *Compendium of Training* counter the false belief that bodied beings possess an intrinsic and eternal essence? It employs an analytical and meditational technique we have already encountered in this chapter. It teaches bodhisattvas to regard their bodied beings as nothing but a collection of impermanent elements. We have already seen that bodied beings are comprised of five impermanent aggregates (*skandha*). Bodied beings are also said to be comprised of another set of impermanent constituent parts, namely, the six elements (*ṣaḍ-ḍhātu*) of earth (*pṛthivī*), water (*ap*), fire (*tejas*), wind (*vāyu*), space (*ākāśa*), and consciousness (*vijñāna*). Earth represents solidity, water represents fluidity, fire represents heat, wind represents motion, space represents any opening or hollow such as the eye socket or mouth, and consciousness represents affective and cognitive processes.[47] Together these six elements comprise bodied beings. Whether breaking bodied being down into its five aggregates or six elements, the point of the exercise is the same. If the constituent parts of bodied being are impermanent, then so too is bodied being. If the constituent parts are empty of any intrinsic nature (*svabhāva*), that is, an intrinsic and eternal essence, then so too is bodied being.

The discussion of the six elements occurs in chapter 14 of the text, which is specifically concerned with eradicating the false belief that bodied beings possess an intrinsic and eternal essence (*satkāyadṛṣṭi*). The discussion is long and I confine myself here to a few salient aspects of it.[48] The discussion proceeds systematically through each of the six elements, taking into account their existence both inside and outside of bodied being. In all cases, the text argues that these elements are empty of intrinsic nature and hence so too are bodied beings. For instance, the discussion begins with the earth element. Earth designates all that is solid in bodies, such as "head hairs, body hairs, nails, teeth, and so forth."[49] Earth also designates all that is solid outside of bodies, such as mountains. Neither solid matter internal to bodies nor solid matter external to bodies is permanent; solid matter thus possesses no intrinsic nature. The discussion then applies the same kind of analysis to the elements of water, fire, wind, space, and consciousness. Again and again bodhisattvas are told that if the six elements that comprise bodied beings have no intrinsic nature, then neither do bodied beings. Bodied beings are empty of any intrinsic and eternal essence.

Contemplating the six elements in this manner has profound ethical implications. Its desired effect is the eradication of the defilements of lust, anger, and delusion. Purified of these defilements, bodhisattvas become less concerned with self-gratification and more concerned with the gratification of others. Thus contemplation of the six elements renders bodhisattvas better able to care for others.

Neither Female nor Male

Contemplation of the six elements that comprise bodied being is not so much a negative discourse on bodies as it is a discourse that seeks to relativize their value. There is a qualitative difference between contemplating bodied being's lack of intrinsic and eternal essence and bodied being's foulness. Ascetic discourse thus displays a range of perspectives on body and bodied being. Nevertheless all the meditations and philosophical reflections discussed in this chapter share the same goal: eliminating the desire for sensual pleasures and eradicating the defilements which are the root cause of attachment to self-gratification. Further, just as meditation on the foulness of bodies is said to be an especially effective antidote to male sexual desire for women, so too is contemplation of the six elements largely focused on eliminating male sexual desire for women. Again, we see that a key aim of the ascetic discourse is producing celibate monks.

Chapter 14, in which is found the discussion of the six elements, indicates at the very outset that male celibacy is its central concern when it declares that one of the good effects of meditation on emptiness is that one avoids falling into the power of women.[50] Strikingly, the discussion of the six elements repeatedly concludes its analysis of particular elements by proclaiming that these elements are neither female nor male. If there is neither female nor male in the elements that comprise bodied beings, then bodied beings too are in some sense neither female nor male. Thus the point of discovering each element's lack of intrinsic nature is ultimately to discover that women and men also possess no intrinsic nature. Rather than teach bodhisattvas to regard women as dangerous and foul, this practice takes a different approach and teaches them to regard both women and men as empty of intrinsic nature, thus undermining the very basis for sexual attraction. For instance, the contemplation of the earth element entails reflecting as follows:

> Great king, there comes a time when a woman imagines concerning herself, "I am a woman." Having imagined with respect to herself, "I am a woman," she imagines concerning a man external to her, "This is a man." Having imagined concerning the man external to her, "This is a man," being aroused [*saṃraktā*], she desires to have sex with the man external to her. The man also imagines concerning himself, "I am a man," as stated previously. Because of their mutual desire for sex, they have sex. Because of having sex, an embryo is created. In this context, great king, both the imagined thought and the one who does the imagining do not exist. A woman does not exist in the woman. A man does not exist in the man.[51]

One ends the contemplation of the earth element by reflecting that the earth element itself is merely a conventional expression; it has no intrinsic or eternal essence. Significantly, the text thus concludes, "This too is a conventional expression. There is no female, there is no male."[52] We find the same conclusion in the discussion of the water, space, and consciousness elements.[53] (Discussion of the fire and wind elements is abbreviated and thus omits this conclusion.) The constant reminder that each element is neither female nor male indicates that the real point of contemplating the six elements is to recognize that bodied beings too are neither female nor male.

What does the *Compendium of Training* mean when it claims that bodied beings are neither female nor male? The text recognizes that although living beings conventionally assume the existence of sexual difference, ultimately these differences are a fiction because, like the self, they have no intrinsic and eternal reality. This is a subtle philosophical point and rests on a distinction Buddhists make between "conventional" (*saṃvṛti*) and "ultimate" (*paramārtha*) perspectives on reality. From a conventional perspective, there are women and men and thus there exists a basis for sexual attraction. From an ultimate perspective, however, since all phenomena are empty of intrinsic and eternal essence, women and men are merely conceptual fictions. Buddhists invoke an "ultimate" perspective on reality in order to challenge habitual patterns of actions, feelings, and thoughts. In this instance, the *Compendium of Training* attempts to break the habit of male sexual desire for women. By demonstrating that the constituent elements of bodied being possess no female or male essence, the practitioner is made to feel that bodied being itself can possess no female or male essence. Hence there can be no basis for sexual attraction.

Contemplation of the six elements that comprise bodied beings is followed by highly technical reflections on the affective and cognitive processes that similarly constitute bodied beings. Eyes, ears, nose, tongue, body, and mind (*manas*) serve as the six bases of sensory contact with the world (*sparśāyatana*). Additionally bodied beings respond to these six forms of sensory stimulus in three different ways—with pleasure, pain, and indifference—thereby producing a total of eighteen spheres of mental activity (*mana-upavicāra*). Bodied beings are thus comprised of six elements, six bases of sensory contact with the world, and eighteen spheres of mental activity. I will limit my analysis of this technical material to one point: the centrality of women to the discussion of the eighteen spheres of mental activity. This discussion lends further support to my argument that the primary goal of the *Compendium of Training*'s meditations and philosophical reflections on body and bodied being is the eradication of male sexual desire for women. These meditations and philosophical reflections are Buddhist technologies of the self designed to create celibate male monastic bodhisattvas.

Discussion of the eighteen spheres of mental activity focuses on eliminating the defilements of lust, anger, and delusion.[54] The text assumes that experiences of pleasure, pain, and indifference respectively give rise to lust, anger, and delusion.[55] The meditation attempts to eradicate the defilements by demonstrating that the objects of lust, anger, and delusion are empty of intrinsic nature. The meditation defines women as the object of lust, enemies as the object of anger, and demons (*piśāca*) as the object of delusion. Women, enemies, and demons appear to be real and therefore evoke a strong and often improper response on our parts, but they are merely like figures in a dream, ultimately devoid of any real essence. What is striking about the discussion of the eighteen spheres of mental activity is that it pays significantly more attention to deconstructing the concept of a woman than it does to the concepts of an enemy or a demon. Even when the meditation focuses on the defilement of delusion, it quickly moves from deconstructing the notion of a demon to deconstructing—once again—the notion of a woman. Women, represented throughout this meditation in idealized form as the most beautiful woman in the country (*janapada-kalyāṇī*), must be regarded like dream figures, without substantial reality. The fact that much of the meditation on the six elements and the eighteen spheres of mental activity concern women is strong indication that the primary purpose of this material is eradication of male sexual desire for women.

Wilson remarks, concerning Mahāyāna Sanskrit Buddhist literature, that "vicious tirades against women" coexist with statements about the irrelevance of gender distinctions, specifically citing the *Compendium of Training* on this point.[56] The *Compendium of Training* engages in radically different discourses on women. On the one hand, meditation on the foulness of women's bodies teaches men to regard women with fear and disgust. On the other hand, meditation on the six elements teaches men to regard sexual differences as ultimately unreal. Thus one and the same text can claim that (a) "women are in every way the root cause of bad realms of rebirth . . ." and (b) there is no such thing as female and male. How are we to reconcile these statements? Some scholars of Buddhism would do so by invoking the notion of conventional and ultimate perspectives on reality. A conventional perspective takes sexual difference seriously, whereas an ultimate perspective challenges the validity of such distinctions since all beings—female and male—are empty of intrinsic and eternal essence. According to this logic, meditations on women's foulness would represent a conventional perspective, and meditations on women's lack of intrinsic nature would represent an ultimate perspective. Further, since an ultimate perspective is often presumed to take precedence over a conventional perspective, the philosophically correct way to view women is not as foul, but as empty of intrinsic and eternal essence. Therefore it would be possible to argue that meditations on women's foulness simply represent a provisional method for eradicating sexual desire; eventually bodhisattvas move on to the more philosophically correct meditations on women's lack of intrinsic nature. The notion of conventional and ultimate perspectives on reality can thus be used by apologists for the text as a way of downplaying its misogynistic statements.

I find this line of argument unconvincing for a number of reasons, most strikingly because nowhere in the text is there any suggestion that the foulness of women's bodies constitutes a conventional perspective on women. Indeed, the conventional perspective is that women's bodies are desirable rather than disgusting, which is why they pose a problem in the first place. Meditations on the foulness of women's bodies are designed to counter a conventional view that women are sexually desirable. A distinction between conventional and ultimate perspectives on reality will not help to reconcile the different discourses on women. A far better approach is to recognize that in the *Compendium of Training* both forms of meditation represent equally valid and valued approaches to the problem of male sexual desire for women. In Foucauldian terms, they are different kinds of disciplinary practices, or technologies of the self, designed to achieve the same end: the production of celibate male monastic bodhisattvas. Radically different discourses on women can coexist in this text because they serve the same purpose.

Ultimate and Conventional Perspectives on Bodies

The *Compendium of Training* offers multiple perspectives on bodies, male and female. Further, it appears to regard radically different perspectives as true and useful. This is the case for its evaluation of women's bodies and its evaluation of bodies in general. I wish now to examine the relationship between ascetic and physiomoral discourses on bodies. The differences between these two discourses could not be more pronounced. First, an ascetic discourse on bodies describes all bodies—although sometimes women's in particular—as impermanent, foul, and without intrinsic and eternal essence. From the standpoint of an ascetic discourse, all bodies, no matter how virtuous, are alike. A physiomoral discourse on bodies, however, is acutely attentive to the details of bodily differences, because body and morality are presumed to be inextricably linked. From the standpoint of a physiomoral discourse, all bodies are not alike. Second, an ascetic discourse appears to devalue bodies, either by making overtly negative comments about them or by invoking an ultimate perspective to relativize their value. A physiomoral discourse, however, values bodies, since bodies play critical roles in the ethical development of oneself and others. Finally, an ascetic discourse regards attachment to bodies as highly problematic, because such attachment is contrary to ethical development. As the first quotation at the start of this chapter indicates, attachment to bodies leads to immoral deeds and rebirths in hell. Yet the second quotation reflects a very different perspective: attachment to certain kinds of bodies such as the virtuous bodies of buddhas and bodhisattvas is valorized. In such instances attachment to bodies is beneficial for ethical development. How do we reconcile these two very different discourses?

Here too, scholars of Buddhism are likely to invoke a notion of conventional and ultimate perspectives on reality in order to account for such radically different kinds of body discourse. Generally speaking, they would be correct in characterizing physiomoral discourse on bodies as representative of a conventional perspective and ascetic discourse as representative of an ultimate perspective on reality. However, as we shall see, characterizing the two discourses in this way still leaves unanswered the troubling question of their relationship to each other. Does an ultimate perspective take precedence over a conventional perspective and, if so, what happens to Buddhist ethics? Are there ways of upholding conventional and ultimate perspectives simultaneously? These questions will be addressed below. First, let us examine why physiomoral and ascetic discourses can be said to represent conventional and ultimate perspectives on reality, respectively.

A physiomoral discourse on bodies represents a conventional perspective because it values and foregrounds bodily differences. An ascetic discourse on bodies represents an ultimate perspective because it negates or relativizes the significance of bodily differences, although, as we have seen, it may still reinscribe a distinction between women and men, as in the case of meditations on the foulness of women's bodies. Ascetic discourse most clearly represents an ultimate perspective on reality when it defines all bodily differences as being empty of intrinsic and eternal essence and thus without real significance. From an ultimate perspective, distinctions of any kind have no substantial reality. For example, chapter 14 explicitly invokes the notion of conventional (*saṃvṛti*) and ultimate (*paramārtha*) perspectives, arguing that distinctions such as those between different realms of rebirth (*gati*), lowly and superior families (*nīca-kula, ucca-kula*), and rich and poor families have significance only from a conventional point of view.[57] The chapter goes on to argue that from an ultimate perspective even the concepts of a buddha, the experience of awakening, a bodhisattva, and a prediction of buddhahood have no substantial reality. These are merely conventional expressions.[58] Even basic conventional distinctions between good and evil have no ultimate significance. Thus chapter 14 maintains there is no ultimate distinction between awakening and the most heinous of deeds.[59] Here it appears that an ultimate perspective calls into question not only the significance of a physiomoral discourse on bodies, but also the very significance of ethical discourse in general. Or does it?

Scholars have observed that an ultimate perspective does not invalidate a conventional perspective; rather it refines that conventional perspective.[60] Thus as Frederick J. Streng argues, "The things of the apparent world are not destroyed, but they are reevaluated in such a way that they no longer have the power emotionally and intellectually to control human life."[61] In the *Compendium of Training* an ultimate perspective on reality serves the purpose of cultivating ethical persons. Meditations and philosophical reflections on the unsatisfactory nature of bodies are technologies of the self designed to eradicate the defilements and more specifically to produce celibate male monastic bodhisattvas. Chapter 14 thus asserts that bodhisattvas who believe in the emptiness of all phenomena are not attracted to worldly matters (*loka-dharma*).[62] Most important, belief in the emptiness of all phenomena, including one's own bodied being, challenges any distinctions bodhisattvas might make between themselves and others. From an ultimate perspective such distinctions have no validity. Thus bodhisattvas learn to take the needs of others as seriously as their own needs. Indeed, the *Compendium of Training* goes a step further: chapter 14 instructs bodhisattvas to regard other living beings with respect (*gaurava*) and themselves with contempt (*avajñā*).[63] In other words, bodhisattvas should put the needs of others ahead of their own. An ultimate perspective on reality thus encourages bodhisattvas to put themselves more fully in the service of others. Ultimate and conventional perspectives are not, in the end, at cross-purposes; they both seek to produce bodhisattvas who are dedicated to the happiness and well-being of others.

Just as an ultimate perspective on reality does not reject ethics, but instead produces ethical persons, so too an ascetic discourse on bodies does not reject bodies, but instead produces bodied beings that can ripen others. Let us recall that the bodhisattva discipline (*saṃvara*) requires that bodhisattvas learn to regard their bodied beings (*ātmabhāva*) as gifts intended for the benefit of others (see chapter 2 of this book). Recall also that in order for bodhisattvas to benefit others with their bodied beings, these must first be protected, purified, and increased. Significantly, although meditations and philosophical reflections on bodies occur throughout the *Compendium of Training*, they occur with greatest concentration in chapters 9 through 14, which are dedicated to teaching bodhisattvas how to purify bodied being (*ātmabhāva*) of defilements. Discussion of women's bodies, in particular, also occurs in chapter 4, which teaches bodhisattvas how to protect bodied being, especially from the horrific karmic consequences of lust for women. The *Compendium of Training*'s ascetic discourse on bodies, no matter how negative, must be interpreted in light of the explicitly articulated goals of the bodhisattva discipline, foremost of which is cultivating bodhisattvas with bodies that benefit others. In light of this larger goal, it becomes difficult to interpret an ascetic discourse on bodies as a rejection of their significance and value. The ascetic discourse must be interpreted differently. It does not represent a rejection of bodies; to the contrary, it affirms their value because it regards bodhisattva bodies as integral to the welfare and happiness of others.

Virtuous Bodied Beings

Bodhisattvas use their bodies as well as their heartminds to please, attract, and ripen living beings. We saw in chapters 3 and 4 of this book how important the maintenance of monastic etiquette and deportment is in enabling monastic bodhisattvas to do so. The ascetic discourse on bodies, however, raises the possibility of materializing different kinds of monastic bodies. Along with a conventional monastic body, shaped by conventional monastic etiquette and deportment, we find indications in the text of an ascetic body, shaped by a range of more extreme ascetic practices. The *Compendium of Training* quotes from a number of Mahāyāna scriptures, such as the *Ugraparipṛcchā*, which urges bodhisattvas to go beyond the "standard requirements of monastic life" and spend long periods of time "performing stringent ascetic practices in the wilderness."[64] These ascetic practices are often referred to in sources as the *dhūtaguṇas* or *dhutaṅgas*. Wilson summarizes these practices as follows:

> In Theravāda contexts, the classical list of ascetic practices (*dhutaṅga*) includes thirteen items: wearing patchwork robes recycled from cast-off cloth, wearing no more than three robes, going for alms, not omitting any house while going for alms, eating at one sitting, eating only from the alms bowl, refusing all further food, living in the forest, living under a tree, living in the open air, living in a cemetery, being satisfied with any humble dwelling, and sleeping in the sitting position (without ever lying down). Mahāyāna texts mention twelve ascetic practices (called *dhūtaguṇa*). They are the same as the Theravāda list except they omit two rules about eating and add a rule about wearing garments of felt or wool.[65]

The *Compendium of Training* makes very few direct references to the *dhūtaguṇas*, but it does repeatedly exhort monastics to repair to the wilderness for solitary practice.[66] It regards solitary retreat in the wilderness as particularly well suited for performing meditations and philosophical reflections on the unsatisfactory nature of bodies. This is so presumably because there are fewer distractions to practice and also because the harsh and sometimes dangerous environment of the wilderness forces monastics to confront both their craving for self-gratification and their fear of death. We do not know how many monastics might have followed the *Compendium of Training*'s advice. Those who did, however, might well have adopted some or all of the *dhūtaguṇas* during the course of a wilderness retreat.

Adoption of extreme ascetic practices such as living in the open air would undoubtedly have produced very different kinds of monastic bodies than those produced in the context of conventional monastic life. At the very least, living in the open air requires significant alteration to one's daily toilet. Modern-day Theravāda practitioners of the *dhutaṅgas* are sometimes regarded with suspicion. As Steven Collins notes, "Although the idea (and practice) of such heroic supererogatory asceticism is often accorded great popular acclaim, in the longer term the cleanliness and decorum expected of monks becomes the greater demand."[67] Collins cites the work of Jane Bunnag, who observes that contemporary Thai Theravāda *dhutaṅga* practitioners are "frequently regarded as being on par with tramps, beggars and other kinds of social derelicts."[68] In the contemporary Theravāda world, the *dhutaṅgas* may produce monastic bodies directly in tension with more conventional monastic ideals. The *Compendium of Training*, however, appears to make room for both conventional and ascetic monastic bodies. Further, both kinds of bodies have the capacity to please, attract, and ripen others. Indeed, the *Compendium of Training* places its chapter on the benefits of wilderness retreats in its section on purifying bodied being. Bodies are not without value or meaning in asceticism; to the contrary they serve as visible symbols of self-discipline.[69] Ascetic practices produce bodies that instantiate for others a bodhisattva's commitment to extraordinary ascetic discipline.

The *Compendium of Training*'s chapter on wilderness retreats urges bodhisattvas to wander alone like a rhinoceros (*khaḍga*).[70] This does not mean, however, that bodhisattvas were to have no contact with other people. Bodhisattvas practicing alone in the wilderness still depend on laity for alms. Therefore the *Compendium of Training* instructs them to live neither too close nor too far from a place where they can collect such alms.[71] Additionally, it provides instructions on how to handle visitors, specifically, kings, royal ministers, members of the *brāhmaṇa* and *kṣatriya* castes, and other visitors from both towns and villages. Bodhisattvas must greet these with respect, offer appropriate seating, and preach a sermon suited to the disposition and capacities of the visitor. Whatever sermon he preaches, it should generate in his audience joy (*prīti*), pleasure (*prasāda*), and delight (*prāmodya*).[72] Thus even when practicing alone in the wilderness, bodhisattvas have the opportunity to ripen others.

Ascetic meditations and philosophical reflections on bodies produce a range of virtuous bodied beings, from conventional monastics to more ascetic monastics. They also produce buddhas. The ultimate goal of the bodhisattva path is buddhahood, and the *Compendium of Training* regards its meditations and philosophical reflections on the unsatisfactory nature of bodies as key to achieving that goal. Chapter 14 is a case in point. As we have seen, this chapter contains an ascetic discourse on bodies that teaches bodhisattvas to reject the false belief that bodied being possesses an intrinsic and eternal essence (*satkāyadṛṣṭi*). This false belief is replaced by the correct belief that bodied being is empty of intrinsic nature (*svabhāva*). At one point the chapter promises the following good effects of meditating on emptiness. We have already encountered one of these good effects: never falling into the power of women. Additionally, the chapter promises that the person who understands the true nature of all phenomena will never land in a bad realm of existence (*durgati*); he will be beautiful (*abhirūpa*) and will display the major and minor marks of a great man (*mahāpuruṣa*).[73] The thirty-two major and eighty minor marks of a great man are key features of both buddhas and world-conquering kings. The *Compendium of Training* is particularly interested in the fact that meditating on emptiness materializes buddhas. It maintains that those who wish to produce a buddha's body (*buddha-kāya*) and who desire to acquire the thirty-two major and eighty minor marks of a great man must study the perfection of wisdom, a text associated in the *Compendium of Training* with the doctrine of emptiness.[74] Meditation and philosophical reflection on the emptiness of bodied being is a liberating insight that, if fully realized, results in the permanent elimination of all defilements and the materialization of a buddha. Acceptance of the emptiness of bodied being and attendant rejection of a false belief that bodied being possesses an intrinsic and eternal essence is, in the end, not a rejection of bodies, but a necessary condition for producing the very best body of all: the irresistibly beautiful body of a buddha. The person who understands the emptiness of bodied being produces a body capable of benefiting others. An ascetic discourse on bodies that denies an ultimate significance to bodies is actually in the service of a physiomoral discourse on bodies that valorizes certain kinds of bodies because it regards these bodies as critical to the ethical transformation of other living beings.

There is a productive paradox at the heart of the *Compendium of Training*'s discourses on bodies. The bodhisattva who realizes that bodies are impermanent, foul, and without intrinsic and eternal essence gets a body so beautiful that living beings are never sated by gazing upon it. Meditations and philosophical reflections on bodies make bodies both the means and objects of transformation. Thus ascetic discourse on bodies does not represent a rejection or repudiation of bodies; instead it represents an effort to transform bodies into something worthwhile for others. This interesting paradox is best summed up by a curious phrase that occurs several times in the *Compendium of Training*. Bodhisattvas are instructed to take the worth or essence (*sāra*) from their worthless or essenceless (*asāra*) bodies (*kāya, śarīra*).[75] Generally, the context for this statement is discussion of bodily sacrifice. Bodhisattvas take the worth from their worthless bodies when they sacrifice themselves for others. Reiko Ohnuma has also come across this curious phrase in her study of Buddhist narratives of bodily sacrifice in *jātaka* and *avadāna* literature.[76] She argues that bodhisattva bodies attain worth precisely when bodhisattvas recognize their bodies' ultimate worthlessness. Insight into the ultimately unsatisfactory nature of bodies has two effects: bodhisattvas attain liberation, and they give their bodies away to others.[77] According to Ohnuma, narratives of bodily sacrifice attribute worth to a worthless body primarily because this body serves as a "locus of enlightenment" for the bodhisattva himself.[78] Ohnuma is less interested than I am in the ways in which bodies become worthwhile for others. According to the *Compendium of Training*, the primary worth of a worthless body is its ability to benefit other living beings. Indeed, the point of protecting, purifying, and increasing bodied beings is to turn bodies into "something for the enjoyment of all living beings." The productive paradox at the heart of this text's discourses on bodies is that the bodhisattva who recognizes the worthlessness of his body produces a body that has great worth for others.

Implications for Analysis of Ascetic Discourse in South Asian Buddhist Literature

The foregoing analysis of the *Compendium of Training* demonstrates that the presence of an ascetic discourse on bodies in a text does not automatically mean that the text denies the significance and value of bodies. A text that characterizes bodies as impermanent, foul, and/or without intrinsic and eternal essence may still valorize particular kinds of bodies. This point has implications for analysis of ascetic discourse more broadly in South Asian Buddhist literature. For example, the Theravāda tradition records the story of Subhā, a Buddhist nun and contemporary of the historical Buddha.[79] According to the story, a layman attempts to seduce Subhā. She tries to extinguish the man's lust by teaching him to regard her body as impermanent and disgusting. The man is particularly attracted to Subhā's beautiful eyes. Consequently, Subhā informs him, "[The eye] is like a ball set in a hollow, with a bubble in the center and tears; / eye secretions are produced there, like various kinds of eyes collected together."[80] When the man continues to press his case, Subhā tears out her eye and presents it to him. Needless to say, his lust for Subhā abates quickly. Wilson discusses this story in her analysis of textual representations of women in Indian literature. She argues that Subhā instantiates for her would-be lover the Buddhist teaching that all bodies are impermanent and disgusting.[81] Thus Subhā literally materializes for him an ascetic perspective on bodies. Subhā's story, however, does not end with her disfigurement, as is noted by Trainor. Subhā goes to the Buddha and, as soon as she sees the Buddha, her eye is restored: "And then that nun, liberated, went before the excellent Buddha; / having seen the one with the marks of excellent merit, [her] eye was restored."[82] According to a commentary on the text, the "marks of excellent merit" (*vara-puñña-lakkhaṇa*) refer to the thirty-two major and eighty minor marks of a great man.[83] Trainor observes that "in contrast to the fundamentally negative characterization of the human body that has dominated the poem's discourse, this verse credits the extraordinary physical appearance of the Buddha's body with the healing of Subhā's eye."[84] Even a text that employs a resolutely ascetic discourse to characterize bodies as impermanent and disgusting may still valorize certain kinds of bodies, such as those of buddhas or bodhisattvas, because these bodies are believed to have transformative effects on others.

The foregoing analysis of the *Compendium of Training* indicates that interpretation of any body discourse in Buddhist literature needs to be sensitive to the fact that a text that appears on the surface to devalue bodies may, on closer scrutiny, offer a very different evaluation of bodies. Buddhist narratives about bodily sacrifice on the part of bodhisattvas are a further case in point. The *Compendium of Training* provides a number of examples of such extreme acts of generosity, although, as we have seen, it regards bodily sacrifice as the prerogative of only the most advanced bodhisattvas (see chapter 2 of this book). Scholars have often interpreted narratives of bodily sacrifice (or the actual performance thereof) as indicative of a general Buddhist rejection of bodies.[85] Yet the matter is far more complex. In Buddhist narrative literature, when bodhisattvas give away their bodies, they often do so specifically in order to produce a better kind of body. These narratives underscore the attention Buddhist traditions pay to bodily transformation.

Ohnuma argues similarly, in her study of Buddhist narratives of bodily sacrifice, that bodhisattvas frequently sacrifice their bodies in order to attain a better kind of body, namely, an "ideal body." She argues that an "ideal body," often called a "dharma-body" in her sources, is best understood as "a body that tends toward non-body" because it appears to be less fully material than ordinary human bodies.[86] Thus when bodhisattvas sacrifice their bodies, they trade in a "physical body for an immaterial 'dharma-body.'"[87] At the same time, however, Ohnuma observes that bodhisattvas also seem to trade in a "physical body for a superior form of physicality."[88] For example, when the bodhisattva King Sivi (a past incarnation of Śākyamuni Buddha) gives away his eyes, he subsequently performs a "declaration of truth" to restore his body to its former condition. Not only does King Sivi get his eyes back, but these eyes are now endowed with supernatural powers.[89] Ohnuma, who discusses this and other such stories, argues that these stories display "a bizarre brand of bodily alchemy wherein the limb offered as gift is not only restored, but becomes greater and more powerful than before."[90] Thus, according to Ohnuma, these stories reveal simultaneously two perspectives on bodies. On the one hand, they seem to privilege an immaterial kind of body—that is, "a body that tends toward non-body"; on the other hand, they also valorize the transformed and decidedly physical bodies of bodhisattvas. Ohnuma reconciles the presence of such different discourses on bodies in her sources by attributing them to different levels of realization—those of bodhisattvas and those of ordinary beings:

> From the bodhisattva's perspective, there is a wish to exchange the debased *rūpa-kāya* [form body] of an ordinary being for the eternal *dharma-kāya* [dharma body] of the Buddha. From the perspective of

> the readers and those who react to the bodhisattva's deed, there is a wish to celebrate the way in which the *dharma-kāya* of the Buddha manifests itself in the world in the form of a glorified *rūpa-kāya*.[91]

The different discourses on bodies in narratives of bodily sacrifice are meant to reflect the different perspectives of awakened and ordinary beings.

Ohnuma's analysis both complements and differs from my own analysis of narratives of bodily sacrifice.[92] Although I disagree that the "ideal bodies" of buddhas or bodhisattvas are less fully material than other kinds of bodies, I do agree that these narratives reflect the desire to exchange one kind of body for another. Bodhisattvas give up their ordinary bodies in order to attain extraordinary bodies. In Mahāyāna *sūtra* literature that extraordinary body is often identified as a buddha's body, which is adorned with the thirty–two major and eighty minor marks of a great man such as golden skin color. For example, the *Aṣṭasāhasrikā Prajñāpāramitā* contains a story that is partially quoted in the *Compendium of Training* about a bodhisattva who engages in an act of bodily sacrifice.[93] This bodhisattva sells his heart, blood, and bone marrow in order to earn the money needed to make an offering to his teacher, Dharmodgata. This story is cited as an example of the intense (*tīvra*) respect (*gaurava*) and affection (*prema*) bodhisattvas owe their beautiful friends (*kalyāṇamitra*).[94] When in the source text the bodhisattva is asked by an onlooker why he inflicts such torment on himself, he explains,

> Dharmodgata will explain to me the perfection of wisdom and the skill in means. In them I shall train myself, and, as a result, I shall become a refuge to all beings; and, after I have known full enlightenment, I shall acquire a body [*kāya*] of golden colour [*suvarṇa-varṇa*], the thirty-two marks of the [great man], the eighty accessory marks, the splendour of a halo the rays of which extend to infinitude.[95]

The bodhisattva sacrifices his current body in order to attain buddhahood. Buddhahood is defined in explicitly corporeal terms; it is a physical as well as affective and cognitive achievement. By sacrificing his current body, this bodhisattva hopes to materialize a buddha's body.

Several similar examples from Mahāyāna *sūtra* literature come immediately to mind. For instance, the *Saddharmapuṇḍarīkasūtra* (*Lotus Sutra*) tells the story of a bodhisattva named Bhaiṣajyarāja. In a past life, Bhaiṣajyarāja intentionally set his arm ablaze as an offering to the relics of another buddha. Subsequently he performs a declaration of truth in which he proclaims that he has sacrificed his arm in order to gain "a body [*kāya*] of gold colour" (*suvarṇa-varṇa*).[96] The *Samādhirājasūtra* contains a similar story.[97] The bodhisattva

Kṣemadatta (a past incarnation of Śākyamuni Buddha) also burns his arm as an offering to the relics of another buddha. He subsequently performs a declaration of truth, after which his arm is restored and his body is adorned with the thirty-two marks of a great man. Further, his transformed body has a transformative effect on women. Those who see him cease to be women and are promised future buddhahood.[98] Finally, the *Śrīmālāsiṃhanādasūtra* states that the well-born son or daughter who renounces his or her body will obtain the body of a buddha.[99] Even narratives of bodily sacrifice do not necessarily represent a rejection of bodies. They may, in fact, represent just the opposite: a desire to produce a particular and better kind of body.

What do we make of the fact that these narratives, like the *Compendium of Training*, offer different kinds of discourses on bodies? Ohnuma points out that the *jātaka* and *avadāna* narratives she studies contain both positive and negative statements about bodies. Bodhisattvas frequently discourse on the unsatisfactory nature of bodies before they engage in an act of bodily sacrifice.[100] In other words, an ascetic discourse on bodies precedes bodily sacrifice. Bodily sacrifice, in turn, is frequently followed by a miraculous bodily transformation, resulting in the production of valorized buddha and bodhisattva bodies. In other words, bodily sacrifice is followed by a physiomoral discourse on bodies. Although both Ohnuma and I discern different kinds of body discourses in Buddhist literature, we interpret them differently. As we have seen, for Ohnuma different discourses in one story are meant to reflect different levels of realization. Bodhisattvas understand the unsatisfactory nature of bodies and hence desire to exchange a physical body for "a body that tends toward non-body." Ordinary beings have not yet attained this insight and thus remain attached to the extraordinary bodies of buddhas and bodhisattvas.[101] The *Compendium of Training* offers another way of making sense of the different body discourses in Buddhist literature. This text assumes that both ascetic and physiomoral discourses are part of a single bodhisattva's conceptual universe. They do not represent different levels of realization. Instead, bodhisattvas embrace an ascetic discourse on bodies in order to cultivate the kinds of bodies that are valorized in physiomoral discourse, namely, bodies that reflect high levels of moral achievement, notably the virtuous bodies of celibate monastic bodhisattvas and ultimately the virtuous body of a buddha. The *Compendium of Training* conceives of progress along the bodhisattva path in bodily as well as affective and cognitive terms. Indeed, as we have seen throughout this book, one of the primary goals of bodhisattva practice is the materialization of bodied beings who use their bodies to benefit others. Thus bodhisattvas do not repudiate their bodies; they transform them into "something for the enjoyment of all living beings." The *Compendium of Training* illumines the central role that South Asian Buddhist literature attributes to bodies in the ripening of living beings.

From Foul to Pure Bodies

Buddhist perspectives on bodies are complex, and analysis thereof requires careful attention to the context of any body discourse. As we have seen, statements that question the significance and value of bodies sit side by side in the *Compendium of Training* with statements that valorize bodies. I close this chapter with one final example from chapter 13 of the text, which describes a meditation commonly called the "application of mindfulness" (*smṛtyupasthāna*). The meditator contemplates in turn body (*kāya*), feelings (*vedanā*), thoughts (*citta*), and phenomena (*dharma*). Applying mindfulness to body entails contemplating its impermanence, foulness, and lack of intrinsic and eternal essence. Surprisingly, in the midst of an ascetic discourse on bodies that calls into question the ultimate significance and value of bodies, we find a passage that offers an alternative perspective. The passage opens by reminding bodhisattvas of the impermanence of bodies and instructs them to refrain from engaging in any immoral conduct for the sake of what is impermanent.[102] Instead bodhisattvas should use their bodies for the benefit of others, making themselves "a servant and student of all beings," "zealous in doing whatever needs to be done" for others.[103] It is at this point that the passage offers an alternative perspective on bodies. I quote it in full:

> Moreover, well-born son, a bodhisattva cultivating mindfulness of body [*kāya*] by observing body [*kāya*] connects [*upanibandh-*] the bodies of all living beings with his own. It occurs to him: I should establish the bodies of all living beings in [the process of] establishing a buddha's body. Just as there are no defilements [*āśrava*] in a tathāgata's [i.e., buddha's] body, so too one should regard the nature of one's own body. One who is skilled in the undefiled nature knows that the bodies of all living beings also have these very features.[104]

This is a dense passage and requires some unpacking before we can explore the alternative perspective on bodies that it offers. The passage instructs bodhisattvas to perform a mindfulness meditation on bodies in such a way that they "connect" their own bodies to those of all other living beings. I interpret this to mean that bodhisattvas must recognize the connections, that is, similarities, between their own bodies and those of others, as well as commit themselves to "connecting" their own transformation to those of others. Hence they resolve to "establish the bodies of all living beings in [the process of] establishing a buddha's body." In other words, they resolve to help living beings materialize a buddha's body.[105] Remarkably, the basis for the connection between, and mutual transformation of, bodhisattva bodies and all other bodies is not their shared impermanence, foulness, and lack of intrinsic and eternal essence. Rather it is their inherent purity. The passage makes the claim that the bodies of all living beings are pure like the body of a buddha. This is a radical claim and is not made elsewhere in the text. Its radical nature is underscored by the fact that the passage occurs in the midst of an ascetic discourse on bodies that draws particular attention to the fact that bodies are "by nature impure, putrid, and fetid" (*aśuci-pūti-durgandha-svabhāva*).[106] Briefly, visions of foul bodies give way to visions of pure bodies.

The passage characterizes the bodies of all living beings as inherently pure, offering an intriguing alternative to both the ascetic and physiomoral discourses more commonly found in the text. As we have seen, an ascetic discourse, which represents an ultimate perspective on reality, regards all bodies as alike, characterizing these in largely negative terms as inherently impermanent, foul, and without intrinsic and eternal essence. A physiomoral discourse, on the other hand, which represents a conventional perspective on reality, displays a fascination with bodily differences, characterizing particular kinds of bodies in positive terms as necessary conditions for the ethical development of oneself and others. A vision of the inherent purity of *all* bodies is an ultimate perspective on reality, but one that offers a decidedly positive evaluation of bodies. The passage shares with the ascetic discourse the assumption that all bodies have the same nature, while at the same time it shares with the physiomoral discourse a positive representation of bodies. The passage therefore provides an alternative to both ascetic and physiomoral discourses, offering a radically transformed vision of bodies and, by implication, bodied beings: all bodied beings have the features of a buddha. The passage, which occurs in a meditation designed to purify bodied being, thus suggests that the process of purifying bodied being requires, in part, an ability to recognize its inherently pure nature. A meditation that begins in standard ascetic style with contemplation of the unsatisfactory nature of all bodies ends with contemplation of bodily perfection.

We have already seen that ascetic and physiomoral discourses share the same goal of producing bodied beings with bodies that benefit others. This alternative discourse on the inherent purity of bodies also asks bodhisattvas to use their bodies as a basis for the transformation of others. The meditation itself is part of a wide range of technologies of the self designed to purify a bodhisattva's bodied being and thus render the bodhisattva's body capable of ripening others. More specifically, however, the meditation indicates that a bodhisattva's physiomoral self-transformation is connected to the physiomoral transformation of all other beings. By connecting his body to those of others, the bodhisattva also commits himself to the materialization of their buddhahood. The passage does not clarify just how a bodhisattva should establish others in the body of a buddha. Jürg Hedinger asks whether the bodhisattva's "spiritual power" has some kind of direct effect on the bodies of other living beings.[107] Certainly the evidence presented in this book would support such an interpretation. We have seen throughout the book that bodhisattvas use their bodies to ripen others. I would, however, want to clarify that it is not just a bodhisattva's "spiritual power" that accounts for such ripening; it is his physiomoral power. Hedinger's observation also raises the question of how literally we are to take the "connection" that bodhisattvas make between their bodies and those of others. As I have interpreted the passage, this connection is a mental one created during the course of meditation. Perhaps, however, in the context of the *Compendium of Training*, which highlights the transformative nature of encounters between bodhisattvas and other living beings, we need to consider the possibility that these connections are also physical. The passage affords no certainty on this matter. Certain only is the fact that the passage supports my larger argument that the various meditations and philosophical reflections on bodies contained in this text seek to transform bodhisattvas physically and morally so that they can do the same for others.

The *Compendium of Training* demonstrates the extraordinary complexity of body discourse in South Asian Buddhist literature. A single text—even a single passage—can display diverse and seemingly contradictory perspectives on bodies. Side by side in the *Compendium of Training* we find both negative and positive statements about bodies. As we have seen, however, even the most negative of statements does not mean that the text dismisses the significance and value of bodies. To the contrary, ascetic, physiomoral, and other forms of body discourse all contribute to the text's larger goal of cultivating bodied beings that can benefit others. Thus meditations and philosophical reflections on bodies, which challenge the ultimate significance and value of these, are actually in the service of producing the conventionally valorized virtuous bodies of buddhas and bodhisattvas. Whether by valorizing these virtuous bodies or even by affirming, however briefly, the ultimate purity of all bodies, the text repeatedly places bodies front and center in bodhisattva training, because it regards these as critical to the ethical development of oneself and others. All forms of body discourse serve the larger purpose of cultivating bodied beings with bodies that can ripen others.

6

Revisioning Virtue

Then noble Sudhana touched his head to the feet of the monk, Sāradhvaja, circumambulated him many hundreds of thousands of times, looked at the monk, Sāradhvaja, prostrated, looking again and again, all the while prostrating, bowing, bowing down, bearing him in mind, thinking about him, meditating on him, soaking him in, making an inspired utterance, exclaiming in admiration, looking at his virtues, penetrating them, not being frightened of them, recollecting them, making them firm in his mind, not giving them up, mentally approaching them, binding them fast to himself, attaining the bodhisattva vow, yearning for his sight, grasping the distinctive characteristic of his voice *and so on until* he departed from his presence.[1]

The *Compendium of Training* serves in this book as a case study of the different roles Buddhists have ascribed to bodies in the ethical development of living beings. It makes for an ideal case study precisely because it is a compendium. It draws on approximately one hundred Buddhist sources, thereby demonstrating that bodies figure prominently in Buddhist ethical discourse. The value of this case study, however, lies not in the fact that it describes *the* Buddhist perspective on bodies, or even *the* medieval Indian Buddhist perspective on bodies. Instead its value lies in the fact that it reveals the presence of a larger conversation on the topic. The *Compendium of Training* is one particular voice in this conversation. To be sure, many of the key themes in it recur across texts. Nevertheless, the *Compendium of Training* represents but one way of articulating these themes. The text reveals an author in conversation with his tradition, choosing and framing quotations to create his own original vision of the bodhisattva discipline, one in which bodies play key roles in the ethical development of oneself and others. In this final chapter I summarize the arguments of the book and consider their ethical implications for both medieval and contemporary readers of the *Compendium of Training.*

The Corporeal Specificity of Buddhist Ethical Ideals

Throughout this book I have argued that there is a physical dimension to morality in Buddhist ethics. The *Compendium of Training* seeks to cultivate bodhisattvas with virtuous bodies as well as virtuous heartminds. The text indicates this goal from the very outset, when it makes *ātmabhāva* a key item in its summary of the vital points of the bodhisattva discipline. As we have seen, *ātmabhāva* is a hard word to translate. It designates "one's whole person," that is, the entire complex of body, feelings, and thoughts.[2] The *Compendium of Training* and its sources underscore the corporeality of the *ātmabhāva* and therefore I have translated the term as "bodied being."[3] According to the text's summary of the vital points of the bodhisattva discipline, bodhisattvas must cultivate bodied beings that benefit others. This means that they must cultivate both virtuous bodies and virtuous heartminds. According to the *Compendium of Training,* the mere sight of a bodhisattva should serve to please, attract, and ripen others. The text brings into sharp relief the extent to which Mahāyāna Buddhist texts portray bodhisattva bodies as key vehicles for the transformation of others.

The *Compendium of Training*'s attention to the transformative effects of bodhisattva bodies sheds new light on the metaphor "ripening living beings." "Ripening" (*paripac-*) is a metaphor for ethical and spiritual maturation. According to the *Compendium of Training* and its sources, bodhisattvas use their bodies as well as their heartminds to ripen others. The *Compendium of Training* prescribes a wide range of practices, or technologies of the self, to make this possible, including various kinds of bodhisattva and monastic vows. These vows produce bodies in present and future lifetimes that have transformative effects on others. Significantly, these transformative effects are both physical and moral. When living beings are ripened, they are changed in physical as well as moral ways. Animals become male gods, women become men, and human beings are alleviated of the torment of the defilements.

The metaphor of ripening living beings illumines a key feature of Mahāyāna Buddhist ethics. Specifically, the metaphor underscores the ethical interdependence of living beings, since it implies both an ethical agent and an ethical patient: one who ripens and one who is ripened. Living beings require the skillful and compassionate intervention of bodhisattvas if they are to be ripened. For bodhisattvas, *self*-transformation is always in the service of the transformation of *others*. Most important, as we have seen, the roles of ethical agent and ethical patient are not mutually exclusive. The *Compendium of Training* envisions monastic communities as places of collective ripening where living beings participate in the mutual transformation of each other. Ripening is a communal enterprise in which living beings enable each other to realize their full ethical and spiritual potential.

The *Compendium of Training* draws on more than one form of body discourse in its description of the bodhisattva discipline. I have examined the presence of both physiomoral and ascetic discourses in the text. The physiomoral discourse posits a close relationship between body and morality. This relationship is complex and construed in different ways. As the effects of morality, bodies serve as markers of past and present moral character. As the conditions for morality, bodies enable or disable particular kinds of moral agency. Most important, the bodies of buddhas, bodhisattvas, arhats, and monastics serve as the conditions for the ethical transformation of others. The close relationship between body and morality begs the question: What are virtues? Are these best described as affective and cognitive aspects of a person's psyche, or can virtues also be described as features, postures, and movements of a person's body? I have argued throughout this book that virtues have both physical and moral dimensions. They are as evident in bodies as in heartminds. Consequently, we can speak of virtuous bodies and their opposite.

Buddhist texts associate a wide range of bodily features with morality. These include realm of rebirth, beauty, health, the absence or presence of physical and mental disabilities, longevity, sex, caste, and family. Additionally, forms of bodily inscription such as monastic dress, posture, and movement are also important markers of moral character. From a Buddhist point of view, virtue and vice are, to some extent, contagious. For example, the mere sight of a well-disciplined monastic who has mastered proper etiquette and deportment can serve to ripen living beings. The sight of an undisciplined monastic, however, may serve to repel living beings and thereby consign them to horrific torment in hell. Hence the *Compendium of Training* repeatedly admonishes monastics to conduct themselves in such a way that they please rather than displease others. The text appears to regard a variety of virtuous monastic bodies as potentially transformative for others. These include bodies formed by conventional monastic etiquette and deportment as well as bodies formed by more extreme ascetic practices.

In spite of the prominence of the physiomoral discourse in Buddhist literature, it is the ascetic discourse that has received most scholarly attention, in part because it is a much more explicit kind of body discourse. The physiomoral discourse frequently operates at the level of implicit assumption rather than explicit discourse in Buddhist texts. Thus it is widely assumed, but rarely overtly argued in these texts, that body and morality are inextricably linked. The ascetic discourse is altogether different. It argues explicitly that all bodies, no matter how virtuous, are impermanent, foul, and without any intrinsic and eternal essence. Physiomoral and ascetic discourses offer very different perspectives on bodies. As we have seen, the difference in their perspectives corresponds more broadly to a difference between conventional and ultimate perspectives on reality. Whereas a physiomoral discourse pays close attention to the details of bodily differences because bodies serve as markers of, and conditions for, ethical development, an ascetic discourse rejects the ultimate validity of any such differences. From an ascetic perspective, all bodies are equally unsatisfactory.

How do we reconcile the presence of such different discourses in one text? The answer lies in how we read the *Compendium of Training*. My approach has been to read it as a coherent text—in other words, to assume that it does, in the end, make sense. Even the most negative statements on bodies must be interpreted in light of the text's overall goal of producing bodhisattvas with bodies that ripen others. Therefore I have argued that the prescribed meditations and philosophical reflections on the unsatisfactory nature of bodies are technologies of the self, in the Foucauldian sense. They are disciplinary practices adopted to transform an individual into an ideal ethical subject. This transformation has physical and moral consequences. As we have seen, the primary goal of these practices is to eradicate male sexual desire for women. Thus these practices materialize celibate monastic bodhisattvas and, eventually when bodhisattvas reach the end of their religious path, buddhas. There is a productive paradox at the heart of the *Compendium of Training*'s discourses on bodies. The bodhisattva who learns to regard his body as impermanent, foul, and without intrinsic and eternal essence, gets the most virtuous body of all: the irresistibly beautiful body of a buddha. Scholars have sometimes mistakenly interpreted the ascetic discourse as evidence that South Asian Buddhists ascribed little value to bodies. The *Compendium of Training* suggests otherwise. Here an ascetic discourse is in the service of producing a range of virtuous bodied beings, valued for their physical as well as moral qualities.

This study of the *Compendium of Training* demonstrates that we cannot fully understand Buddhist ethics until we explore the significance of bodies in ethical thought and practice. For feminist scholars such as myself, the importance of bodies in Buddhist ethical discourse raises questions about the gendering of Buddhist ethical ideals. There is no such thing as a generic body, and therefore ethical ideals such as that of the bodhisattva are embodied in very particular kinds of ways. Mahāyāna Buddhists believe that as bodhisattvas progress along the path to buddhahood they eventually gain the ability to manifest bodies of magical transformation (*nirmāṇakāya*). In theory, there is no limit to the kinds of bodies bodhisattvas can assume in order to help living beings. In reality, the *Compendium of Training* displays a strong preference for male bodies. The bodies that ripen others are almost exclusively male in this text. The one female bodhisattva to appear in the text occupies at best an ambiguous position, since her beauty poses a threat to male celibacy. The *Compendium of Training* displays again and again a male ascetic fear of women. By placing body at the center of ethical inquiry, this study of the *Compendium of Training* illumines the centrality of bodies to the bodhisattva ideal as well as the corporeal specificity of that ideal as envisioned by the text.

A Hermeneutics of Recovery and Suspicion

I had two broad goals in this book. First, I wanted to set the historical record straight by demonstrating that South Asian Buddhists took bodies very seriously and that one of the reasons they did so was because they believed that bodies played critical roles in the ethical development of living beings. Second, I wanted to explore the ethical implications, for medieval as well as contemporary audiences, of a text that constantly draws attention to the corporeal specificity of ethical ideals. There is thus a constructive component to my analysis which takes this study of the *Compendium of Training* beyond the confines of more traditional historical textual studies. In this final section of the book I create a dialogue between medieval and modern worlds in order to see how each can illumine, enrich, and challenge the other. My objectives are twofold: First, I wish to investigate what a medieval Indian Buddhist text, however distant its cultural assumptions are from our own, can teach us today about the place of bodies in ethical life. Second, I wish to consider how a contemporary critique of the *Compendium of Training* can make possible the recognition of more diversely bodied Buddhist ethical ideals.

In order to meet these objectives I employ a hermeneutical method first espoused by Paul Ricoeur: a hermeneutics of recovery and suspicion. In his book *Freud & Philosophy*, Ricoeur describes a hermeneutics of recovery—a term that he himself does not use but that has become associated with him—as the effort to recollect or restore meaning.[4] His language is explicitly theological. The recollection of meaning takes the form of kerygma or revelation;[5] it is a disclosure of the sacred.[6] A hermeneutics of recovery requires that we take seriously the truth claims of the texts we study. It requires, in Ricoeur's words, a "willingness to listen"[7] and, above all, an admission that we ourselves are personally addressed by these texts. Ricoeur writes,

> The philosopher as such cannot and must not avoid the question of the absolute validity of his object. For would I be interested in the object, could I stress concern for the object . . . if I did not expect, from within understanding, this something to "address" itself to me? Is not the expectation of being spoken to what motivates the concern for the object?[8]

A willingness to listen to the *Compendium of Training* means that we approach this text as something more than a historical record of a particular moment in Mahāyāna Buddhist history. From the standpoint of a hermeneutics of recovery, the *Compendium of Training*'s value transcends the fact that it provides insight into the medieval past. Instead, its value lies also, and perhaps even more so, in the fact that its ethical vision may provide insight into the present.

If a hermeneutics of recovery requires a willingness to listen, a hermeneutics of suspicion requires a "willingness to suspect."[9] It calls into question the very truth claims that a hermeneutics of recovery reveals. Ricoeur defines Marx, Nietzsche, and Freud as the three "masters of suspicion," because their analyses of class struggle, the will to power, and the unconscious, respectively, challenge normative conceptions of human beings and their societies. For these masters of suspicion, reality is not as it appears. Truth as we know it is but illusion. Ricoeur's list of masters of suspicion can and should be expanded to include feminist scholars whose analyses of gender have fundamentally changed the ways in which all kinds of people evaluate human relationships and institutions. The hermeneutics of suspicion I employ in my analysis of the *Compendium of Training* is largely a feminist one. I use a feminist hermeneutics of suspicion in order to reveal the gendered nature of the bodhisattva ideal in this text and, more broadly, to problematize the text's hierarchical ranking of bodies and bodily differences.

These two hermeneutical approaches of recovery and suspicion can be characterized respectively as an effort to *re*cover truth and an effort to *un*cover truth. A hermeneutics of recovery enables me to recover a medieval Indian Buddhist ethical vision—one that I believe offers important resources to contemporary scholars and practitioners. A hermeneutics of suspicion enables me to uncover the limitations of this ethical vision—limitations that must be addressed if the *Compendium of Training* is indeed going to be useful for scholars and practitioners today. Like Ricoeur, I believe that each hermeneutical approach, when taken by itself, is insufficient for interpretation. A hermeneutics of recovery takes too much at face value. A hermeneutics of suspicion fails to recognize that there is anything of value at hand. Therefore my method, following Ricoeur, is to combine both approaches—to listen and to suspect.

Those of us writing within the discipline of religion are frequently faced with the question of whether our work represents an "insider's" perspective or an "outsider's" perspective on a particular religious tradition. For several reasons, I find this question deeply troubling. First, notions of "insider" and "outsider" generally rest on essentialistic definitions of a tradition, as if all "insiders" had identical beliefs and practices. Second, simplistic categories like "insider" and "outsider" fail to do justice to the complex identities of bodied beings. Third, it is sometimes incorrectly assumed that a hermeneutics of recovery could be practiced only by an "insider," whereas a hermeneutics of suspicion could be practiced only by an "outsider." Ricoeur asks that a single individual employ both hermeneutical methods. He assumes that any text worth considering is capable of speaking to bodied beings with varied allegiances and commitments. Nowhere in *Freud & Philosophy* is there a suggestion that only Christians can appreciate the Gospels or that only Freudians can appreciate Freud. Nor is it suggested that Christians are incapable of criticizing the Gospels or that Freudians are incapable of criticizing Freud. Ricoeur assumes that all persons can engage critically with both the Gospels and Freud. Thus Ricoeur would ask that we, whether Buddhist or not, approach the *Compendium of Training* with a willingness to listen and a willingness to suspect. His hermeneutical approach renders problematic simplistic distinctions between "insider" and "outsider." As one listens to a text, allowing it to speak to one as truth, one is altered by it. Such alteration, however, does not imply a suspension of critical thinking. For Ricoeur, engagement with a text is always a form of critical engagement.

How, then, have I gone about implementing the two hermeneutical approaches of recovery and suspicion? I have listened to the *Compendium of Training* by engaging in a close reading of this Sanskrit text. What do I mean by a close reading? Most obviously, I mean paying careful attention to the text's language, such as its vocabulary for body and bodied being, and its metaphors for ethical development, notably, that of ripening. A close reading also entails paying attention to the narrative and descriptive details of the text, which reveal, among other things, an implicit assumption that body and morality are interrelated. Additionally, a close reading necessitates attending to the text's internal organization, especially as outlined in the verse summary of the bodhisattva discipline. Finally, a close reading requires treating this text as a coherent work and therefore trying to make sense of the different forms of body discourse in it.

A close reading of the Sanskrit *Compendium of Training* also forms the basis of my feminist critique. I have paid careful attention to the presence in this text of very different kinds of bodied beings and the relative value these have in a Buddhist cosmological hierarchy. I have been especially interested in the different representations and evaluations of men's and women's bodies. The *Compendium of Training*'s focus on bodies and bodily differences makes it impossible for an attentive reader to ignore the corporeal specificity of its ethical ideals and especially the gendered nature of its bodhisattva ideal. Thus a close reading of the text serves to problematize a frequently made claim that Indian Mahāyāna Buddhism invariably represented an improvement in the status of Buddhist women.

According to Ricoeur, a hermeneutics of recovery requires that we approach our texts with "the expectation of being spoken to." I would add that a hermeneutics of suspicion also requires that we speak back to these same texts. Herein lies the possibility of a dialogue between medieval and modern worlds. Like Ronald Inden, I wish to treat the texts I study as "living arguments" not only in "their historic usages" but also in "our reenactment" of these arguments in the present.[10] One of the legacies of colonialism is that the Indian past often appears to scholars as quite a bit more "dead" than the European past.[11] Dipesh Chakrabarty, who makes this point, argues that whereas it is common to find social scientists engaged in passionate debate with figures such as Marx and Weber, it is rare to find one who "would argue seriously" with comparable figures in Indian intellectual history.[12] Indian intellectual traditions are treated as "matters of historical research."[13] European intellectual traditions, on the other hand, hold an interest for scholars that transcends the historical. In a postcolonial world it is no longer acceptable to treat European intellectual traditions alone as "living arguments" that are pertinent to our own times and problems. Chakrabarty's remarks are directed specifically at social scientists, but they are pertinent for other scholars as well. I am committed to reading the *Compendium of Training* as a living argument. In doing so, I hope to encourage scholars in diverse disciplines as well as religious practitioners to enter into its argument, and the arguments of other South Asian Buddhist texts, since these offer valuable intellectual resources for those interested in the place of bodies in ethical life.

Neither the effort to recover a medieval Indian Buddhist ethical vision nor the effort to uncover the limitations of that vision corresponds to traditional notions of scholarly neutrality. A neutral methodological stance—should such even be possible—is deeply problematic, because it fails to take its subject matter seriously enough to argue with it. The measure of my esteem for the *Compendium of Training* and those who produced and used this text can be gauged by the extent to which I am committed to critical engagement with the text. It is only through such critical engagement that the *Compendium of Training* can move out from the medieval past and become part of the living arguments of the present.

Toward More Diversely Bodied Ethical Ideals

The *Compendium of Training* presents a holistic vision of ethical persons, addressing itself at all times to a decidedly bodied being. Its bodhisattva discipline is meant to transform bodies as much as heartminds. In this text, as in so many Buddhist texts, ethical maturation manifests in physical as well as moral ways. Ethical ideals such as that of the bodhisattva are embodied ideals. Thus living beings encounter these ethical ideals in concrete corporeal forms. The *Compendium of Training* is extraordinarily conscious of the impact such encounters can have on living beings. Seeing a bodhisattva whose features, gestures, and movements instantiate a high level of moral discipline can be as transformative as hearing this bodhisattva preach. Recall the example of Sudhana in chapter 2 of this book. The relevant passage is quoted again at the head of this chapter. Sudhana is inspired to formulate the bodhisattva vow upon seeing his beautiful friend (*kalyāṇamitra*), the monk Sāradhvaja. It is common in Buddhist literature for living beings to convert to Buddhism or commit to Buddhist ethical principles at the sight of a buddha, bodhisattva, arhat, or monastic. The *Compendium of Training* is not alone in underscoring the transformative power of bodies. Nor is this phenomenon confined to texts. Contemporary Buddhists also frequently comment on the positive effects they experience at the sight of religious figures. For instance, Georges B. J. Dreyfus, a scholar of Buddhism and a former Buddhist monk in the Tibetan tradition, mentions in the course of a discussion of Buddhist monastic decorum that his own initial interest in Buddhism was inspired by seeing monastics in North India.[14] I myself have observed lay Buddhists in Sri Lanka take great pleasure in seeing monastics walk in ceremonial procession, such as when entering a temple to receive alms.

The fact that Buddhists display such a strong interest in seeing monastics and religious teachers should come as no surprise, given the significance of *darśan*, or seeing the divine, in South Asian religions. Diana L. Eck has demonstrated that seeing the divine—whether in the form of a sacred image, sacred place, or holy person—is "the central act of Hindu worship."[15] Seeing the divine in the form of holy persons such as bodhisattvas is also a central act in Buddhist ethics. Of course, the *Compendium of Training* does not speak just about *seeing* bodhisattvas. It maintains that various forms of contact with bodhisattvas have physically and morally transformative effects on living beings. It points more broadly to the importance of *physical proximity* to bodhisattvas. Living beings are ripened through physical proximity to bodhisattvas, who literally materialize the bodhisattva ideal in their very appearance and conduct. Hence the text devotes most of its second chapter to the role of the beautiful friend. It warns bodhisattvas that they must never abandon their beautiful friends, because beautiful friends keep them from committing sins and earning bad rebirths. Thus bodhisattvas should cultivate affection and intense respect for their beautiful friends, they should follow their instructions, and they should spend time in their presence, like a good son "looking at the face of the beautiful friend."[16] Along with advising bodhisattvas to associate with beautiful friends, the *Compendium of Training* also advises them to avoid association with sinful or ugly friends (*pāpamitra, akalyāṇamitra*), and it provides on occasion specific lists of those who should be avoided. One such list includes members of the ruling elite, various kinds of entertainers, alcoholics, heretics, monks making false claims about their spiritual achievements, non-normatively sexed persons (*strīpaṇḍaka*), members of certain low castes, butchers, and courtesans.[17] Virtue and vice are indeed to some extent contagious in a Buddhist worldview. Those who materialize virtue help to ripen others, while those who materialize vice may lead others to hell.

The focus on proximity to those who materialize the bodhisattva ideal is not limited to the need for proximity to one's religious superiors. One also needs proximity to peers who are committed to a similar ethical path. Recall that the *Compendium of Training* regards monastic communities as places of mutual ripening. Monastic bodhisattvas are, to borrow Derris's terms, simultaneously "benefactors" and "beneficiaries" of each other.[18] Many of the instructions in the *Compendium of Training* are aimed at creating ideal communities of monastic bodhisattvas who ripen each other. Such communities are not easy to create. The *Compendium of Training* is cognizant of the opportunities as well as the challenges that monastic life presents to bodhisattvas. It is particularly aware of how difficult it can be to get along with one's monastic companions. Thus the text devotes a great deal of attention to instructing bodhisattvas how to behave toward each other. As we have seen, bodhisattvas are repeatedly admonished to conduct themselves in such a way that they please, rather than displease, others. It is equally important for bodhisattvas to learn how to take pleasure themselves in their monastic companions. Accordingly, the *Compendium of Training* promises incalculable amounts of merit to those who can behold, with a pleased heartmind (*prasanna-citta*), another bodhisattva committed to Mahāyāna Buddhism.[19] At the same time the text warns that anyone who so much as speaks harshly to another bodhisattva will incur incalculable amounts of sin.[20] The very fact that the *Compendium of Training* makes such promises and delivers such warnings indicates that pleasure in one's monastic companions does not necessarily come naturally. It may take considerable work, just as it takes considerable work to conduct oneself in such a way that one pleases others. The tensions inherent in monastic life may be one of the reasons why the *Compendium of Training* urges periodic solitary retreats in the wilderness. It should be noted, however, that even in the wilderness bodhisattvas are never entirely without community. As we saw in chapter 5 of this book, they must be prepared to receive visitors. Additionally, Harrison suggests that wilderness-dwelling monastics may actually have congregated in groups.[21] But even if a bodhisattva had no companions, the *Compendium of Training* insists that he is never really alone. The text closes its chapter on wilderness retreats with the following advice to bodhisattvas:

> While dwelling in that wilderness abode, he should think thus: Although I came to the wilderness alone, unaccompanied, with no friend who might admonish me about things I have done well or done wrong, still there are these gods, nāgas, yakṣas, and buddhas, blessed ones, who know my mental disposition. They are my witnesses: [They know whether] while I am dwelling here in this wilderness retreat I will come under the influence of bad thoughts.[22]

Even alone in the wilderness, bodhisattvas are surrounded by various kinds of divine beings. The passage concludes by warning bodhisattvas that should they give rise to any bad feelings or thoughts, they will have broken their word to the gods, nāgas, and yakṣas (presumably to maintain the bodhisattva discipline); they will also have displeased the buddhas.[23]

The *Compendium of Training* urges bodhisattvas to regard all other bodhisattvas as their teachers (*śāstṛ*).[24] Indeed it urges bodhisattvas to regard living beings in general as their teachers on the off chance that one of them might be a bodhisattva. The rationale behind this advice is that bodhisattvas must be careful never to disrespect another bodhisattva—whether in deed, word, or thought—since they would thereby incur great sin. The problem is that bodhisattvas may not always be able to tell that another individual is also a bodhisattva, especially if that individual is at the very early stages of his or her practice. Hence it is best to regard all living beings with the respect due a teacher to make sure one does not unwittingly disrespect a bodhisattva.[25] This advice comes in the form of a quotation from the *Śūraṅgamasamādhisūtra*. Significantly, the *Compendium of Training* follows this quotation with a piece of advice from the author of the *Compendium of Training* himself. Śāntideva adds that if it is the case that one should guard against disrespect of those who might or might not be bodhisattvas, how much more is this the case for those who "certainly" (*niyatam*) "have the mark of having attained awakening" (*bodhi-prāpti-cihna*).[26] As always, the *Compendium of Training* is attentive to the physical as well as moral consequences of the bodhisattva discipline. Awakening produces a visible mark.

The *Compendium of Training* seeks to cultivate bodhisattvas with virtuous bodies as well as virtuous heartminds. Consequently, the text offers instruction on how to comport oneself in a pleasing and attractive manner. Producing virtuous bodied beings, however, takes considerable time and effort. Therefore the text also offers instruction on how to respond to one's monastic companions, who may or may not always comport themselves in a pleasing and attractive manner. Thus on the one hand bodhisattvas must learn how to comport themselves in a manner conducive to the ripening of others, and on the other hand they must learn how to overlook any faults in the comportment of others so that they remain open to being ripened themselves. The *Compendium of Training* seeks to create monastic communities conducive to the mutual ripening of its members and it underscores that such mutual ripening involves bodies as much as it does heartminds.

As compelling as such a holistic ethical vision might be, it is also problematic. The problem, of course, is that bodhisattvas in the *Compendium of Training* assume a limited range of material forms. Not all bodies are equal. The *Compendium of Training* adheres to a hierarchical ranking of bodies in which some are better than others. For instance, men are better than women, high castes are better than low castes, and humans are better than animals. In this hierarchical universe, only certain kinds of bodies are deemed capable of ripening others. As a feminist I am especially concerned with the gendered nature of the bodhisattva ideal in this text. Male bodhisattva bodies ripen others; female bodies do not.

The gendered nature of the bodhisattva ideal in the *Compendium of Training* calls into question modern representations of Mahāyāna Buddhism that stress its egalitarian nature. Modern scholars as well as practitioners of Buddhism often characterize Mahāyāna traditions as egalitarian because they offer a universal path to buddhahood. In other words, they make buddhahood accessible to all living beings, including women. For this reason, they named themselves the Mahāyāna, which means "great vehicle," and called their Buddhist rivals the Hīnayāna, or "inferior vehicle." The Mahāyāna polemic against the Hīnayāna goes as follows: Hīnayāna Buddhists believe that the highest goal a person can aspire to is that of the arhat, or saint. Buddhahood is too difficult a goal for most living beings. This was a general belief among the various Mainstream Buddhist schools that arose within the first few centuries following the death of the historical Buddha. Mahāyāna Buddhists, however, encourage all living beings to embark on the bodhisattva path to buddhahood. By opening up the goal of buddhahood to all living beings, Mahāyāna Buddhist traditions earned a reputation for being more inclusive than their rivals. Scholars and practitioners frequently emphasize a perceived improvement in the status of women in Mahāyāna traditions, because even women can pursue the ultimate goal of buddhahood.

There is no doubt that, in theory at least, Mahāyāna traditions today embrace egalitarian ideals, including gender equality. A few scholars, however, have questioned whether this has always been the case.[27] In a study of one Mahāyāna scripture called *The Inquiry of Ugra (Ugraparipṛcchā)*—a scripture heavily quoted in the *Compendium of Training*—Jan Nattier maintains that "the emergence of the goal of Buddhahood (as opposed to Arhatship) brought with it a perceptible drop in women's status in those circles that embraced it."[28] Why? As Nattier argues, Mainstream Buddhism (Nattier prefers the term "early Buddhism") and Mahāyāna Buddhism record the existence of both male and female arhats. Theoretically at least, this goal has always been open to men and women alike. However, Mainstream and Mahāyāna Buddhism uniformly conceptualized buddhahood as exclusively male. It is well known that all buddhas possess a set of thirty-two marks (see chapter 4 of this book), one of which is a "sheathed" or "retractable" penis.[29] Thus one of the conditions a bodhisattva must meet before he or she can become a buddha is male sex. Nattier suggests that this requirement may be one reason that the words "buddha" and "bodhisattva" have no feminine forms in Sanskrit or Prākrit languages, whereas there are feminine forms for other kinds of Buddhist practitioners, notably, arhats, monastics, and laypersons.[30] The gendered nature of buddhahood caused some Mahāyāna Buddhists in ancient and medieval India to wonder whether women really could become buddhas.[31] They speculated at times that women first had to become men, through either rebirth or miraculous transformation. Nattier concludes, "It is ironic, then, that while the 'Mahāyāna' is often portrayed in twentieth-century publications as more welcoming of women than earlier Buddhism had been, the reality appears to have been the opposite. While the highest goal of Arhatship was, in early Buddhism, completely accessible to women, the goal of Buddhahood was not."[32]

Whether *all* premodern forms of Mahāyāna Buddhism were equally unwelcoming toward women is debatable. Alan Sponberg rightly observes the presence of a "multiplicity of voices" on women in Buddhist literature.[33] Thus we find a mix of positive, negative, and downright ambiguous representations of women in Mahāyāna texts. Such a "multiplicity of voices" suggests that Mahāyāna Buddhists historically held a range of opinions concerning women's full participation in their tradition. Mahāyāna Buddhists were neither uniformly misogynist nor uniformly egalitarian. Instead they made different kinds of choices about how to represent women. The *Compendium of Training* constitutes one such choice. Like other Mahāyāna scriptures, the *Compendium of Training* contains no female buddhas. It also contains only one female bodhisattva, who, as we have seen, occupies an ambiguous position in the text since she instills lust in men. One could argue, however, that in the case of the *Compendium of Training* at least, the gendered nature of the bodhisattva ideal is neither surprising nor problematic, since this text was written primarily for a male monastic audience. The problem, however, is that the text itself actually claims that its bodhisattva discipline is also accessible to *some* women (see chapter 2 of this book). What is troubling for feminists is not so much that texts represent a male perspective, but that these same texts sometimes claim to represent a more universal perspective. Subsequent generations of readers, misled by such seemingly universalistic claims, fail to acknowledge the gendered nature of Buddhist ethical ideals. They thus carry these ideals into the present without subjecting them to critical reflection. We need to interrogate the universalistic claims of Mahāyāna Buddhist texts, because only when we acknowledge the gendered perspectives of these texts can we begin to generate more inclusive interpretations and uses of them. Only by unmasking the gendered nature of Buddhist ethical ideals can we create the possibility of more diversely bodied ethical ideals.

Given the fact that the *Compendium of Training* affirms a hierarchical rather than egalitarian society and cosmos, some might feel that its ethical vision is too problematic to offer any useful intellectual resources to contemporary scholars and practitioners. When the *Compendium of Training* foregrounds the embodied nature of the bodhisattva ideal, it draws our attention to the fact that living beings are different from one another. Difference, however, implies hierarchy in this text and more broadly in premodern South Asian Buddhist literature. Not surprisingly, to date, scholars and practitioners of Buddhism committed to egalitarian ideals have generally chosen to emphasize those aspects of Buddhism that affirm living beings' commonalities rather than their differences. For instance, some point to the fact that Buddhist traditions endow all living beings with the same capacity for liberation, although some living beings will have to wait until they achieve a more favorable rebirth to actualize that capacity. Others emphasize that living beings have the same basic nature. For instance, Śāntideva observes in his *Understanding the Way to Awakening* that all living beings desire happiness and fear suffering.[34] East Asian Mahāyāna Buddhists commonly assert that all living beings possess "buddha nature." Another common approach, especially in studies of Mahāyāna Buddhism, is to invoke the philosophical distinction between conventional and ultimate perspectives on reality in order to argue for the ultimate insignificance or "emptiness" of all conventionally valued differences. For example, some scholars and practitioners of Buddhism have argued for men's and women's equality by denying the ultimate significance of sexual differences. Thus in a variety of ways modern scholars and practitioners have sought resources for an egalitarian ethic in those strands of Buddhism that claim that living beings are essentially the same.

Although I am no less committed to egalitarian ideals than other modern scholars and practitioners of Buddhism, I nevertheless turn to a discourse on bodies and ethics that emphasizes difference rather than commonality. Why? If Buddhist traditions offer such obvious resources for an egalitarian ethic, why not avail myself of them? Why especially do I not make more of the Mahāyāna philosophical doctrine of emptiness, which usually occupies pride of place in studies of Mahāyāna Buddhist ethics? I choose to focus on difference rather than commonality because, like many contemporary scholars outside the field of Buddhist studies, I am suspicious of ethical theories and perspectives that efface the fact of human differences. A growing number of contemporary scholars have argued that we should take body as the very starting point for any ethical inquiry. For example, one sociologist has suggested that all ethics should "take the body as its fundamental point of departure."[35] Feminist scholars in particular have been extremely suspicious of ethical theories that presume a generic universal subject, because that subject is frequently implicitly male. Feminist theory itself has been criticized for its common presumption of a Western, white, middle- or upper-middle-class, heterosexual subject, who masquerades as the generic woman. Consequently contemporary feminist theorists such as Grosz, among others, have begun to investigate how a variety of human differences such as sex, race, ethnicity, class, sexuality, and physiognomy shape our identities and experiences.[36] The *Compendium of Training* offers the opportunity to study a text that foregrounds the corporeal specificity of ethical ideals. As such, it may serve as a useful corrective to ethical discourses that efface the fact of human differences.

I am especially concerned about the potential misuse of the doctrine of emptiness. In my professional and personal experience, this doctrine is as frequently invoked to dismiss charges of sexism in Buddhism as it is to address the problem. Rita M. Gross puts it well when she says, "But if mind is truly beyond gender, why make such a fuss about gender? That is an argument I have often heard, usually from those who do not favor changes in liturgies or institutions that would make them more gender-inclusive, gender-free and gender-neutral."[37] Bernard Faure has recently argued that attempts to address sexism by invoking an ultimate perspective on reality are problematic because the "denial of gender at the ultimate level presupposes its preservation at the conventional level."[38] Thus it is possible to assert at one and the same time that men and women are the same from an ultimate perspective but different from a conventional perspective. Faure maintains that feminist scholars, in particular, too often take a Buddhist "rhetoric of equality" at face value without examining the effects this rhetoric actually has on the lives of women.[39] Undoubtedly, recourse to an ultimate perspective on sexual difference has been, and will continue to be, empowering for many men and women committed to gender equality. For others, however, this approach has proved problematic precisely because an ultimate perspective can be used to mask the conventional gendering of Buddhist ideals. Indeed it can be used to mask a variety of inequities. Hilda Ryūmon Gutiérrez Baldoquín has recently expressed concern that an emphasis on ultimate reality can sometimes serve to mask the presence of racism in Buddhist communities, especially in the predominantly white convert Buddhist communities of North America.[40] Thus it may be helpful to consider a range of approaches to sexism and other forms of inequality in Buddhist traditions.

I focus on difference rather than commonality because this is where a hermeneutics of recovery and suspicion leads me. When I practice a hermeneutics of recovery, I take seriously the embodied nature of Buddhist ethical ideals. I also take seriously the fact of human differences. There is no such thing as a generic body, thus there is no such thing as a generic materialization of virtue. The *Compendium of Training* may present us with a range of virtuous bodied beings, but these are always specific kinds of bodied beings. As we have seen, the bodied being of choice is a male monastic bodhisattva. Thus when I practice a hermeneutics of suspicion, I question the limited and limiting forms virtue assumes in the *Compendium of Training*. Instead of addressing sexism and other inequalities by invoking an ultimate perspective that effaces the fact of human differences, I prefer to operate within a conventional perspective and work toward rendering culturally legible and legitimate more diversely bodied ethical ideals.[41] A hermeneutics of recovery and suspicion offers modern readers of the *Compendium of Training* an opportunity to revision virtue. It prompts us to ask what kinds of bodied beings are present in our texts as well as in our communities. It challenges us to examine our own assumptions about what virtue should look like. It encourages us to cultivate, in Hallisey's words, a "grateful openness"[42] to the many bodied beings whose physical proximity to us is key to our own ripening. Thus a hermeneutics of recovery and suspicion reveals the rich resources the *Compendium of Training* and Buddhist ethical discourse, more broadly, may offer to those committed to a vision of human flourishing that values human differences.

Notes

CHAPTER I

1. Bendall, *Śikshāsamuccaya*, 299.1–2 (quotation from the *Avalokana-sūtra*): *na jātu so 'ndhaḥ khañjo vā kalpānām api koṭibhiḥ | utpādya bodhicittaṃ yaḥ śāstu stūpaṃ hi vandate* ||

2. Following Margaret R. Miles, I avoid the expression "the body" because this implies a generic body. There is no such thing as a generic body, as bodies are always marked by a variety of physical differences (whether genetic or environmental). See Miles, *Plotinus on Body and Beauty*, xii; and "Sex and the City (of God)," 308. I discuss this point in further detail in chapter 2.

3. I use the term "heartmind" because, as Sid Brown has observed, "In Buddhism, as in most Asian religions, the heart and mind are one; thoughts and feelings often are located in one place, called the 'heartmind'" (Brown, *The Journey of One Buddhist Nun*, 9). The Sanskrit word for heartmind is *citta*.

4. Keown, *Buddhism & Bioethics*, 39.

5. See Harvey, "Vinaya Principles for Assigning Degrees of Culpability," 271–291.

6. de Silva, "Buddhist Ethics," 61.

7. *Cetanāhaṃ bhikkhave kammaṃ vadāmi; cetayitvā kammaṃ karoti kāyena vācāya manasā* (Hardy, *The Aṅguttara-Nikāya*, pt. III, 415. Peter Harvey quotes this passage in his *An Introduction to Buddhist Ethics*, 17; see also de Silva, "Buddhist Ethics," 61; and Gombrich, *Buddhist Precept and Practice*, 288.

8. See Harrison, "Who Gets to Ride in the Great Vehicle?" 67–89; and Nattier, *A Few Good Men*.

9. See Foucault, *Discipline and Punish, The Use of Pleasure*, and *The Care of the Self.*

10. Hallisey, "In Defense of Rather Fragile and Local Achievement," 150.

11. Inden, "Introduction: From Philological to Dialogical Texts," 14.

12. For instance, Frank, "For a Sociology of the Body," 95.

13. I thank Jens Braarvig and Jonathan A. Silk for making a copy of the manuscript available to me.

14. Schopen, "The Manuscript of the *Vajracchedikā* Found at Gilgit," 95–98.

15. Klaus, "Einige Textkritische und exegetische Bemerkungen zu Śāntidevas Śikṣāsamuccaya (Kapitel XII und XIII)," 397–398; see also Nattier, *A Few Good Men*, 19–20.

16. Nattier, *A Few Good Men*, 19.

17. See, for instance, de Jong, review of *Aspekte der Schulung in der Laufbahn eines Bodhisattva*, 233.

18. Daniel, *Fluid Signs*; Inden and Nicholas, *Kinship in Bengali Culture*; Marriott, "Hindu Transactions," 109–142; and Marriott and Inden, "Toward an Ethnosociology of South Asian Caste Systems," 227–238.

19. Inden and Nicholas, *Kinship in Bengali Culture*, 65.

20. Grosz, *Volatile Bodies.*

21. Hallisey lectured extensively on this subject in his graduate and undergraduate courses at Harvard University.

22. Bendall, *Śikshāsamuccaya*, vii–viii.

23. Matics, *Entering the Path of Enlightenment*, 28.

24. Harrison, "The Case of the Vanishing Poet," forthcoming.

25. Ibid.

26. Ibid.

27. Heim, *Theories of the Gift in South Asia*, 23.

28. Ibid.

29. Blackburn, *Buddhist Learning and Textual Practice in Eighteenth-Century Lankan Monastic Culture*, 117.

30. Heim, *Theories of the Gift in South Asia*, 23. Jens Braarvig remarks, concerning "anthologies" such as the *Compendium of Training*, that these "probably replaced the original sūtras as canonical sources being shorter and more systematic" (Braarvig, *The Tradition of Imperishability in Buddhist Thought*, vol. 2 of *Akṣayamatinirdeśasūtra*, lvi).

31. Schopen, "Vinaya," 889.

32. The text calls itself a *vinaya* at Bendall, *Śikshāsamuccaya*, 366.4.

33. Nattier, *A Few Good Men*, 63.

34. Prajñākaramati quotes extensively from the *Compendium of Training* in his commentary on the *Bodhicaryāvatāra* (see La Vallée Poussin, *Prajñākaramati's Commentary to the Bodhicaryāvatāra of Śāntideva*). Atīśa quotes the *Compendium of Training* in his *Bodhipathapradīpa* (see Sherburne, *A Lamp for the Path and Commentary of Atīśa*).

35. Tsong-kha-pa, *The Great Treatise on the Stages of the Path to Enlightenment.*

36. See Huntington and Huntington, *Leaves from the* Bodhi *Tree*, 86–87.

37. Thapar, *A History of India*, vol. 1, 154.

38. Ibid.; Huntington and Huntington, *Leaves from the* Bodhi *Tree*, 87.

39. Beal, *Si-Yu-Ki*, ii.170.

40. Bendall, *Catalogue of the Buddhist Sanskrit Manuscripts in the University Library, Cambridge*, 106; Bendall, *Śikshāsamuccaya*, xxiv–xxvii.

41. On the classification of Bengali scripts, see Dimitrov, "Tables of the Old Bengali Script," 27–78.

42. Bendall, *Catalogue of the Buddhist Sanskrit Manuscripts in the University Library, Cambridge*, 109; see also Bendall, *Śikshāsamuccaya*, xxvii.

43. According to D. D. Kosambi and V. V. Gokhale, during the Pāla period (ca. eighth to twelfth centuries) monasteries awarded the title *paṇḍita* by royal decree to those scholars who had extensive formal education (Kosambi and Gokhale, *The Subhāṣitaratnakoṣa Compiled by Vidyākara*, xxxvi).

44. Hara Prasad Shastri makes a suggestion to this effect in his *A Descriptive Catalogue of Sanscrit* [sic] *Manuscripts in the Government Collection*, 22. On Vibhūticandra, see Stearns "The Life and Tibetan Legacy of the Indian *Mahāpaṇḍita* Vibhūticandra," 127–171.

45. Stearns, "The Life and Tibetan Legacy of the Indian *Mahāpaṇḍita* Vibhūticandra," 158–159.

46. Ibid., 158.

47. Ibid., 137.

48. I am using Kate Crosby and Andrew Skilton's translation of the title of the *Bodhicaryāvatāra* (Śāntideva, *The Bodhicaryāvatāra*, xxx).

49. The text is the *Bodhicaryāvatāratātparyapañjikā Viśeṣadyotanī* (*Byang chub kyi spyod pa la 'jug pa'i dgongs pa'i 'grel pa khyad par gsal byed*). See Stearns, "The Life and Tibetan Legacy of the Indian *Mahāpaṇḍita* Vibhūticandra," 160; and Williams, *Altruism and Reality*, 4.

50. de Jong, "La Légende de Śāntideva," 164.

51. Kosambi and Gokhale, *The Subhāṣitaratnakoṣa*, xxxvi–xxxvii, including n. 6–7.

52. Huntington and Huntington, *Leaves from the* Bodhi *Tree*, 76–77. See also Kosambi and Gokhale, *The Subhāṣitaratnakoṣa*, xxxvii, nn. 6–7.

53. Kosambi and Gokhale, *The Subhāṣitaratnakoṣa*, xxxvii. Approximate dates of Rāmapāla are from Huntington and Huntington, *Leaves from the* Bodhi *Tree*, 542.

54. See Huntington and Huntington, op. cit., 88; and Dutt, *Buddhist Monks and Monasteries of India*, 376–380.

55. Sāṅkṛityāyana, "Second Search of Sanskrit Palm-Leaf Mss. in Tibet," 32.

56. Majumdar, Raychaudhuri, and Datta, *An Advanced History of India*, 1053. I thank David E. Pingree and Kim L. Pflofker for their generous help in interpreting this colophon.

57. Huntington and Huntington, *Leaves from the* Bodhi *Tree*, 542. Unfortunately, not much is known about Kumārapāla of Bengal (Huntington, *The "Pāla-Sena" Schools of Sculpture*, 69).

58. See Williams, "General Introduction," to Śāntideva, *The Bodhicaryāvatāra*, viii.

59. For instance, Vibhūticandra of Jagaddala does so in the brief biography of Śāntideva included in his commentary on *Understanding the Way to Awakening* (de Jong, "La Légende de Śāntideva," 171).

60. See Pāsādika,"Tib J 380, a Dunhuang Manuscript Fragment of the Sūtrasamuccaya," 483.

61. Pagel, *The Bodhisattvapiṭaka*, 71.

62. It should be noted that the Dunhuang recension of *Understanding the Way to Awakening* (*Bodhicaryāvatāra*) names Akṣayamati, rather than Śāntideva, as the author of this text (Crosby and Skilton's "Translators' Introduction" to Śāntideva, *The Bodhicaryāvatāra*, xxxi).

63. Crosby and Skilton, "Translators' Introduction" to Śāntideva, *The Bodhicaryāvatāra*, xxxi. Crosby and Skilton cite the work of Akira Saito (Saito, *A Study of Akṣayamati (= Śāntideva)'s* Bodhisattvacaryāvatāra *as Found in the Tibetan Manuscripts from Tun-huang*, and "On the Difference between the Earlier and the Current Versions of Śāntideva's *Bodhi(sattva)caryāvatāra*"; see also Saito, "Śāntideva in the History of Mādhyamika Philosophy," 258.)

64. Crosby and Skilton, "Translators' Introduction" to Śāntideva, *The Bodhicaryāvatāra*, xli; see also xxxiii.

65. For instance, see de Jong, review of *Aspekte der Schulung in der Laufbahn eines Bodhisattva*, 230, 233.

66. Recent studies of the *Compendium of Training* include Clayton, "Ethics in the *Śikṣāsamuccaya*"; Clayton, *Moral Theory in Śāntideva's* Śikṣāsamuccaya; Hedinger, *Aspekte der Schulung in der Laufbahn eines Bodhisattva*; Mahoney, "Of the Progresse of the Bodhisattva"; and Mrozik, "The Relationship between Morality and the Body in Monastic Training According to the *Śikṣāsamuccaya*."

CHAPTER 2

1. Bendall, *Śikshāsamuccaya*, 21.23–22.4 (quotation from the *Akṣayamatisūtra*): *ayam eva mayā kāyaḥ sarvasatvānaṃ kiṃkuruṇīyeṣu kṣapayitavyaḥ* | *tad yathāpi nāmemāni bāhyāni catvāri mahābhūtāni pṛthivīdhātur abdhātus tejodhātur vāyudhātuś ca nānā[mukhair] nānāparyāyair nānārambaṇair nānopakaraṇair nānāparibhogaiḥ satvānāṃ nānopabhogaṃ gacchanti* | *evam evāham imaṃ kāyaṃ caturmahābhūtasamucchrayaṃ nānā[mukhair] nānāparyāyair nānārambaṇair nānopakaraṇair nānāparibhogair vistareṇa sarvasatvānāṃ upabhogyaṃ kariṣyāmīti* ' *sa imam arthavaśaṃ saṃpaśyan kāyaduṣkhatāṃ ca pratyavekṣate kāyaduṣkhatayā ca na parikhidyate satvāvekṣayeti* || Please note that the half-*daṇḍa*, which resembles an apostrophe with a blank space on either side, occurs throughout Bendall's edition. The manuscript itself had employed a "single point level with the middle of the letters as a minor stop, the equivalent of our comma or semicolon, often without causing a break in the *sandhi*." Bendall thought, however, that readers might confuse the single point with a *visarga* and thus replaced it with the half-*daṇḍa* (Bendall, "Introduction [preliminary]" to *Śikshāsamuccaya*, v). Please note that Bendall's edition contains *two* introductions, one

at the opening of the book and the other at the end; the preliminary introduction can be found at the *end* of the book. Please note as well that Bendall regularly spells *sattva* as *satva*, in accordance with the manuscript. Unless otherwise stated, I follow Bendall's punctuation and spelling. In this passage I have replaced "sukhair" with "mukhair" in accordance with Bendall's notes (Bendall, *Śikshāsamuccaya*, 398, n. 22.1, 2). My translation of the Sanskrit passage is partially based on the translation from the Tibetan given in Braarvig, *The Tradition of Imperishability in Buddhist Thought*, vol. 2 of *Akṣayamatinirdeśasūtra*, 485–486.

2. Grosz, *Volatile Bodies*, ix.

3. Ibid., 22. Recently Anne Carolyn Klein has argued that Buddhist traditions, in particular, foreground the extent to which subjectivity is rooted in body (Klein, "Buddhist Understandings of Subjectivity," 23–34).

4. The relevant passage occurs at Bendall, *Śikshāsamuccaya*, 17.5–15 (quoted in part from the *Ratnamegha*). I discuss the verse summary below.

5. Thus argued Bendall in his introduction to the Sanskrit text (Bendall, *Śikshāsamuccaya*, i–iii). This remains the position of current scholarship (see Harrison, "The Case of the Vanishing Poet: New Light on Śāntideva and the *Śikṣā-samuccaya*," forthcoming).

6. To the best of my knowledge Jürg Hedinger was the first to illumine the significance of the verse summary of the vital points of the bodhisattva discipline (Hedinger, *Aspekte der Schulung in der Laufbahn eines Bodhisattva*, 10–13). I discussed the verse summary in my 1998 dissertation (Mrozik, "The Relationship between Morality and the Body in Monastic Training According to the *Śikṣāsamuccaya*," chapter 1). Subsequently Barbra R. Clayton and Richard Mahoney have also argued for the importance of the verse summary. Clayton does so in *Moral Theory in Śāntideva's* Śikṣāsamuccaya, 39–40, which is based on her Ph.D. dissertation, "Ethics in the *Śikṣāsamuccaya*." Mahoney does so in his master's thesis, "Of the Progresse of the Bodhisattva," 16–21.

The numerous references to the verse summary throughout the text and especially at the opening of chapters clearly indicate that it provides the organizational and conceptual framework of the entire text. For example, Bendall, *Śikshāsamuccaya*, 17.13–14, 18.8–9, 26.4, 34.11–13, 34.18, 41.9–10, 44.19–20, 118.2, 127.8–9, 127.14–15, 131.13, 143.1–3, 143.14–15, 143.19–20, 146.21–22, 158.13–15, 160.2–3, 267.7, 267.10–11, 269.10, 270.8, 273.11–16, 275.9–10, 276.1–5, 284.6, 286.6, 289.11, 297.9, 311.5–6, 316.3–4, 348.3, 350.20–22, and 356.1.

7. Bendall, *Śikshāsamuccaya*, 17.13–14 (with emendation): *ātmabhāvasya bhogānāṃ tryadhvavṛtteḥ śubhasya ca* | *utsargaḥ sarvasatvebhyas tadrakṣāśuddhivarddhanam* || The *Śikṣāsamuccaya* restates its summary of the bodhisattva's *saṃvara* at Bendall, *Śikshāsamuccaya*, 18.8–9: *tasmād evam ātmabhāvabhogapuṇyānām aviratam utsargarakṣāśuddhivṛddhayo yathāyogaṃ bhāvanīyāḥ* || The passage at 18.8–9 clarifies that *śubha* should be understood as *puṇya*. The passage also reveals that Bendall's reading of the verse (17.13–14) and its translation are incorrect. Bendall splits the compound, *tadrakṣāśuddhivarddhanam*, which I translate as "protecting, purifying, and increasing these," after *rakṣā*, which yields "guard each and grow in holiness."

His translation reads in full: "Give freely for all creatures' sake thy person, thy enjoyments too[,] thy merit's store throughout all time; guard each and grow in holiness" (Bendall, *Śikshāsamuccaya*, xl). But the *Śikṣāsamuccaya* regards giving away, protecting, purifying, and increasing as four *separate* activities undertaken with respect to bodied being, goods, and merit. The compound, *tadrakṣāśuddhivarddhanam*, is clearly a *tatpuruṣa* compound whose second member is a *dvandva* compound.

8. Less frequently the text uses *deha, samucchraya, rūpa*, and *gātra*. Rarely we find *vapus/vapu* and *kaḍevara*. One quotation from the *Dharmasaṃgītisūtra* lists the following as synonyms for *kāya: deha, bhoga, āśraya, śarīra, kuṇapa*, and *āyatana* (Bendall, *Śikshāsamuccaya*, 229.9–10).

9. *Ātmabhāva* is inconsistently translated as "frame," "self," and "person" in Cecil Bendall and W. H. D. Rouse's translation of the *Compendium of Training* (Bendall and Rouse, *Śikṣā Samuccaya*, e.g., 19 and 37). It is also sometimes translated as "body" (Bendall and Rouse, *Śikṣā Samuccaya*, 251). Clayton translates *ātmabhāva* as "self" (*Moral Theory in Śāntideva's* Śikṣāsamuccaya, 39–40).

10. Hedinger, *Aspekte der Schulung in der Laufbahn eines Bodhisattva*, 10, 165.

11. Eckel, *To See the Buddha*, 99. Elsewhere in this same text Eckel also translates *ātmabhāva* as "body" (82).

12. Thurman, *The Holy Teaching of Vimalakīrti*, 127, n. 21.

13. Steven Collins translates the Pāli form *attabhāva* as "individuality" (Collins, *Selfless Persons*, 156–160).

14. Filliozat, "Self-Immolation by Fire and the Indian Buddhist Tradition," 102.

15. Vaidya, *Daśabhūmikasūtra*, 7.

16. Gómez, "Two Tantric Meditations," 320.

17. E.g., *Buddhist Hybrid Sanskrit Grammar and Dictionary*, s.v. *Ātmabhāva* is a compound made up of two elements—*ātman* ("self") and *bhāva* ("the state" or "condition" of being something) (Collins, *Selfless Persons*, 156)—each of which is semantically complex in its own right.

18. The corporeality of *ātmabhāva* is also suggested by the Tibetan translation of the term as *bdag gi lus* and *rang gi lus*, which are also sometimes abbreviated as *lus*. See Śāntideva, *Śikṣāsamuccaya; Bslab pa kun las btus pa*, 25.3, 26.4, and 48.5, which correspond to Bendall, *Śikshāsamuccaya*, 17.13, 18.8, and 34.3, respectively. The Tibetan translation of *ātmabhāva* in the verse summary of the bodhisattva discipline is *bdag gi lus* (25.3). I am indebted to Holly Gayley for help with the Tibetan materials.

19. Bendall, *Śikshāsamuccaya*, 21.21 (quotation from the *Nārāyaṇaparipṛcchā*). The *Nārāyaṇaparipṛcchā* is Śāntideva's way of referring to the *Sarvapuṇyasamuccayasamādhisūtra*, now extant only in Chinese and Tibetan (Harrison, "Mediums and Messages," 125).

20. Ibid., 21.6–10 (quotation from the *Nārāyaṇaparipṛcchā*).

21. Ibid., 84.11–12 (quotation from the *Praśāntaviniścayaprātihāryasūtra*).

22. In one passage animals eat the dead *ātmabhāva* of a bodhisattva (Ibid., 158.16–159.6 [quotation from the *Tathāgataguhyasūtra*]). In another passage a king is instructed to reflect on the transience of life by considering that his own *ātmabhāva*

will lie one day in a cemetery (Ibid., 208.1–209.2 [quotation from the *Rājāvavādakasūtra*]).

23. Ibid., 302.5 (quotation from the *Avalokanasūtra*).

24. Ibid., 303.8 (quotation from the *Avalokanasūtra*).

25. See chapter 4 of my book for a more detailed discussion of the thirty-two marks.

26. Luis O. Gómez translates *ātmabhāva* as "one's whole person" in his "Two Tantric Meditations," 320.

27. See Bendall, *Śikshāsamuccaya*, 192.11, 193.3, 264.19. Hedinger also argues that *ātmabhāva* includes mental factors ("geistige Gegebenheiten") but opts therefore to translate the term as "Persöhnlichkeit/personality" (Hedinger, *Aspekte der Schulung in der Laufbahn eines Bodhisattva*, 10, n. 39; 165).

28. See Bendall, *Śikshāsamuccaya*, 160.2.

29. Miles, *Plotinus on Body and Beauty*, 14.

30. In my initial study of the *Compendium of Training* I proposed "embodied subject" as a translation for *ātmabhāva* (Mrozik, "The Relationship between Morality and the Body in Monastic Training According to the *Śikṣāsamuccaya*," chapter 1). The concept of embodiment, however, is still problematic since, as Grosz herself observes, it can reinscribe the very dualism it seeks to refute (*Volatile Bodies*, xii). Thus I now translate *ātmabhāva* as "bodied being." This has a slightly less dualistic ring and also has the added advantage of working better in translation of passages.

31. See Ohnuma, "*Dehadāna*"; Ohnuma, "The Gift of the Body and the Gift of Dharma," 323–359; Ohnuma, "Internal and External Opposition to the Bodhisattva's Gift of His Body," 43–75; Ohnuma, "The Story of Rūpāvatī," 103–145; and Mrozik, "Materializations of Virtue," 15–47.

32. Bendall, *Śikshāsamuccaya*, 21.17–21.22 (quotation from the *Nārāyaṇaparipṛcchā*): *tad yathāpi nāma kulaputra bhaiṣajyavṛkṣasya mūlato vā hriyamāṇasya gaṇḍataḥ śākhātaḥ tvaktaḥ patrato vā hriyamāṇasya puṣpataḥ phalataḥ sārato vā hriyamāṇasya naivaṃ bhavati vikalpo ' mūlato me hriyate yāvat sārato me hriyata iti* ǁ *api tu khalu punar avikalpa eva hīnamadhyotkṛṣṭānāṃ satvānāṃ vyādhīn apanayati* | *evam eva kulaputra bodhisatvena mahāsatvenāsmiṃś cāturmahābhautike ātmabhāve bhaiṣajyasaṃjñotpādayitavyā yeṣāṃ yeṣāṃ satvānāṃ yena yenārthaḥ tat tad eva me harantu hastaṃ hastārthinaḥ pādaṃ pādārthina iti pūrvavat* ǁ Please note that the text regularly abbreviates quotations through the use of *yāvat*, which, following Paul Harrion, I translate here as "and so on until."

33. For instance, Bendall, *Śikshāsamuccaya*, 11.6.

34. Ibid., 51.7–13.

35. There is no exact equivalent of *bhoga* in English. I have chosen to translate *bhoga* as "goods" rather than as "belongings" because the concept of "goods" better conveys to readers the enjoyable nature of a bodhisattva's belongings.

36. Bendall, *Śikshāsamuccaya*, 34.3–4: *tena cātmabhāvād[i]nā vaḍiṣāmiṣeṇeva svayam anabhigatopabhogenāpy ākṛṣya parān api tārayati* ǁ I have emended what appears to be a typographical error in Bendall's edition in accordance with the manuscript (folio 22b, line 7). The printed edition reads *tena cātmabhāvādanā*. . . .

37. Nattier, *A Few Good Men*, 232.

38. Bendall, *Śikshāsamuccaya*, 271.12–13: *madyapānād api nairāśyakṛte bodhisatve pratigho garīyān* | *satvasaṃgrahahāniś cāto* ' *'nyaprasādanopāyāsaṃbhave madyaṃ deyam ity abhiprāyaḥ* |

39. Matics, *Entering the Path of Enlightenment*, 28.

40. The story of Jyotis occurs at Bendall, *Śikshāsamuccaya*, 167.3–10. The concluding point follows at Bendall, *Śikshāsamuccaya*, 167.11–13. The text does not explicitly say that Jyotis marries the woman. It says only that he permits her to do what she pleases with him. The text, however, refers to the fact that he takes seven steps and grasps the woman in his right hand, which may refer to the ritual actions of an Indian marriage ceremony. I am indebted to Stephanie Jamison for pointing this out to me (on this point, see also Tatz, *The Skill in Means [Upāyakauśalya] Sūtra*, 95, n. 46). The full story, preserved in the Tibetan translation of the *Upāyakauśalyasūtra* indicates that Jyotis enters into the householder life with the woman (Tatz, *The Skill in Means [Upāyakauśalya] Sūtra*, 34–35; see also 33).

41. Bendall, *Śikshāsamuccaya*, 164.8–165.1 (quotation from the *Upālipariprcchā*). Please note that Bendall regularly spells *sattva* as *satva*, in accordance with the manuscript.

42. Ibid., 34.11–13: *paribhogāya satvānām ātmabhāvādi dīyate* | *arakṣite kuto bhogaḥ* | *kiṃ dattaṃ yan na bhujyate* || *tasmāt satvopabhogārtham ātmabhāvādi pālayet* || (Printed edition reads *satvā nāmātmabhāvādi*, which is clearly a typographical error.) I thank Andy Rotman for help in rendering this passage into readable English.

43. Ibid., 141.4–142.4.

44. References to *akalyāṇamitra* and *pāpamitra* occur at Bendall, *Śikshāsamuccaya*, 51.22 and 52.4 (quotation from the *Ratnameghasūtra*).

45. Ibid., 160.2.

46. I translate *rāga* as lust because of the associations the English word has with sexual desire. Although bodhisattvas can lust after many things, the *Compendium of Training* spends most of its energy warning bodhisattvas of the dangers of sexual desire.

47. See Bendall, *Śikshāsamuccaya*, 209.6–7, 212.9, and 219.9.

48. Ibid., 273.13–14. The passage reads: "Those who take are very many and this is but a trifle. What is the use of it? It does not produce great satisfaction. Therefore it must be increased" (*gṛhītāraḥ subahavaḥ svalpaṃ cedam anena kiṃ* | *na cātitṛptijanakaṃ vardhanīyam idaṃ tataḥ* ||). I have borrowed portions of Richard Mahoney's translation of this passage (Mahoney, "Of the Progresse of the Bodhisattva," 161–162).

49. Bendall, *Śikshāsamuccaya*, 297.10–309.4.

50. Ibid., 318.5–322.4. I discuss this passage in chapter 4 of this book.

51. Grosz, *Volatile Bodies*, 142.

52. Ibid.

53. See ibid.

54. Ibid., 190.

55. Butler, *Bodies That Matter*, 9 and passim.

56. For example, this is the case in the Sadāprarudita story of the *Prajñāpāramitā Aṣṭasahasrikā*, which is quoted at length in the *Compendium of Training*. The story employs both *ātmabhāva* and *kāya* to speak of body. Both terms may refer to body in the present lifetime, but only *ātmabhāva* is placed in the plural to refer to bodies throughout the cycle of rebirth. This passage occurs at Bendall, *Śikshāsamuccaya*, 37.13–41.6 (see especially 40.14–41.6). Similarly a passage from another text also employs *ātmabhāva* and *kāya* for body. Here too *ātmabhāva*, in the plural, refers to bodies throughout the cycle of rebirth, whereas *kāya*, in the singular, refers to body in one's present rebirth. The passage occurs at Bendall, op. cit., 287.14–16 (quotation from the *Daśabhūmikasūtra*). I discuss both passages at length in Mrozik, "The Relationship between Morality and the Body in Monastic Training According to the *Śikṣāsamuccaya*," 22–26. Prajñākaramati seems to have something similar in mind when he glosses *ātmabhāva* in the *Bodhicaryāvatāra* as "all bodies in the passing out of and arising in all realms of existence" (*ātmabhāvān iti sarvagaticyutyupapattiṣu sarvakāyān*) (La Vallée Poussin, *Prajñākaramati's Commentary to the Bodhicaryāvatāra of Śāntideva*, 80). See also Collins, *Selfless Persons*, 159.

57. See Price and Shildrick, *Feminist Theory and the Body*, 218.

58. Payutto, *Buddhadhamma*, 224–225.

59. Bendall, *Śikshāsamuccaya*, 36.8–13 (quotation from the *Vācanopāsikāvimokṣa*, which is found in the *Gaṇḍavyūha*): *ata evāryasudhanaḥ sāradhvajasya bhikṣoḥ pādau śirasābhivandyānekaśatasahasrakṛtvaḥ pradakṣinīkṛtya sāradhvajaṃ bhikṣum avalokya praṇipatya punaḥ punar avalokayan niyataṃ praṇipatan namasyann avanaman manasi kurvan cintayan bhāvayan paribhāvayann udānam udānayan hākkāraṃ kurvan ' guṇān abhimukhīkurvan nigamayann atrasann anusmaran dṛḍhīkurvann avijahan manasāgamayann upanibadhnan praṇidhiṃ samavasaran darśanam abhilaṣan svaranimittam udgṛhṇan yāvat tasyāntikāt prakrāntaḥ* | It is difficult to know how to interpret *atrasann*. I have read this as *a* plus a present participle of the verbal root *tras-* (to be frightened), but it could also be read as *atra* plus a present participle of the verbal root *as-* (to be), yielding "while he stood there" (Bendall and Rouse, *Śikṣā Samuccaya*, 39).

60. Bendall, *Śikshāsamuccaya*, 36.13–14 (quotation from the *Vācanopāsikāvimokṣa*): *tathā kalyāṇamitrāgatāṃ sarvajñatāṃ saṃpaśyann*. I thank Andy Rotman for help in rendering this passage into readable English.

61. See Ibid., 37.13–14 (quotation from the *Prajñāpāramitā Aṣṭasahasrikā*).

62. See Miles, *Plotinus on Body and Beauty*, xii; and Miles, "Sex and the City (of God)," 308.

63. Miles, *Plotinus on Body and Beauty*, xii.

64. Griffiths, *Religious Reading*, 137.

65. Bendall, *Śikshāsamuccaya*, 14.13–21 urges renunciation; chapter 4 of the *Compendium of Training* devotes considerable attention to warning men away from women.

66. Bendall, *Śikshāsamuccaya*, 78.9–10 (quotation from the *Ugradattaparipṛcchā*).

67. Richard H. Robinson introduces the notion of an asceticizing laity in his "The Ethic of the Householder Bodhisattva," 25–56. See also Silk, "What, If Anything, Is Mahāyāna Buddhism?" 377.

68. Bendall, *Śikshāsamuccaya*, 11.10–11: *ayaṃ ca saṃvaraḥ strīṇām api mṛdukleśānāṃ bodhyabhilāṣacittānāṃ labhyate |*

CHAPTER 3

1. Bendall, *Śikshāsamuccaya*, 124.6–8 (quotation from the *Dharmasaṃgītisūtra*): *tathā tathā bhagavan bodhisatvena pratipattavyaṃ yat sahadarśanenaiva satvāḥ prasīdeyuḥ | tat kasmād dhetoḥ | na bhagavan bodhisatvasyānyat karaṇīyam asty anyatra satvāvarjanāt | satvaparipāka eveyaṃ bhagavan bodhisatvasya dharmasaṃgītir iti ||*

2. See Eckel, *To See the Buddha*, 84–90; Gómez, "The Bodhisattva as Wonder-Worker," 221–261; Guang Xing, *The Concept of the Buddha*, 136–146; and McMahan, *Empty Vision*, 114–116.

3. Mainstream Buddhism refers to the various non-Mahāyāna schools, such as the Theravāda, Sarvāstivāda, and Dharmaguptaka, that arose in India within a few centuries of the Buddha's death. According to tradition, there were eighteen such schools; however, scholars note that more than thirty Mainstream school names have been recorded (Cox, "Mainstream Buddhist Schools," 503). I follow current scholarly convention in designating these non-Mahāyāna schools as Mainstream, rather than Hīnayāna, Buddhist schools. The term Hīnayāna appears in Mahāyāna texts as a general pejorative label for anyone who does not follow Mahāyāna Buddhism. The term, however, does not refer to a particular Buddhist sect or group of sects any more than the pejorative label "redneck" refers to a particular U.S. political party. Thus it is historically inaccurate to use the term Hīnayāna as a synonym for Mainstream Buddhism.

4. For example, the *Visuddhimagga* describes how to create a mind-made body (Ñānamoli, *The Path of Purification* [Visuddhimagga] *by Bhadantācariya Buddhaghosa*, chapter 12, section 139, p. 444). Guang Xing discusses this passage in *The Concept of the Buddha*, 136.

5. McMahan, *Empty Vision*, 115. See also Gómez, "The Bodhisattva as Wonder-Worker," 221–222.

6. Gómez characterizes the bodhisattva as "wonder-worker" in his "The Bodhisattva as Wonder-Worker," 221–261.

7. LaFleur, *Buddhism*, 82.

8. McMahan, *Empty Vision*, 115. See also Gómez, "The Bodhisattva as Wonder-Worker," 225.

9. Bendall, *Śikshāsamuccaya*, 346.1 (quotation from the *Ratnolkādhāraṇī*): *acintiya darśiyi rūpaṃ sarvadaśaddiśi.*

10. Bendall, *Śikshāsamuccaya*, 324.13 (quotation from the *Vimalakīrtinirdeśa*). Gómez characterizes the thaumaturgical displays of buddhas and bodhisattvas as an "iconic preaching" about the true nature of reality ("The Bodhisattva as Wonder-Worker," 231).

11. Bendall, *Śikshāsamuccaya*, 326.1–2 (quotation from the *Vimalakīrtinirdeśa*).

12. Ibid., 325.5–8 (quotation from the *Vimalakīrtinirdeśa*).

13. Ibid., 331.3–4 (quotation from the *Ratnolkādhāraṇī*).

14. See references to the miracles resulting from meditation (*samādhi-vikurvā*) in the *Ratnolkādhāraṇī* (Bendall, *Śikshāsamuccaya*, 327.20; 333.12; 343.14).

15. Bendall, *Śikshāsamuccaya*, 334.1–4 (quotation from the *Ratnolkādhāraṇī*).

16. Ibid., 335.3–4; 336.3–6; 337.13–14; 338.5–8, 9–10, 13–14 (quotation from the *Ratnolkādhāraṇī*).

17. Ibid., 341.5–8; 341.15–16; 341.21–22; 342.1–2 (quotation from the *Ratnolkādhāraṇī*).

18. Witness the frequent use of *dehin* as a synonym for *sattva*.

19. On several occasions in chapter 18 the *Compendium of Training*'s sources indicate that bodhisattvas manifest these physical forms specifically in order to ripen living beings. These occur at Bendall, *Śikshāsamuccaya*, 324.14 and 326.10 (quotation from the *Vimalakīrtinirdeśa*); and 328.16 (quotation from the *Ratnolkādhāraṇī*).

20. Ibid., 158.14–15: *śodhitasyātmabhāvasya bhogaḥ pathyo bhaviṣyati* | *samyaksiddhasya bhaktasya niṣkaṇasyeva dehinām* || Concerning the term *niṣkaṇa*: *Kaṇa* refers to "the fine red powder between the husk and the grain of rice, husk-powder"; *akaṇa* means "free from the coating of red powder, characteristic of the best rice" (*The Pali Text Society's Pali-English Dictionary*, s.v. *kaṇa*). *Niṣkaṇa* is a synonym for *akaṇa* (*Buddhist Hybrid Sanskrit Grammar and Dictionary*, s.v. *niṣkaṇa*).

21. Bendall, *Śikshāsamuccaya*, 158.16–159.6 (quotation from the *Tathāgataguhyasūtra*): *yāni ca tāni mahānagareṣu mahāśmaśānāni bhavanty anekaprāṇiśatasahasrākīrṇāni* ' *tatrāpi sa bodhisatvo mahāsatvo mahāntam ātmabhāvaṃ mṛtaṃ kālagatam upadarśayati* | *tatra te tiryagyonigatāḥ satvā yāvadarthaṃ māṃsaṃ paribhujyāyuḥparyante mṛtāḥ kālagatāḥ sugatau svargaloke deveṣūpapadyante* | *sa caiva teṣāṃ hetur bhavati yāvat parinirvāṇāya* | *yad idaṃ* ' *tasyaiva bodhisatvasya pūrvapraṇidhānapariśuddhyā* ' *yena dīrgharātram evaṃ praṇidhānaṃ kṛtam* ' *ye me mṛtasya kālagatasya māṃsaṃ paribhuñjīran* | *sa eva teṣāṃ hetur bhavet svargotpattaye yāvat parinirvāṇāya tasya śīlavataḥ* | *ṛdhyati cetanā* ' *ṛdhyati prārthanā* ' *ṛdhyati praṇidhānam iti* || I am reading against the *daṇḍa* that follows *tasya śīlavataḥ*. My translation of this passage is closely based on a working translation by Paul Harrison, who, together with Jens-Uwe Hartmann, is preparing a new English translation of the *Compendium of Training*.

Holly Gayley has recently noted parallels between this passage and the Tibetan Buddhist practice of ingesting *kyedun* pills (Gayley, "Soteriology of the Senses in Tibetan Buddhism").

22. Ibid., 159.7–8 (quotation from the *Tathāgataguhyasūtra*).

23. See Ibid., 245.9–10 for a similar use of *saṃyuj-*.

24. *Nirvikāra* means "unchanged," "unchangeable," "immutable," "uniform," or "normal." I believe it has the sense here of maintaining one's natural balanced state. W. S. Karunatillake suggested to me that it may refer to the balance of bodily humors (personal communication, Sri Lanka, 1997).

25. Bendall, *Śikshāsamuccaya*, 159.7–18 (quotation from the *Tathāgataguhyasūtra*): *sa dharmakāyaprabhāvito darśanenāpi satvānām arthaṃ karoti* | *śravaṇenāpi sparśanenāpi satvānām arthaṃ karoti* | *tad yathāpi nāma śāntamate jīvakena vaidyarājena sarvabhaiṣajyāni samudānīya bhaiṣajyatarusaṃhātamayaṃ dārikārūpaṃ [kṛtaṃ]*

prāsādikaṃ darśanīyaṃ sukṛtaṃ suniṣṭhitaṃ suparikarmakṛtaṃ | sāgacchati gacchati tiṣṭhati niṣīdati śayyāṃ ca kalpayati | tatra ye āgacchanty āturā mahātmāno rājāno vā rājamātrā vā śreṣṭhigṛhapatyamātyakoṭṭarājāno vā ' tān sa jīvako vaidyarājas tayā bhaiṣajyadārikayā sārddhaṃ saṃyojayati ' teṣāṃ samanantarasaṃyogam āpannānāṃ sarvavyādhayaḥ prasrabhyante 'rogāś ca bhavanti sukhino nirvikārāḥ | paśya śāntamate jīvakasya vaidyarājasya laukikavyādhicikitsājñānaṃ yady anyeṣāṃ vaidyānāṃ saṃvidyate | evam eva śāntamate tasya dharmakāyaprabhāvitasya bodhisatvasya yāvantaḥ satvāḥ strīpuruṣadārakadārikā rāgadoṣamohasaṃtaptāḥ kāyaṃ spṛśanti ' teṣāṃ saṃspṛṣṭamātrāṇāṃ sarvakleśāḥ prasrabhyante vigatasaṃtāpaṃ ca kāyaṃ saṃjānanti || yad idaṃ tasyaiva bodhisatvasya pūrvapraṇidhānasupariśuddhatvāt | etad artham ātmabhāvaḥ śodhyaḥ ||

26. On the different meanings of dharma body, see Eckel, *To See the Buddha*, esp. 97–109; Griffiths, *On Being Buddha*, esp. 147–180; Guang Xing, *The Concept of the Buddha*, esp. 69–100; Harrison "Is the *Dharma-kāya* the Real 'Phantom Body' of the Buddha?" 44–94; Makransky, "Buddhahood and Buddha Bodies," 76–79, and *Buddhahood Embodied*; Williams, *Mahāyāna Buddhism*, 167–184; and Williams with Tribe, *Buddhist Thought*, 172–176.

27. Guang Xing, *The Concept of the Buddha*, 145. According to a Mahāyāna text called the *Avataṃsaka*, the dharma body of a bodhisattva has the same nature as the dharma body of a buddha, but its merits and powers are not as fully developed (Guang Xing, 145).

28. See Williams with Tribe, *Buddhist Thought*, 173.

29. McMahan, *Empty Vision*, 159.

30. Ibid., 160.

31. Williams with Tribe, *Buddhist Thought*, 174.

32. Paul Harrison cautions against assuming that any reference to a dharma body implies the very particular concept of dharma body in the three-body doctrine (Harrison, "Is the *Dharma-kāya* the Real 'Phantom Body' of the Buddha?" esp. 75).

33. Bendall, *Śikshāsamuccaya*, 168.5–8 (quotation from the *Upāyakauśalyasūtra*): *priyaṃkarasya praṇidheḥ punaḥ punar yā istri prekṣeta sarāgacittā | sā istribhāvaṃ parivarjayitvā puruṣo bhavet yādṛg udārasatvaḥ || paśyasva ānanda guṇās ya īdṛśāḥ ' yenānyasatvā nirayaṃ vrajanti | tenaiva śūreṣu janitva rāgaṃ gacchanti svargaṃ puruṣatvam eva ca ||*

34. The *Compendium of Training* is quoting from the *Upāyakauśalyasūtra*. In the Tibetan recension of the *Upāyakauśalyasūtra*, a woman is clearly reborn as a male god (Tatz, *The Skill in Means [Upāyakauśalya] Sūtra*, 39–45).

35. The *Compendium of Training* makes no bones about the fact that male sex is superior to female sex: Bendall, *Śikshāsamuccaya*, 175.14–16 (quotation from the *Bhaiṣajyaguruvaiḍūryaprabharājasūtra*), 176.1–2 (quotation from the *Mañjuśrībuddhakṣetraguṇavyūhālaṃkārasūtra*), 219.3–4 (quotation from the *Suvarṇabhāsa*). Please note, I cite titles as given in the *Compendium of Training*. Jan Nattier has noted the extreme fluidity of titles of Indian Buddhist *sūtras* (Nattier, *A Few Good Men*, 26).

36. Bendall, *Śikshāsamuccaya*, 14.13–21; ibid., 78.9–10.

37. Ibid., 305.5 (quotation from the *Avalokanasūtra*): *durgandhikāmān aśucijugupsanīyān varjeti.*

38. Ibid., 168.9–10 (quotation from the *Upāyakauśalyasūtra*): *bhaiṣajyarājeṣu mahāyaśeṣu ˈ ko bodhisatveṣu janayeta dveṣam | yesāṃ kileśo 'pi sukhasya dāyakaḥ ˈ kiṃ vā punar yaḥ tān satkareyā ˈ iti ||*

39. Ibid., 22.3 (quotation from the *Akṣayamatisūtra*). For a discussion of this passage, see chapter 2 of this book.

40. The *Compendium of Training*'s focus on "enjoying" bodhisattva bodies brings to mind the concept of the enjoyment body (*saṃbhogakāya*) in the three-body theory. Scholars of the three-body theory, and its variations, have defined the enjoyment body as one that enables the communal enjoyment of the Dharma in the pure lands where the enjoyment body is manifest (Griffiths, *On Being Buddha*, 128; Makransky, *Buddhahood Embodied*, e.g., 6, 59, 88). The *Compendium of Training* contains no references to the concept of the enjoyment body, nor does it engage in any discussion of three-body theory, yet its focus on "enjoying" bodhisattva bodies points to a larger interest in the productive uses of pleasure in Mahāyāna traditions. Interestingly, whereas the object of enjoyment in the three-body theory is the Dharma, in the *Compendium of Training* it is often the bodhisattva's body itself.

41. Williams, "Some Mahāyāna Buddhist Perspectives on the Body," 213–216.

42. Ibid., 228.

43. Williams cites the *Compendium of Training* in his article. He does not, however, discuss the passages that are in chapter 8, which demonstrate that bodhisattva bodies have physically as well as morally transformative effects on living beings, nor does he discuss the bodhisattva discipline (*saṃvara*) outlined in this text, which places bodied being (*ātmabhāva*) at the center of bodhisattva practice. Consequently he also does not discuss the concept of *ātmabhāva*. Thus our analyses of the *Compendium of Training* complement each other without actually overlapping.

44. Bendall, *Śikshāsamuccaya*, 177.14–178.8 (quotation from the *Maitreyavimokṣa*, which is now found in the *Gaṇḍavyūha*). It is not entirely clear what *Pātāla* refers to in this passage. Pātāla is sometimes a general name for the lower regions and hells. According to Hindu mythology, it also has a more specific meaning. The god Śiva released a fiery liquid from his third eye when he incinerated Kāma, the god of love. This fire would have consumed the entire world had Śiva not placed it in the mouth of a "submarine mare" at the bottom of a southern sea. The submarine mare's mouth is located in an underworld region called Pātāla (White, *The Alchemical Body*, 232 and 233, n. 79). For a more complete account of this myth, see O'Flaherty, *Women, Androgynes, and Other Mythical Beasts*, chapter 7.

45. *Hāṭaka* is a type of gold. According to David Gordon White, it is the highest quality gold produced in alchemy and has "in addition to the density of gold and gold's other properties, the quality of nearly being *alive*. So charged is *hāṭaka* with subtleness and power that it has a rosy quality to it, is sweet-smelling, and shines 'like a newly risen sun' " (White, "Why Gurus Are Heavy," 53).

46. Bendall, *Śikshāsamuccaya*, 177.15–178.2 (quotation from the *Maitreyavimokṣa*): *tad yathā kulaputra hāṭakaprabhāsaṃ nāma rasajātaṃ | tasyaikaṃ palaṃ lohapalasahasraṃ suvarṇīkaroti | na ca tatra tat palaṃ śakyate tena lohapalasahasreṇa paryādātuṃ ˈ na lohīkartuṃ | evam evaikaḥ sarvajñatācittotpādarasadhātuḥ*

kuśalamūlaparīṇāmanājñānasaṃgṛhītaḥ sarvakarmakleśāvaraṇalohāni paryādāya sarvadharmān sarvajñatāvarṇān karoti | *na ca sarvajñatācittotpādarasadhātuḥ śakyaḥ sarvakarmakleśalohaiḥ saṃkleśayituṃ paryādātuṃ vā* | The Tibetan translation clarifies the meaning of the compound *sarvajñatācittotpādarasadhātu; rasa* is short for *rasajāta*, as indicated by the fact that both terms are rendered by *dngul chu* (Śāntideva, *Śikṣāsamuccaya; Bslab pa kun las btus pa*, 198.5, 198.6). Likewise the Tibetan clarifies the grammar of the compound *sarvakarmakleśāvaraṇaloha*, which it renders as *las dang nyon mongs pa'i sgrib pa'i lcags thams cad* (Śāntideva, *Śikṣāsamuccaya; Bslab pa kun las btus pa*, 198.6). I am indebted to Holly Gayley for help with the Tibetan materials.

47. Bendall, *Śikshāsamuccaya*, 177.14.

48. White, *The Alchemical Body*, 269.

49. Foucault, *The Care of the Self*, 51. Foucault dedicates volumes 2 and 3 of *The History of Sexuality* to the study of technologies of the self. Volume 2 is titled *The Use of Pleasure*. On technologies of the self, see also Martin, Gutman, and Hutton, *Technologies of the Self*.

50. Foucault, *The Care of the Self*, esp. 56–57, 118–123, 133–134.

51. For instance, in the *Sukhāvatīvyūhasūtra*, living beings reborn in Amitābha's pure land possess golden-colored bodies, the divine eye and ear; they have limitless life spans, and not even the word "nonmeritorious conduct" is heard in this realm. See Gómez, *The Land of Bliss*, 69–71 and 166–167.

52. Tatz, *Buddhism and Healing: Demiéville's Article "Byō" from Hōbōgirin*, 44–50.

53. Quoted in ibid., 47.

54. Quoted in ibid., 47–48.

55. Quoted in ibid., 48–49.

56. Quoted in ibid., 49.

57. Collins discusses some of these Buddhist agricultural metaphors in his *Selfless Persons*, 218–224. Paul J. Griffiths also discusses the agricultural imagery underlying the Yogācāra concept of the *ālayavijñāna*, or store-consciousness, in his *On Being Mindless*, 91–96.

58. Heimann, *The Significance of Prefixes in Sanskrit Philosophical Terminology*, 54. In the *Compendium of Training* and its sources, *paripac-* is reserved for the ripening/cooking of living beings, whereas *vipac-* is reserved for the ripening of karma (the latter is always an agricultural metaphor). We will see below that when *pac-* occurs without a prefix, it generally refers to the cooking of living beings in the fires of hell.

59. See Hopkins, *The Hindu Religious Tradition*, 26; Malamoud, "Cooking the World," 48; and Zimmermann, *The Jungle and the Aroma of Meats*, 129.

60. White, *The Alchemical Body*, 20. For a recent study of cooking imagery in Vedic religion see Patton, *Bringing the Gods to Mind*, esp. chapter 4.

61. Malamoud, "Cooking the World," 23–53.

62. Ibid., 46–48.

63. White, *The Alchemical Body*, 20.

64. The *Compendium of Training* spells *sattva* as *satva*.

65. Bendall, *Śikshāsamuccaya*, 124.5–11: *etad eva ca bodhisatvasya kṛtyaṃ yad uta satvāvarjanaṃ* | *yathāryadharmasaṃgītisūtre* ' *āryapriyadarśanena bodhisatvena*

paridīpitaṃ | tathā tathā bhagavan bodhisatvena pratipattavyaṃ yat sahadarśanenaiva satvāḥ prasīdeyuḥ | tat kasmād dhetoḥ | na bhagavan bodhisatvasyānyat karaṇīyam asty anyatra satvāvarjanāt | satvaparipāka eveyaṃ bhagavan bodhisatvasya dharmasaṃgītir iti || evaṃ punar akriyamāṇe ko doṣa ity āha | anādeyaṃ tu taṃ lokaḥ paribhūya jināṅkuraṃ | bhasmachann[aṃ] yathā vahni[ṃ] pacyeta narakādiṣu || Bendall has emended *bhasmachannaṃ yathā vahniṃ* so that it reads *bhasmachanno yathā vahniḥ*. Bendall's notes indicate that he believes the manuscript actually reads *bhasmachannā* rather than *bhasmachanno* (*Śikshāsamuccaya*, 124, n. 4). I myself read *bhasmachannaṃ*, however, it must be noted that this *akṣara* is difficult to read in the manuscript. Bendall also emends *vahniṃ* to *vahniḥ* even though the manuscript clearly reads *vahniṃ*, as he himself indicates in his notes (*Śikshāsamuccaya*, 124, n. 4). Prajñākaramati's commentary to the *Bodhicaryāvatāra* supports a reading of *bhasmachannaṃ yathā vahniṃ*: *anādeyaṃ tu taṃ lokaḥ paribhūya jināṅkuraṃ | bhasmachannaṃ yathā vahniṃ pacyeta narakādiṣu ||* (La Vallée Poussin, *Prajñākaramati's Commentary to the Bodhicaryāvatāra of Śāntideva*, 136). At issue is whether it is the nascent Jina or the world that is likened to a fire hidden by ash. Prajñākaramati's reading and the manuscript of the *Compendium of Training* itself indicates that it is the nascent Jina, rather than the world. I am indebted to Paul Harrison for clarifying this point for me.

66. Paul Harrison, personal communication, January 6, 2006.

67. Zimmermann, writing on Malamoud's essay "Cooking the World," characterizes the Vedic sacrifice as "cooking to perfect the world" (*The Jungle and the Aroma of Meats*, 207). He also describes the cooking of food itself as a twofold process of mixing (*saṃyoga*) ingredients and perfecting (*saṃskāra*) them through cooking (Zimmermann, *The Jungle and the Aroma of Meats*, 129; and Zimmermann, *Le discours des remèdes au pays des épices*, 62–63). Similarly, H. L. Seneviratne characterizes the cooking of food over the digestive fires as a process of refining food (Seneviratne, "Food Essence and the Essence of Experience," 181). In addition to yogic austerities, cremation provides yet another example of cooking to perfection. In Vedic religion the crematory fire transforms the corpse into a sacrificial oblation, tempering it to perfection so that it can enter into the afterlife (O'Flaherty, *The Rig Veda*, 46; see also Malamoud, "Cooking the World," 42–44).

68. Bendall, *Śikshāsamuccaya*, 366.4.

69. Ibid., 124.18.

70. Ibid., 124.18, 125.13–127.5.

71. Ibid., 124.19.

72. Ibid., 125.2–3.

73. Ibid., 125.11–12, 127.16–131.12.

74. Interestingly, the Sarvāstivāda-Vaibhāṣika Mainstream Buddhist school defined the *prātimokṣa* vows as a subtle form of matter, providing a different perspective on the connection between vows and materiality. The Sarvāstivāda-Vaibhāṣika differentiate between eight different kinds of *prātimokṣa* vows: the discipline (*saṃvara*) observed by monks (*bhikṣu*), nuns (*bhikṣuṇī*), female probationers (*śikṣamāṇā*), male novices (*śrāmaṇera*), female novices (*śrāmaṇerī*), male lay Buddhists (*upāsaka*), female lay Buddhists (*upāsikā*), and those observing a temporary period of fast (*upavāsa*)

(Shastri, *Abhidharmakośa & Bhāṣya of Acharya Vasubandhu with Sphutārthā Commentary of Acharya Yaśomitra*, part 2, 606 [4.14]; Pruden, *Abhidharmakośabhāṣyam*, vol. 2, 581. Pruden's translation is an English translation of Louis de La Vallée Poussin's French translation of the text: La Vallée Poussin, *L'Abhidharmakośa de Vasubandhu*, 1971). Some scholars have argued that the categories of *upāsaka* and *upāsikā* do not refer to all laymen and laywomen, but only to a subgroup of these who live more committed Buddhist lives (e.g., Nattier, "Monks in the Mahāyāna," 270).

It is the *prātimokṣa* vows observed by monastics that pertain to my analysis, since these include the rules concerning etiquette and deportment. The issue is discussed in Vasubandhu's *Abhidharmakośabhāṣya* where the question arises: What accounts for the continuity of the monastic *prātimokṣa* vows when a monastic is either (a) distracted (*vikṣipta*) or (b) in a deep state of meditation (*asaṃjñi-nirodha-samāpatti*)? (Shastri, op. cit., part 1, 38 [1.11]; Pruden, op. cit., vol. 1, 67–68). The Sarvāstivāda-Vaibhāṣika posit the existence of a subtle (*sūkṣma*) form of matter (*dravya, rūpa*), called *avijñapti-rūpa* (Shastri, op. cit., part 2, 589 [4.4]; Pruden, op. cit., vol. 2, 567–568). The *avijñapti-rūpa* arises when one first takes a vow and lasts until one either gives up the vow or dies (see Lopez, Jr., *The Story of Buddhism*, 167; Hopkins, *Meditation on Emptiness*, 234; I am also grateful to Janet Gyatso for first bringing this matter to my attention, personal communication July 2003). The *avijñapti-rūpa* thus constitutes the serial continuity (*anubandha, pravāha*) of the vow (Shastri, op. cit., part 1, 38 [1.11]; Pruden, op. cit., vol. 1, 67). The Sarvāstivāda-Vaibhāṣika position was rejected by the Sautrāntika Mainstream Buddhist school who argued that there is no such thing as *avijñapti-rūpa*. Vows are not subtle forms of matter; they are volition (*cetanā*) and their continuity is guaranteed by the memory of the vow (Shastri, op. cit., part 2, 588 [4.4]; Pruden, op. cit., vol. 2, 567). For further discussion of *avijñapti-rūpa* see Gokhale, "What Is Avijñaptirūpa (Concealed Form of Activity)?" 69–73; Gombrich, "Merit Detached from Volition," 427–440; Lamotte, *Karmasiddhiprakaraṇa*, 19–20; Sanderson, "The Sarvāstivāda and Its Critics," 33–48. I am grateful to Prof. M. G. Dhadphale for reading the *Abhidharmakośabhāṣya's* material on *avijñapti-rūpa* with me.

75. I borrow the term "ethical patient" from Charles Hallisey, who lectured extensively on ethical agency and patiency in his undergraduate and graduate courses at Harvard University.

76. Bendall, *Śikshāsamuccaya*, 197.6–17 and 201.12–19. I discuss these passages further in chapters 5 and 6 of this book. I follow Nattier in translating *araṇya* as "wilderness" rather than as "forest," which is its literal meaning. As Nattier observes, the forest was a harsh and dangerous environment; "it was viewed as a frightful place and not as a site for pleasant encounters with nature" (Nattier, *A Few Good Men*, 94).

77. Foucault, *The Care of the Self*, 53; Foucault, *The Use of Pleasure*, 27.

78. Hallisey lectured extensively on this topic in his undergraduate and graduate courses at Harvard University.

79. Derris, "Virtue and Relationships in a Theravādin Biography of the Bodhisatta," 7–8.

80. Ibid., 193–194.

81. Ibid., 193.

82. Ibid., 253.

83. Hallisey, "Buddhism," 124. On the centrality of gratitude in Buddhist ethics, see also Berkwitz, "History and Gratitude in Theravāda Buddhism," 579–604 and *Buddhist History in the Vernacular.*

84. The *Compendium of Training*'s excerpt from the *Candrottarādārikāparipṛcchā* does not identify the members of the crowd that is chasing Candrottarā, but we can infer from the nature of her remarks to this crowd that they are men sexually attracted to her (Bendall, *Śikshāsamuccaya*, 78.19–80.12). The Chinese version of the text, as translated by Diana Y. Paul, also supports this conclusion (Paul, *Women in Buddhism*, 194), as do Jens Braarvig and Paul Harrison in their "Candrottarādārikāvyākaraṇa," 51.

85. Bendall, *Śikshāsamuccaya*, 79.3 (quotation from the *Candrottarādārikāparipṛcchā*).

86. Ibid., 79.9 (quotation from the *Candrottarādārikāparipṛcchā*).

87. Ibid., 79.10 (quotation from the *Candrottarādārikāparipṛcchā*).

88. Ibid., 80.1–3, 7–8 (quotation from the *Candrottarādārikāparipṛcchā*).

89. See Harrison, "Who Gets to Ride in the Great Vehicle?" 67–89; and Nattier, *A Few Good Men*, esp. 96–100.

90. Cleary, *The Flower Ornament Scripture*, 1272. Williams also discusses Vasumitrā in his "Some Mahāyāna Buddhist Perspectives on the Body," 215.

91. Cleary, op. cit., 1272.

92. Thurman, *The Holy Teaching of Vimalakīrti*, 61–62. The *Compendium of Training* actually cites from the very chapter in which this exchange takes place (chapter 7) but does not cite the exchange itself.

93. See Paul's partial translation of the Chinese version of the text in her *Women in Buddhism*, 195–197.

94. Shaw, *Buddhist Goddesses of India*, 6.

95. Kinnard, *Imaging Wisdom*, 142.

96. On this point see chapter 2 of this book.

CHAPTER 4

1. Bendall, *Śikshāsamuccaya*, 34.3–4: *tena cātmabhāvād[i]nā vaḍiṣāmiṣeṇeva svayam anabhigatopabhogenāpy ākṛṣya parān api tārayati* || I have emended what appears to be a typographical error in Bendall's edition in accordance with the manuscript (folio 22b, line 7). The edition reads *tena cātmabhāvādanā*. . . .

2. These monastic regulations were probably compiled in the first or second century C.E. in northwest India (Schopen, "Mūlasarvāstivāda-vinaya," 573).

3. Gnoli, *The Gilgit Manuscript of the Saṅghabhedavastu*, 163: *mayā tvaṃ rājye pratiṣṭhāpitaḥ; māṃ api tvam buddhatve pratiṣṭhāpaya iti.*

4. Ibid.: *bhagavataḥ suvarṇavarṇaḥ kāyaḥ; ādau tāvat tava suvarṇavarṇataiva nāsti iti.*

5. The entire story can be found in ibid., 163–164.

6. The entire story can be found in ibid.

7. On the relationship between body and morality, see also Susanne Mrozik, "The Value of Human Differences," 1–33; and Mrozik, "Materializations of Virtue."

8. Daniel, *Fluid Signs*; Inden and Nicholas, *Kinship in Bengali Culture*; Marriott, "Hindu Transactions," 109–142; and Marriott and Inden, "Toward an Ethnosociology of South Asian Caste Systems," 227–238.

9. Inden and Nicholas, *Kinship in Bengali Culture*, 65.

10. Ibid., 38.

11. Hemacandra, *The Lives of the Jain Elders*, 114 (4.49).

12. See Wimalaratana's *Concept of Great Man (Mahāpurisa) in Buddhist Literature and Iconography* for a thorough discussion of the origins and significance of the concept of the great man in Buddhist traditions.

13. Wimalaratana, *Concept of Great Man*, 7.

14. Some of the most famous accounts of this episode in the Buddha's life can be found in the *Buddhacarita, Lalitavistara, Mahāvastu*, and *Nidāna-kathā* of the *Jātakaṭṭhakathā*. See Johnston, *Aśvaghoṣa's Buddhacarita or Acts of the Buddha*; Goswami, *Lalitavistara*; Jones, *The Mahāvastu*, vol. 2; Jayawickrama, *The Story of Gotama Buddha*.

15. Egge, "Interpretive Strategies for Seeing the Body of the Buddha," 191. See also Wimalaratana, *Concept of Great Man*, 184–185.

16. Egge, "Interpretive Strategies for Seeing the Body of the Buddha," 194.

17. Ibid., 193.

18. Ibid., 196.

19. Griffiths, *On Being Buddha*, 99–100. I quote only Griffiths's English translation of the marks; his list includes the Sanskrit terms as well. He translates from Dutt, *Bodhisattvabhūmiḥ*, 259–260.

20. Wimalaratana, *Concept of Great Man*, 74. Wimalaratana also observes that the *Gaṇḍavyūha*, a Mahāyāna text, mentions both a set of twenty-eight and thirty-three marks (*Concept of Great Man*, 74).

21. Wimalaratana, op. cit., 9.

22. For succinct overviews of Buddhist iconography, see Brown, "Buddha Images," 79–82; and Kinnard, "Iconography: Buddhist Iconography," 4327–4331. The imprint of the wheel on the palms of the hands appears in some, but not all, lists of the thirty-two marks.

23. Endo, *Buddha in Theravada Buddhism*, 141.

24. For a comparative chart of the major and minor marks, see Guang Xing, *The Concept of the Buddha*, 29–31. See Wimalaratana, *The Concept of Great Man*, 193–195, for a complete list of the eighty minor marks. Among the most famous of the minor marks are the elongated earlobes, which are a standard feature in visual images of the Buddha.

25. Strong discusses rupalogical versus dharmalogical dimensions in *The Legend of King Aśoka*, 105–109; see also his "The Transforming Gift," 221–237.

26. Bendall, *Śikshāsamuccaya*, 318.5–319.2 (quotation from the *Rāṣṭrapālasūtra*).

27. Ibid., 319.3–4 (quotation from the *Rāṣṭrapālasūtra*): *kāyaś ca lakṣaṇacito bhagavan sūkṣma chavī kanakavarṇanibhā | nekṣañ jagad vrajati tṛptim idaṃ rūpaṃ tavāpratimarūpadhara ||*

28. Kemper, "Wealth and Reformation in Sinhalese Buddhist Monasticism," 167.

29. Ibid., 167–168.

30. Bendall, *Śikshāsamuccaya,* 80.2 (quotation from the *Candrottarādārikāparipṛcchā*).

31. I am grateful to James Andrew McHugh for drawing my attention to the importance of beauty of scent in Buddhist literature.

32. Bendall, *Śikshāsamuccaya,* 298.3–4, 299.1, 304.6, 307.5 (quotation from the *Avalokanasūtra*).

33. Ibid., 79.9 (quotation from the *Candrottarādārikāparipṛcchā*).

34. Ibid., 132.18 (quotation from the *Laṅkāvatārasūtra*).

35. For example, ibid., 153.20–22 (quotation from the *Vimalakīrtinirdeśa*).

36. Ibid., 175.14–16 (quotation from the *Bhaiṣajyaguruvaiḍūryaprabhārājasūtra*), 176.1–2 (quotation from the *Mañjuśrībuddhakṣetraguṇavyūhālaṃkārasūtra*).

37. Ibid., 219.4 (quotation from the *Suvarṇabhāsasūtra*).

38. I take this list of terms from Gyatso, "One Plus One Makes Three," 94–95, esp. nn. 10–11.

39. Ibid., 95.

40. Sweet and Zwilling, "The First Medicalization," 592. See also Leonard Zwilling, "Homosexuality as Seen in Indian Buddhist Texts," 203–214.

41. Gyatso, "One Plus One Makes Three," 94.

42. Ibid., 97–98.

43. References to *ṣaṇḍaka* and *paṇḍaka* occur at Bendall, *Śikshāsamuccaya,* 69.6 (quotation from the *Pravrajyāntarāyasūtra*); reference to *strīpaṇḍaka* occurs at ibid., 48.7 (quotation from the *Saddharmapuṇḍarīkasūtra*); reference to *napuṃsaka* occurs at ibid., 221.11, 13 (quotation from the *Śālistambasūtra*).

44. Ibid., 133.1 (quotation from the *Laṅkāvatārasūtra*).

45. Ibid., 133.8–9 (quotation from the *Laṅkāvatārasūtra*).

46. Ibid., 298.7; 298.11, 300.3, 301.5 (quotations from the *Avalokanasūtra*).

47. Carter and Palihawadana, *The Dhammapada,* 66–71 (chapter 26).

48. Gombrich, *Theravāda Buddhism,* 30.

49. Bendall, *Śikshāsamuccaya,* 80.1–3, 7–8 (quotation from the *Candrottarādārikāparipṛcchā*).

50. Ibid., 69.5–7 (quotation from the *Pravrajyāntarāyasūtra*).

51. For a list of the eight conditions, see Endo, *Buddha in Theravada Buddhism,* 253.

52. For an overview of pertinent primary sources on the question of whether women can become buddhas, see Paul, *Women in Buddhism,* 166–243. For a range of scholarly perspectives on this issue, see Faure, *The Power of Denial,* esp. chapters 3 and 4; Hae-ju Sunim (Ho-Ryeon Jeon), "Can Women Achieve Enlightenment?" 123–141; Hsieh, "Images of Women in Ch'an Buddhist Literature of the Sung Period," 148–187; Levering, "The Dragon Girl and the Abbess of Mo-Shan," 19–35; Mrozik, "Materializations of Virtue," 15–47; Nattier, *A Few Good Men,* 96–100; Ohnuma, "*Dehadāna,*" 244–253; Peach, "Social Responsibility, Sex Change, and Salvation,"

50–74; Schuster, "Changing the Female Body," 24–69; and Sponberg, "Attitudes Toward Women and the Feminine in Early Buddhism," 3–36.

53. Buddhist monastic literature records instances of spontaneous sex change. See Gyatso, "One Plus One Makes Three," 97, 110–111.

54. Endo, *Buddha in Theravada Buddhism*, 260–264.

55. Shastri, *Abhidharmakośa & Bhāṣya of Acharya Vasubandhu with Sphutārthā Commentary of Acharya Yaśomitra*, part 2, 735 (4.108); Pruden, *Abhidharmakośabhāṣyam*, v. 2, 690.

56. Nattier translates *gṛhapati* as "eminent householder." She argues that the term refers to wealthy male householders who are leading figures in their communities, although not members of the *kṣatriya* or *brāhmaṇa* castes (Nattier, *A Few Good Men*, 22–25, 208, n. 12). The term appears in Buddhist literature "in a list of caste names, either in a threefold list of which the first two members are *kṣatriya* and *brāhmaṇa* (in that order) or in a twofold list where the first element is *brāhmaṇa*" (ibid., 23). The *gṛhapati* is frequently said to be a merchant or guild leader (Skt. *śreṣṭhin*, Pāli, *seṭṭhi*) (ibid., 23).

57. *sugatiḥ kulajo 'vyakṣaḥ pumān jātismaro 'nivṛt* (Shastri, *Abhidharmakośa & Bhāṣya of Acharya Vasubandhu with Sphutārthā Commentary of Acharya Yaśomitra*, part 2, 735 (4.108); Pruden, *Abhidharmakośabhāṣyam*, vol., 2, 691.

58. Gyatso, "One Plus One Makes Three," 93.

59. Ibid., 92–93.

60. Karma Lekshe Tsomo, personal communication, March 31, 2004.

61. The *Abhidharmakośabhāṣya* lists three different kinds of *saṃvaras*: *prātimokṣa saṃvara*, the *saṃvara* born of meditation (*dhyānaja saṃvara*), and the pure *saṃvara* (*anāsrava saṃvara*) (Shastri, *Abhidharmakośa & Bhāṣya of Acharya Vasubandhu with Sphutārthā Commentary of Acharya Yaśomitra*, part 2, 605 [4.13]; Pruden, *Abhidharmakośabhāṣyam*, v. 2, 580). On the eight different types of *prātimokṣa saṃvara*, see chapter 3 of this book, n. 74.

62. Shastri, op. cit., part 2, 651 (4.43); Pruden, op. cit., v. 2, 620.

63. *api khalv āśraya eva sa teṣāṃ tādṛśa ūṣarakṣetrabhūtaḥ ṣaṇḍhapaṇḍakobhayavyañjanottarakauravāpāyikānāṃ, yatrāśraye saṃvaro 'pi na virohati, asaṃvaro 'pi, ūṣara iva kṣetre śasyam apy atimātraṃ [kattṛṇa] apīti* | (Shastri, ed., *Abhidharmakośa & Bhāṣya of Acharya Vasubandhu with Sphutārthā Commentary of Acharya Yaśomitra*, part 2, 651 [4.43]; see also Pruden, *Abhidharmakośabhāṣyam*, v. 2, 620). The Tibetan translation of *āśraya* in this passage is *lus*, or body (*Abhidharmakośabhāṣya*, Gelugpa Student Welfare Committee, ed., 362.2). *Āśraya* is frequently used for "body" in the *Abhidharmakośabhāṣya*. For example, just prior to this passage the text discusses the conditions under which living beings lose the *prātimokṣa saṃvara*. The first seven kinds of *prātimokṣa saṃvara* are lifelong vows; the eighth is taken only for the duration of a fast, which lasts one day and one night. Living beings lose their lifelong *prātimokṣā saṃvaras* when one of the following occurs: they abandon the discipline (*śikṣā*), they die (*cyuti*), they become hermaphrodites (*ubhayavyañjana*), or they "cut" their meritorious roots (*kuśalamūla*). Death is glossed as the abandonment of the *āśraya* (*āśraya-tyāga*), and hermaphroditism is glossed as the

simultaneous appearance of both male and female sexual characteristics (*yugapad-ubhayavyañjana-prādurbhāva*), which, in turn, produces a disturbance of the *āśraya* (*āśraya-vikopana*) (Shastri, op. cit., part 2, 643 [4.38]; Pruden, op. cit., vol. 2, 613). Death and hermaphroditism are similarly defined a few verses later, where death (*mṛtyus*) is glossed as the abandonment of the *āśraya* and hermaphroditism (*dvi-vyañjana*) is glossed as the disturbance of the *āśraya* (Shastri, op. cit., part 2, 648 [4.41]; Pruden, op. cit., vol. 2, 617). The term *āśraya* literally means support. In the context of the passages cited, body is defined as the physical support of both discipline and undiscipline. There are other instances in the *Abhidharmakośabhāṣya* of *āśraya* designating "body." For example, body (*āśraya*) is defined as the support of mind (*āśrita*). Whereas body grows by ingesting food, mind grows by contact with the sensory world (Shastri, op. cit., part 2, 496 [3.41]; Pruden, op. cit., vol. 2, 443–444).

Shastri's edition reads *kakvam* rather than *kattṛṇa*. Chinese and Tibetan translations of the text lend support to P. Pradhan's suggestion that *kakvam* be emended to *kattṛṇa* (P. Pradhan, *Abhidharm[a]koshabhāṣya of Vasubandhu*, 226). The Chinese translation reads 穢草 (*hui cao*) (T 1558: 29.80c12, T 1559: 29.237a1; see also La Vallée Poussin, *L'Abhidharmakośa de Vasubandhu*, vol. 3, 104). The Tibetan reads *rtswa* (*Abhidharmakośabhāṣya*, Gelugpa Student Welfare Committee, ed., 362.4). I am indebted to Jay Garfield for help with the Tibetan and to Mark Blum for help with the Chinese translations. I am also indebted to Mark Blum for proposing "weeds" as a translation of the term in question.

64. Gyatso, "One Plus One Makes Three," 98.

65. Bendall, *Śikshāsamuccaya*, 132.13 (quotations from *Laṅkāvatārasūtra*).

66. Ibid., 132.17–133.7 (quotation from *Laṅkāvatārasūtra*). Note that in the *Laṅkāvatārasūtra*, *ḍākinīs* are not the positive figures they are in Buddhist Tantra. Note also that the term *ṛkṣa* can also refer to nilgai, a variety of antelope. See Zimmerman, *The Jungle and the Aroma of Meats*, 225 and 226.

67. Bendall, *Śikshāsamuccaya*, 133.8–9 (quotation from *Laṅkāvatārasūtra*).

68. Ibid., 298.7–8 (quotation from the *Avalokanasūtra*).

69. An English translation can be found in Stephen C. Berkwitz, *The History of the Buddha's Relic Shrine*, 137–140; the original Sinhala can be found in W. S. Karunatillake, *Sinhala Thūpavaṃsa*, 88–93. I am grateful to Stephen C. Berkwitz for bringing the story to my attention and for providing references to the Sinhala version of the text.

70. Aśoka is predisposed to feel affection for Nigrōdha because in a previous lifetime Nigrōdha had been his elder brother. The text underscores that Nigrōdha's appearance and deportment trigger these affectionate feelings in Aśoka in his present lifetime (Berkwitz, *The History of the Buddha's Relic Shrine*, 138–139).

71. Ibid., 139, Karunatillake, *Sinhala Thūpavaṃsa*, 91.

72. Berkwitz, *The History of the Buddha's Relic Shrine*, 137.

73. Ibid., 140.

74. Strong, *The Experience of Buddhism*, 49.

75. Ibid., 49.

76. Ibid., 50.

77. Collins, "The Body in Theravāda Buddhist Monasticism," 198.

78. Prebish, *Buddhist Monastic Discipline,* 97–103.

79. Griffiths, *On Being Buddha,* 73.

80. References to avoiding that which generates *aprasāda* occur at Bendall, *Śikshāsamuccaya,* 124.13, 17; 125.5, 9, 13 (two references); and 127.6. These references are part of a larger discussion of monastic etiquette and deportment that occurs at Bendall, *Śikshāsamuccaya,* 124.2–127.7.

81. See Trainor, *Relics, Ritual, and Representation in Buddhism,* 166–168, and Carter, *Dhamma,* 105, n. 173.

82. Trainor, *Relics, Ritual, and Representation in Buddhism,* 167.

83. Ibid.

84. Ibid., 169.

85. Ludowyk-Gyömröi, "Note on the Interpretation of 'Pasīdati,' " 82, quoted in Trainor, *Relics, Ritual, and Representation in Buddhism,* 167.

86. Ludowyk-Gyömröi, "Note on the Interpretation of 'Pasīdati,' " 77. She cites T. W. Rhys Davids on this point.

87. Rotman, "The Erotics of Practice," 556, 557.

88. Ibid., passim.

89. Ibid., 557 and passim; Trainor, *Relics, Ritual, and Representation in Buddhism,* 169. Jeffrey Samuels and Jonathan S. Walters have also noted the ethical importance of *prasāda* together with a range of other emotions of pleasure and joy in the context of Theravāda Buddhism. See Samuels, "Merit and the Heart," forthcoming; and Walters, "*Stūpa,* Story, and Empire," 179–180.

90. Berkwitz, *The History of the Buddha's Relic Shrine,* 137.

91. Ibid., 138–139.

92. According to another text, the *Aśokāvadāna,* Aśoka became a Cakravartin and patron of Buddhism because in a previous lifetime he had made a vow to this effect when he offered the Buddha his famous gift of dirt. The vow was motivated by an experience of *prasāda* at the sight of the Buddha's beauty (Mukhopadhyaya, *The Aśokāvadāna,* 31). As was discussed above, Steven Kemper argues that laypeople are attracted to monks with the " 'look' of merit" (*pin pāṭa*) because they are *saumya,* that is, "moonlike and, hence, beautiful" (Kemper, "Wealth and Reformation in Sinhalese Buddhist Monasticism," 167). It should be noted that to be *saumya* is not only to be beautiful, but also to have a cooling or calming effect on others. Such an effect bears a resemblance to the calming effect of *prasāda.*

93. Bendall, *Śikshāsamuccaya,* 87.14–21 (quotation from the *Niyatāniyatāvatāramudrāsūtra*).

94. For an instructive comparative example in the Confucian context, see Csikszentmihalyi, *Material Virtue.*

95. Yearley, *Mencius and Aquinas,* 13.

96. Fear and shame are regarded as virtues in Buddhist ethical discourse when, for instance, one fears the karmic consequences of misdeeds or feels shame at having violated monastic vows. For a discussion of these virtues see Heim, "The Aesthetics of Excess," 531–554, and "Shame and Apprehension," forthcoming.

97. Bendall, *Śikshāsamuccaya*, 122.6 (quotation from the *Dharmasaṃgītisūtra*).

98. Ibid., 123.13: *cittaparikarmaiva bodhisatvaśikṣeti* I

99. Ibid., 123.15–124.2.

100. Ibid., 36.13–14 (quotation from the *Vācanopāsikāvimokṣa*, which is found in the *Gaṇḍavyūha*): *tathā kalyāṇamitrāgatāṃ sarvajñatāṃ saṃpaśyann*

101. Ibid., 67.19–68.7 (quotation from the *Kṣitigarbhasūtra*).

102. Strong, *The Legend of King Aśoka*, 81.

103. Among those who have not overlooked this fact are Gregory Schopen, who remarked over twenty years ago that "the 'physical' and 'spiritual' are irredeemably interlocked" in Buddhist traditions (Schopen, "The *Bhaiṣajyaguru-Sūtra* and the Buddhism of Gilgit," 208).

104. Keown, *Buddhism & Bioethics*, 39.

105. Caroline A. F. Rhys Davids, a pioneer in the field of Pāli Abhidhamma literature, argues that *rūpa* is morally neutral or "unmoral" (Rhys Davids, *A Buddhist Manual of Psychological Ethics of the Fourth Century B.C.*, xxxi).

106. I have emended the translation of Tin, *The Expositor (Atthasālinī)*, vol. 1, 18. The Pali reads: *Saṇhasukhumadhammaṃ pana sammasato Lokanāthassa lohitaṃ pasīdi, vatthurūpaṃ pasīdi, chavivaṇṇo pasīdi* (Müller, *The Atthasālinī*, 15).

CHAPTER 5

1. Bendall, *Śikshāsamuccaya*, 18.11–14 (quotation from the *Candrapradīpasūtra*): *adhyavasitā ye bālāḥ kāye 'smin pūtike samyag* I *jīvite cañcale 'vaśye māyāsvapna-nibhopame* II *atiraudrāṇi karmāṇi kṛtvā mohavaśānugāḥ* I *te yānti narakān ghorān mṛtyuyānagatābudhā 'iti* II

2. Ibid., 319.3–4 (quotation from the *Rāṣṭrapālasūtra*): *kāyaś ca lakṣaṇacito bhagavan sūkṣma chavī kanakavarṇanibhā* I *nekṣañ jagad vrajati tṛptim idaṃ rūpaṃ tavāpratimarūpadhara* II

3. A translation of the full story can be found in Woodward, *The Book of the Kindred Sayings (Saṃyutta-Nikāya) or Grouped Suttas*, part 3, 101–106; the Pāli can be found in Feer, *Saṃyutta-Nikaya*, part 3, 119–124.

4. Woodward, *The Book of the Kindred Sayings (Saṃyutta-Nikāya) or Grouped Suttas*, part 3, 103. I have have made minor changes to Woodward's translation. The Pāli reads: *Cirapaṭikāham bhante Bhagavantaṃ dassanāya upasaṅkamitukāmo natthi ca me kāyasmiṃ tāvatikā balamattā* II *yāyāhaṃ Bhagavantaṃ dassanāya upasaṅkameyyan ti* II (Feer, *Saṃyutta Nikaya*, part 3, 120).

5. Here I have used Trainor's translation rather than Woodward's (Trainor, *Relics, Ritual, and Representation in Buddhism*, 181). The Pāli reads: *Alaṃ Vakkali kiṃ te iminā pūtikāyena diṭṭhena* II *Yo kho Vakkali dhammam passati so mam passati* I *yo maṃ passati so dhammam passati* II (Feer, *Saṃyutta Nikaya*, part. 3, 120).

6. Buddhaghosa argues in his commentary to this story that Vakkali was conceited. Vakkali stabbed himself thinking that he had already attained nirvāṇa. When he experiences severe pain from the knife wound, he realizes that he was wrong. Vakkali then makes a great effort in the moments before death and does indeed attain

nirvāṇa (for the Pāli, see Woodward, *Sārattha-ppakāsinī: Buddhaghosa's Commentary on the Saṃyutta-Nikāya*, vol. 2, 314–315).

7. This version of the Vakkali story is contained in the commentary to the *Dhammapada*. For the English translation, see Burlingame, *Buddhist Legends*, part 3, 262–263; for the Pāli, see Norman, *The Commentary on the Dhammapada*, vol. 4, 117–119. Trainor discusses the Vakkali story in his *Relics, Ritual, and Representation in Buddhism*, 181–183. See also McMahan, *Empty Vision*, 155–156. Joel Tatelman has recently published a translation of yet another version of the story (Tatelman, *The Glorious Deeds of Pūrṇa*, 74–75).

8. See again Trainor, *Relics, Ritual, and Representation in Buddhism*, 181. The Pāli reads: *kiṃ te Vakkali iminā pūṭikāyena diṭṭhena, yo kho Vakkali dhammaṃ passati so maṃ passati* (Norman, *The Commentary on the Dhammapada*, vol. 4, 118).

9. Burlingame, *Buddhist Legends*, 263. The Pāli reads: *Ehi Vakkali mā bhāyi olokento Tathāgataṃ | ahaṃ taṃ uddharissāmi pañke sannaṃ va kuñjaraṃ* (Norman, *The Commentary on the Dhammapada*, vol. 4, 119).

10. Trainor draws a similar conclusion (Trainor, *Relics, Ritual, and Representation in Buddhism*, 183).

11. For example, Schmithausen, "Die Vier Konzentrationen der Aufmerksamkeit," 261.

12. BeDuhn, *The Manichaean Body in Discipline and Ritual*; Brown, *The Body and Society*; Bynum, *Holy Feast and Holy Fast*; and Fine, "Purifying the Body in the Name of the Soul," 117–142.

13. Bynum, *Holy Feast and Holy Fast*, 294, see also 6 and 295.

14. Ibid., 3.

15. Ibid., 295, quoted in Fine, "Purifying the Body in the Name of the Soul," 118.

16. Chapter 11 urges bodhisattvas to engage in solitary retreats in the wilderness.

17. Bendall, *Śikshāsamuccaya*, 200.9–11 (quotation from the *Ugradatta-paripṛcchā*).

18. Ibid., 207.19–209.2 (quotation from the *Rājāvavādakasūtra*).

19. Ibid., 77.11–78.6 (quotation from the *Kāmāpavādakasūtra*): *kāyo hyayaṃ bahvādīnavaḥ | asthisaṃghātaḥ snāyusaṃbaddho māṃsenānuliptaḥ carmaṇā paryavanaddhaḥ chavyā praticchannaḥ chidravicchidraḥ kṛmisaṃghaniṣevitaḥ satvānām anarthakaḥ kleśakarmaṇāṃ vastu || asmin kāye vividhā ābādhā utpadyante | tad yathā cakṣūrogaḥ śrotrarogo yāvad arśāṃsi piṭako bhagandaraḥ || pe || kāyikāḥ santāpāḥ kāyikaṃ duṣkhaṃ | kāyasya jīrṇatā bhagnatā kubjatā | khālityaṃ pālityaṃ valipracuratā | indriyāṇāṃ paripākaḥ paribhedaḥ saṃskārāṇāṃ purāṇībhāvo jarjarībhāvaḥ | yāvan nārhasy evam udgharantaṃ pragharantaṃ jugupsanīyaṃ kāyaṃ pratiṣevituṃ || pe || kā tava bhikṣo kāmāśāntiḥ | kaś ca tvāṃ pralobhayati | kathaṃ ca tvaṃ prāhito mūrchito 'dhyavasito 'dhyavasānam āpannaḥ | yadāhaṃ parinirvṛto bhavāmi ' saddharmaś cāntarhito bhavati ' tvaṃ ca kāmān pratisevya vinipātagato bhaviṣyasi | kadā jarāmaraṇād ātmānaṃ parimocayiṣyasi || alaṃ bhikṣo nivāraya cittaṃ kāmebhyaḥ | akālaḥ kāma-paryeṣaṇāyāḥ ' kālo 'yaṃ dharmaparyeṣaṇāyā iti ||* Please note that the *Compendium of Training* regularly spells *duḥkha* as *duṣkha*. The text also regularly abbreviates quo-

tations through the use of *yāvat* (rendered as *and so on until*) and *pe* (rendered as ellipses).

20. For standard lists, see Collins, "The Body in Theravāda Buddhist Monasticism," 192–193; Hamilton, *Identity and Experience,* 185; Khantipalo, *Bag of Bones,* 11–13.

21. Bendall, *Śikshāsamuccaya,* 229.2–3 (quotation from the *Dharmasaṃgītisūtra*): *keśaromanakhadantāsthicarmapiśitavapāsnāyu medovasālasīkāyakṛnmūtra-purīṣāmāśayarudhirakheṭapittapūyasiṅghāṇakamastakaluṅgāni* (See Ibid., 209.7–11 [quotation from the *Ratnamegha*]).

22. Ibid., 210.14–212.8 (quotation from the *Bhagavatī*).

23. Ibid., 209.7 (quotation from the *Ratnamegha*).

24. Wilson, *Charming Cadavers.*

25. Ibid., 93.

26. Bendall, *Śikshāsamuccaya,* 80.14–17 (quotation from the *Udayanavatsa-rājaparipṛcchā*).

27. Ibid., 81.1–4 (quotation from the *Udayanavatsarājaparipṛcchā*).

28. Ibid., 82.10–13 (quotation from the *Udayanavatsarājaparipṛcchā*): *uccāra iva durgandhāḥ striyo buddhaiḥ prakīrtitāḥ* ǁ *tasmād dhīnasya hīnābhiḥ strībhir bhavati saṅgatiḥ* ǀ *uccārabhastrāṃ yo gṛhya bālāvāsaṃ nigacchati* ǁ *yādṛśaṃ kurute karma tādṛśaṃ labhate phalam* ǁ This is a difficult passage to translate, since it is unclear what is meant by *bālāvāsaṃ,* which could mean "dwelling of a fool" or "dwelling of a young woman." P. L. Vaidya emends *bālāvāsaṃ* to *bālo vāsaṃ* (Vaidya, *Śikṣāsamuccaya of Śāntideva,* 49). This emendation yields the following translation: "The fool, who grabs a bag of excrement and enters a home, earns fruit [i.e., karma] in accordance with his actions."

29. Wilson, *Charming Cadavers,* 15.

30. For example, see Faure, *The Red Thread,* 36–37. See also Brown's ethnographic account of a nun who has a vision of her husband as a skeleton (Brown, *The Journey of One Buddhist Nun,* 73–75).

31. Bendall, *Śikshāsamuccaya,* 71.12–72.3 (quotation from the *Sad-dharmasmṛtyupasthāna*).

32. Ibid., 72.4–7 (quotation from the *Saddharmasmṛtyupasthāna*): *striyo mūlam apāyasya dhananāśasya sarvathā* ǀ *strīvidheyā narā ye tu kutas teṣāṃ bhavet sukham* ǁ *pe* ǁ *yāvat* ǀ *strī vināśo vināśānām iha loke paratra ca* ǀ *tasmāt striyo vivarjyāḥ syur yadīcchet sukham ātmana iti* ǁ Abbreviations are indicated by the use of *pe* (rendered as an ellipsis) and *yāvat* (rendered as *and so on until*).

33. Bendall, *Śikshāsamuccaya,* 78.10, 15–18 (quotation from the *Ugradatta-paripṛcchā*). I translate *badhaka* as "murderer," as do Bendall and Rouse (Bendall and Rouse, *Śikṣā Samuccaya,* 83). *Badhaka* is, of course, equivalent to *vadhaka,* which means "murderer."

34. Sponberg, "Attitudes toward Women and the Feminine in Early Buddhism," 18–24.

35. Olivelle, *Saṃnyāsa Upaniṣads,* 78.

36. Collins, *Selfless Persons,* 99.

37. Miller, *The Bhagavad-Gita*, 32–33.

38. For an in-depth discussion of this point, see Collins, *Selfless Persons*.

39. Bendall, *Śikshāsamuccaya*, 242.5.

40. Collins states that the literal translation of the Pāli form *sakkāya-diṭṭhi* is "belief in a (really) existing body." He observes that in this context the term *kāya* refers not just to the physical body but to the collection of five aggregates (Pāli: *khanda*, Sanskrit: *skandha*) (Collins, *Selfless Persons*, 93).

41. LaFleur, *Buddhism*, 81.

42. See ibid.

43. Lewis, "*Samsara* and the Soul," 58.

44. Ibid., 59.

45. Bendall, *Śikshāsamuccaya*, 242.7–9 (quotation from the *Tathāgataguhya-sūtra*): *tad yathāpi nāma śāntamate vṛkṣasya mūlachinnasya sarvaśākhāpatrapalāśāḥ śuṣyanti | evam eva śāntamate satkāyadṛṣṭyupaśamāt sarvakleśā upaśāmyantīti* || Bendall mistakenly breaks the compound *sarvaśākhāpatrapalāśāḥ*. I have emended his edition in accordance with the manuscript. I thank Paul Harrison for pointing out Bendall's error to me.

46. LaFleur, *Buddhism*, 81.

47. See Tatz, *Buddhism and Healing: Demiéville's Article "Byō" from Hōbōgirin*, 68–69. For further discussion of some of these elements, see Hamilton, *Identity and Experience*, 10–14.

48. Discussion of the six elements occurs at Bendall, *Śikshāsamuccaya*, 244.11–250.14 (quotation from the *Pitṛputrasamāgama*).

49. Ibid., 245.2–3 (quotation from the *Pitṛputrasamāgama*).

50. Ibid., 242.12–13 (quotation from the *Candrapradīpasūtra*).

51. Ibid., 245.6–12 (quotation from the *Pitṛputrasamāgama*): *bhavati mahārāja sa samayo yat strī adhyātmam ahaṃ strīti kalpayati | sādhyātmam ahaṃ strīti kalpayitvā bahirdhā puruṣaṃ puruṣa iti kalpayati | sā bahirdhā puruṣaṃ puruṣa iti kalpayitvā saṃraktā satī bahirdhā puruṣena sārdhaṃ saṃyogam ākāṇkṣate | puruṣo 'pyadhyātmaṃ puruṣo 'smīti kalpayatīti pūrvavat | tayoḥ saṃyogākāṇkṣayā saṃyogo bhavati | saṃyoga-pratyayāt kalalaṃ jāyate | tatra mahārāja yaś ca saṃkalpo yaś ca saṃkalpayitā ' ubhayam etan na saṃvidyate | striyāṃ strī na saṃvidyate | puruṣe puruṣo na saṃvidyate |*

52. Ibid., 246.14–15 (quotation from the *Pitṛputrasamāgama*): *so 'pi vyavahāro na strī na puruṣaḥ |*

53. Ibid., 248.1–2, 250.1–4, 250.13 (quotation from the *Pitṛputrasamāgama*).

54. The discussion occurs at ibid., 251.15–255.3 (quotation from the *Pitṛputrasamāgama*).

55. See especially ibid., 251.15–252.1 (quotation from the *Pitṛputrasamāgama*).

56. Wilson, *Charming Cadavers*, 8.

57. Bendall, *Śikshāsamuccaya*, 256.4–18.

58. Ibid., 257.5–8.

59. Ibid., 257.10–11. The most heinous of deeds are the five *ānantarya* deeds, that is, deeds that bring immediate karmic retribution. These deeds are killing one's mother, father, or an arhat; causing dissension in the monastic order; and deliberately

causing a buddha's blood to flow (*Buddhist Hybrid Sanskrit Grammar and Dictionary*, s.v. *ānantarya*).

60. For example, Eckel, *Jñānagarbha's Commentary on the Distinction between the Two Truths*, 40–43; Eckel, *To See the Buddha*, 29; Streng, *Emptiness*, 96.

61. Streng, *Emptiness*, 96.

62. Bendall, *Śikshāsamuccaya*, 264.12 (quotation from the *Dharmasaṃgītisūtra*).

63. Ibid., 265.4.

64. Nattier, "Monks in the Mahāyāna," 270; see also Nattier, *A Few Good Men*, 94–96.

65. Wilson, "Ascetic Practices," 33. For further information on the *dhūtaguṇas*/*dhutaṅgas*, see Bunnag, *Buddhist Monk, Buddhist Layman*, 54–57; Carrithers, *The Forest Monks of Sri Lanka*, esp. 62–66; Tambiah, "Purity and Auspiciousness at the Edge of the Hindu Context—in Theravāda Buddhist Societies," 97–99; and Tiyavanich, *Forest Recollections*, esp. 62–71.

66. References to the *dhūtaguṇas* occur at Bendall, *Śikshāsamuccaya*, 98.20, 135.15, 137.1, and 328.1. The *Compendium of Training* devotes one entire chapter to advocating solitary retreat in the wilderness (chapter 11).

67. Collins, "The Body in Theravāda Buddhist Monasticism," 197.

68. Bunnag, *Buddhist Monk, Buddhist Layman*, 55; quoted in Collins, "The Body in Theravāda Buddhist Monasticism," 197.

69. Harpham, *The Ascetic Imperative in Culture and Criticism*, xiv–v.

70. Bendall, *Śikshāsamuccaya*, 194.15, 195.16, and 196.4.

71. Ibid., 196.16–197.1.

72. Ibid., 197.6–17.

73. Ibid., 243.11–12 (quotation from the *Candrapradīpasūtra*). See chapter 4 of this book for a discussion of the great man.

74. Ibid., 243.15–244.9 (quotation from the *Bhagavatī*).

75. See ibid., 23.13, 25.12–13, 26.2 (quotation from the *Vajradhvajasūtra*), 200.17 (quotation from the *Ratnarāśisūtra*); cf. 229.14–230.1 (quotation from the *Ratnacūḍa*).

76. *Avadāna* literature describes the great deeds of individuals, often bodhisattvas; *jātaka* literature describes the deeds of one particular individual, Śākyamuni Buddha in his many past incarnations as a bodhisattva.

77. Ohnuma, "*Dehadāna*, 161–171. Strong also discusses this curious phrase in his *The Legend of King Aśoka*, 148–161.

78. Ohnuma, "*Dehadāna*," 162, 166, 169–170.

79. The original Pāli version of the story is found in Oldenberg and Pischel, *Thera- and Therī-gāthā*, 158–162. For a translation, see Rhys Davids and Norman, *Poems of Early Buddhist Nuns (Therīgāthā)*, 126–133, 212–215.

80. Translated in Trainor, "In the Eye of the Beholder," 66.

81. Wilson, *Charming Cadavers*, 165–169.

82. Translated in Trainor, "In the Eye of the Beholder," 66. The Pāli reads: *muttā ca tato sā bhikkhunī agami buddhavarassa santikaṃ* | *passiya varapuññalakkhaṇaṃ cakkhu āsi yathāpurāṇakan ti* || (Oldenberg and Pischel, 162 [v. 399]).

83. Trainor, "In the Eye of the Beholder," 67.

84. Ibid.; see also Trainor, *Relics, Ritual, and Representation in Buddhism,* 186.

85. For example, Filliozat, "Self-Immolation by Fire and the Indian Buddhist Tradition," 109, 110, 113, and 116–117. It is unknown to what extent Buddhist practitioners engaged in bodily sacrifice in South Asia. On this subject see Filliozat, "Self-Immolation by Fire and the Indian Buddhist Tradition," 91–125; and Filliozat, "The Giving Up of Life by the Sage," 135–159. Bodily sacrifice, especially through autocremation, branding, and burning, has been extensively documented in premodern and modern East Asia. On this see Benn, "Where Text Meets Flesh," 295–322; Chân Không, *Learning True Love,* esp. 33–48, 96–108; Gernet, *Buddhism in Chinese Society,* 231–247; Jan, "Buddhist Self-Immolation in Medieval China," 243–268; LaFleur, *Buddhism,* 137–143; and Stone, "By the Power of One's Last Nenbutsu," 101–104. Buddhist narratives extolling the virtues of bodily sacrifice notwithstanding, the propriety of such acts is and has been a controversial issue for Buddhists (see King, "They Who Burned Themselves for Peace," 127–150; Orzech, " 'Provoked Suicide' and the Victim's Behavior," 137–160; Sege, "Suicide or Sacrifice?"; and Takakusu, *A Record of the Buddhist Religion as Practised in India and the Malay Archipelago (AD 671–695) by I-Tsing,* 197–198).

86. Ohnuma, "*Dehadāna,*" 191, see also 175. She attributes her concept of "a body that tends toward non-body" to Vernant, "Dim Body, Dazzling Body," 19–47.

87. Ohnuma, "*Dehadāna,*" 184.

88. Ibid., 185.

89. Ibid., 180.

90. Ibid.

91. Ibid., 186.

92. I discuss the differences between Ohnuma's analysis and mine more fully in my dissertation ("The Relationship between Morality and the Body in Monastic Training According to the *Śikṣāsamuccaya,*" 94–101). As this book goes to press, Reiko Ohnuma's *Head, Eyes, Flesh, and Blood: Giving Away the Body in Indian Buddhist Literature* is due to be released shortly by Columbia University Press. I regret that the timing of our books makes it impossible for me to address the ways in which her analysis may have changed since we completed our dissertations.

93. See Bendall, *Śikshāsamuccaya,* 37.13–41.6 (title given in text is *Prajñāpāramitā Aṣṭasahasrikā*).

94. Ibid., 37.13–14 (quotation from the *Prajñāpāramitā Aṣṭasahasrikā*).

95. Conze, *The Perfection of Wisdom in Eight Thousand Lines and Its Verse Summary,* 285. This passage appears in extremely abbreviated form in the *Compendium of Training,* omitting any reference to the type of body the sacrifice will produce (Bendall, *Śikshāsamuccaya,* 39.5–6). The Sanskrit of the *Prajñāpāramitā Aṣṭasahasrikā* can be found in Vaidya, *Aṣṭasāhasrikā Prajñāpāramitā with Haribhadra's Commentary Called* Āloka, 246.13–16.

96. The declaration of truth is as follows: "All the Lords Buddhas who be, exist, live in the endless, limitless worlds in every direction of space, have I taken to witness. Before their face have I pronounced a vow of truth, and by that truth, by that word of truth shall I, after the sacrifice of my own arm in honour of the Tathāgata, have a body of gold colour" (Kern, *Saddharma-Puṇḍarīka or The Lotus of the True Law,*

384; for the Sanskrit, see Vaidya, *Saddharmapuṇḍarīkasūtra*, 240.1–4). The declaration of truth also contains the request (immediately fulfilled) that the bodhisattva's body be restored to its previous presacrifice condition. In this story the bodily sacrifice and declaration of truth thus produce two chronologically distinct sets of transformation, one immediate and one in the distant future.

97. The story can be found in Filliozat's "Self-Immolation by Fire and the Indian Buddhist Tradition," 92–98.

98. Ibid., 97–98.

99. Wayman and Wayman, *The Lion's Roar of Queen Śrīmālā*, 75.

100. Ohnuma, "*Dehadāna*," 167–171, 176–177.

101. Ibid., 184–186.

102. Bendall, *Śikshāsamuccaya*, 229.13–230.5 (quotation from the *Ratnacūḍa*)

103. Ibid., 230.1–2 (quotation from the *Ratnacūḍa*): *sarvasatvānāṃ dāsatvaśiṣyatvam abhyupagamya kiṅkaraṇīyatāyai utsuko bhavati* |

104. Ibid., 230.5–9 (quotation from the *Ratnacūḍa*): *punar aparaṃ kulaputra bodhisatvaḥ kāye kāyānudarśanasmṛtyupasthānaṃ bhāvayan sarvasatvakāyāṃs tatra svakāya upanibadhnāti* | *evaṃ cāsya bhavati* | *sarvasatvakāyā mayā buddhakāyapratiṣṭhānapratiṣṭhitāḥ kartavyāḥ* | *yathā ca tathāgatakāye nāśravas tathā svakāyadharmatāṃ pratyavekṣate* | *so nāśravadharmatākuśalaḥ sarvasatvakāyān api tallakṣaṇān eva prajānātīty ādi* ||

105. The Tibetan reads: *bdag gi lus de la sems can thams cad kyi lus nye bar 'dogs shing bdag gis sems can thams cad kyi lus sangs rgyas kyi sku'i gnas la gnas par bya'o snyam ste* / (Śāntideva, *Śikṣāsamuccaya; Bslab pa kun las btus pa*, 257.2–3). (Affixing the body of all sentient beings to one's [own] body, think "I should establish the body of all sentient beings in the state of a buddha body.") I am indebted to Holly Gayley for the translation of the Tibetan.

106. Bendall, *Śikshāsamuccaya*, 229.11 (quotation from the *Dharmasaṃgītisūtra*).

107. Hedinger, *Aspekte der Schulung in der Laufbahn eines Bodhisattva*, 111.

CHAPTER 6

1. Bendall, *Śikshāsamuccaya*, 36.8–13 (quotation from the *Vācanopāsikāvimokṣa*, which is found in the *Gaṇḍavyūha*): *ata evāryasudhanaḥ sāradhvajasya bhikṣoḥ pādau śirasābhivandyānekaśatasahasrakṛtvaḥ pradakṣinīkṛtya sāradhvajaṃ bhikṣum avalokya praṇipatya punaḥ punar avalokayan niyataṃ praṇipatan namasyann avanaman manasi kurvan cintayan bhāvayan paribhāvayann udānam udānayan hākkāraṃ kurvan* ' *guṇān abhimukhīkurvan nigamayann atrasann anusmaran dṛḍhīkurvann avijahan manasāgamayann upanibadhnan praṇidhiṃ samavasaran darśanam abhilaṣan svaranimittam udgṛhṇan yāvat tasyāntikāt prakrāntaḥ* | I discuss this passage in detail in chapter 2.

2. Gómez translates *ātmabhāva* as "one's whole person" in his "Two Tantric Meditations," 320.

3. As was noted in chapter 2, I borrow the phrase "bodied being" from Miles's *Plotinus on Body and Beauty*, 14.

4. Ricoeur, *Freud and Philosophy*, 28–32.

5. Ibid., 27, 36.

6. Ibid., 29; see also 7–8.

7. Ibid., 27.

8. Ibid., 29.

9. Ibid., 27.

10. Inden, "Introduction: From Philological to Dialogical Texts," 14.

11. Chakrabarty, *Provincializing Europe*, 5–6.

12. Ibid.

13. Ibid., 6.

14. Dreyfus, *The Sound of Two Hands Clapping*, 35.

15. Eck, *Darśan*, 3.

16. Bendall, *Śikshāsamuccaya*, 36.1 (quotation from the *Gaṇḍavyūha*): *suputrasadṛśena kalyāṇamitramukhavīkṣaṇatayā* |

17. Ibid., 47.13–49.4 (quotation from the *Saddharmapuṇḍarīka*).

18. Derris, "Virtue and Relationships in a Theravādin Biography of the Bodhisatta," 193.

19. Bendall, *Śikshāsamuccaya*, 87.14–21 (quotation from the *Niyatāniyatāvatāramudrāsūtra*).

20. Ibid., 86.7–9 (quotation from the *Śraddhābalādhānāvatāramudrāsūtra*).

21. Harrison, "Mediums and Messages," 132.

22. Ibid., 201.12–15 (quotation from the *Ratnarāśisūtra*): *tena tatrāraṇyāyatane viharatā evaṃ cittam utpādayitavyaṃ* | *yady apy aham araṇyam āgata eko 'dvitīyo* ' *na me kaścit sahāyo yo māṃ sukṛtaṃ duṣkṛtaṃ vā codayet* | *api tu khalu punaḥ santīme devanāgayakṣā buddhāś ca bhagavanto ye mama cittāśayaṃ jānanti* | *te mama sākṣiṇaḥ* | *so 'ham ihāraṇyāyatane prativasann akuśalacittasya vaśaṃ gacchāmi* | I am using Jonathan Alan Silk's translation of this passage (Silk, "The Origins and Early History of the *Mahāratnakūṭa* Tradition of Mahāyāna Buddhism with a Study of the *Ratnarāśisūtra* and Related Materials," 341, n. 1).

23. Bendall, *Śikshāsamuccaya*, 201.15–19 (quotation from the *Ratnarāśisūtra*).

24. Ibid., 53.1–2 (quotation from the *Ratnakūṭa*).

25. Ibid., 91.14–92.6 (partially quoted from the *Śūraṅgamasamādhisūtra*).

26. Ibid., 92.4–7. The entire passage reads: *etena kāśyapa nirdeśena bodhisatvena vā śrāvakeṇa vā sarvasatvānām antike śāstṛsaṃjñotpādayitavyā* | *mātra kaścid bodhisatvayānikaḥ pudgalo bhavet tena tatrātmā rakṣitavya iti* | *yasya tu niyatam eva bodhiprāpticihnam asti tatra sutarām avamanyanā rakṣitavyā* ||

27. Harrison, "Who Gets to Ride in the Great Vehicle?" 67–89; Schopen, "On Monks, Nuns, and 'Vulgar' Practices," 238–257. See also Davidson, *Indian Esoteric Buddhism*, 91–98.

28. Nattier, *A Few Good Men*, 99.

29. See ibid., 217.

30. Ibid., 99.

31. For example, see the "Devadatta" chapter of the *Lotus Sutra*. There are many translations of this text. One of the most readable is Burton Watson's translation

of Kumārajīva's Chinese version (Watson, *The Lotus Sutra*, 182–189). For an overview of pertinent primary sources on the question of whether women can become buddhas, see Paul, *Women in Buddhism*, 166–243.

32. Nattier, *A Few Good Men*, 100.

33. Sponberg, "Attitudes toward Women and the Feminine in Early Buddhism," 3–4.

34. Śāntideva, *The Bodhicaryāvatāra*, 96 (8.95–96). Verse 96 also appears in *The Compendium of Training* at Bendall, *Śikshāsamuccaya*, 2.10–11.

35. Frank, "For a Sociology of the Body: An Analytical Review," 95.

36. For instance, Butler, *Bodies That Matter*; Halberstam, *Female Masculinity*; hooks, *Ain't I a Woman*; Mohanty, Russo, and Torres, *Third World Women and the Politics of Feminism*; Moraga and Anzaldúa, *This Bridge Called My Back*; and Visweswaran, *Fictions of Feminist Ethnography*.

37. Gross, "The *Dharma* of Gender," 11; see also McClintock, "Gendered Bodies of Illusion," 261; and Mrozik, "Materializations of Virtue: Buddhist Discourses on Bodies."

38. Faure, *The Power of Denial*, 141.

39. Ibid., 119.

40. Gregory and Mrozik, *Women Practicing Buddhism*, 2007.

41. This goal bespeaks the influence of Butler's *Bodies That Matter*, 3 and passim.

42. Hallisey, "Buddhism," 124.

Bibliography

Abhidharmakośabhāṣya. Ed. Gelugpa Student Welfare Committee. Sarnath, India: Central Institute of Higher Tibetan Studies, 1997.

Beal, Samuel, trans. *Si-Yu-Ki: Buddhist Records of the Western World, Translated from the Chinese of Hiuen Tsiang (A.D. 629)*. 1884. Reprint, Delhi: Motilal Banarsidass, 1981.

BeDuhn, Jason David. *The Manichaean Body in Discipline and Ritual*. Baltimore: Johns Hopkins University Press, 2000.

Bendall, Cecil. *Catalogue of the Buddhist Sanskrit Manuscripts in the University Library, Cambridge*. Publications of the Nepal-German Manuscript Preservation Project 2. 1883. Reprint, Stuttgart: Franz Steiner Verlag, 1992.

———, ed. *Śikshāsamuccaya: A Compendium of Buddhistic Teaching Compiled by Śāntideva Chiefly from Earlier Mahāyāna-Sūtras*. Bibliotheca Buddhica 1. 1897–1902. Reprint, Osnabrück: Biblio Verlag, 1970.

Bendall, Cecil, and W. H. D. Rouse, trans. *Śikṣā Samuccaya: A Compendium of Buddhist Doctrine Compiled by Śāntideva Chiefly from Earlier Mahāyāna Sūtras*. 2nd ed. 1922. Reprint, Delhi: Motilal Banarsidass, 1990.

Benn, James A. "Where Text Meets Flesh: Burning the Body as an Apocryphal Practice in Chinese Buddhism." *History of Religions* 37:4 (May 1998): 295–322.

Berkwitz, Stephen C. *Buddhist History in the Vernacular: The Power of the Past in Late Medieval Sri Lanka*. Leiden: Brill, 2004.

———. "History and Gratitude in Theravāda Buddhism." *Journal of the American Academy of Religion* 71:3 (September 2003): 579–604.

———. *The History of the Buddha's Relic Shrine: A Translation of the Sinhala Thūpavaṃsa*. New York: Oxford University Press, 2007.

Blackburn, Anne M. *Buddhist Learning and Textual Practice in Eighteenth-Century Lankan Monastic Culture.* Princeton, N.J.: Princeton University Press, 2001.

Braarvig, Jens, ed. and trans. *Akṣayamatinirdeśasūtra.* 2 vols. Oslo: Solum Forlag, 1993.

Braarvig, Jens, and Paul Harrison. "Candrottarādārikāvyākaraṇa." In *Manuscripts in the Schøyen Collection 3: Buddhist Manuscripts,* ed. Jens Braarvig, 51–68. Vol. 2. Oslo: Hermes Publishing, 2002.

Brown, Peter. *The Body and Society: Men, Women, and Sexual Renunciation in Early Christianity.* New York: Columbia University Press, 1988.

Brown, Robert L. "Buddha Images." In *Encyclopedia of Buddhism,* ed. Robert E. Buswell, Jr. Vol. 1. New York: Macmillan Reference, 2004.

Brown, Sid. *The Journey of One Buddhist Nun: Even Against the Wind.* Albany: State University of New York Press, 2001.

Buddhist Hybrid Sanskrit Grammar and Dictionary, ed. Franklin Edgerton. Vol. 2. 1953. Reprint, Delhi: Motilal Banarsidass, 1993.

Bunnag, Jane. *Buddhist Monk, Buddhist Layman: A Study of Urban Monastic Organization in Central Thailand.* Cambridge, U.K.: Cambridge University Press, 1973.

Burlingame, Eugene Watson, trans. *Buddhist Legends: Translated from the Original Pali Text of the Dhammapada Commentary.* 3 vols. Cambridge, Mass.: Harvard University Press, 1921.

Butler, Judith. *Bodies That Matter: On the Discursive Limits of "Sex."* New York: Routledge, 1993.

Bynum, Caroline Walker. *Holy Feast and Holy Fast: The Religious Significance of Food to Medieval Women.* Berkeley: University of California Press, 1987.

Carrithers, Michael. *The Forest Monks of Sri Lanka: An Anthropological and Historical Study.* Delhi: Oxford University Press, 1983.

Carter, John Ross. *Dhamma: Western Academic and Sinhalese Buddhist Interpretations, A Study of a Religious Concept.* Tokyo: Hokuseido Press, 1978.

Carter, John Ross, and Mahinda Palihawadana, trans. *The Dhammapada.* New York: Oxford University Press, 2000.

Chakrabarty, Dipesh. *Provincializing Europe: Postcolonial Thought and Historical Difference.* Princeton, N.J.: Princeton University Press, 2000.

Chân Không [Cao Ngoc Phuong]. *Learning True Love: How I Learned and Practiced Social Change in Vietnam.* Berkeley, Calif.: Parallax Press, 1993.

Clayton, Barbra R. "Ethics in the *Śikṣāsamuccaya*: A Study in Mahāyāna Morality." Ph.D. diss., McGill University, 2002.

———. *Moral Theory in Śāntideva's* Śikṣāsamuccaya*: Cultivating the Fruits of Virtue.* London: Routledge, 2006.

Cleary, Thomas, trans. *The Flower Ornament Scripture: A Translation of the* Avatamsaka Sutra. 1984. Reprint, Boston: Shambhala, 1993.

Collins, Steven. "The Body in Theravāda Buddhist Monasticism." In *Religion and the Body,* ed. Sarah Coakley, 185–204. Cambridge, U.K.: Cambridge University Press, 1997.

———. *Selfless Persons: Imagery and Thought in* Theravāda *Buddhism.* Cambridge, U.K.: Cambridge University Press, 1982.

Conze, Edward, trans. *The Perfection of Wisdom in Eight Thousand Lines and Its Verse Summary*. San Francisco: Four Seasons Foundation, 1973.

Cox, Collet. "Mainstream Buddhist Schools." In *Encyclopedia of Buddhism*, ed. Robert E. Buswell, Jr. Vol. 2. New York: Macmillan Reference, 2004.

Csikszentmihalyi, Mark. *Material Virtue: Ethics and the Body in Early China*. Leiden: Brill, 2004.

Daniel, E. Valentine. *Fluid Signs: Being a Person the Tamil Way*. Berkeley: University of California Press, 1984.

Davidson, Ronald M. *Indian Esoteric Buddhism: A Social History of the Tantric Movement*. New York: Columbia University Press, 2002.

Derris, Karen Anne. "Virtue and Relationships in a Theravādin Biography of the Bodhisatta: A Study of the *Sotaṭṭhakīmahānidāna*." Ph.D. diss., Harvard University, 2000.

de Silva, Padmasiri. "Buddhist Ethics." In *A Companion to Ethics*, ed. Peter Singer, 58–68. Oxford: Blackwell Publishers Ltd., 1991. Reprint, with corrections, 1993.

Dimitrov, Dragomir. "Tables of the Old Bengali Script (on the basis of a Nepalese manuscript of Daṇḍin's *Kāvyādarśa*)." In *Śikhisamuccayaḥ: Indian and Tibetan Studies (Collectanea Marpurgensia Indologica et Tibetica)*, ed. Dragomir Dimitrov, Ulrike Roesler, and Roland Steiner, 27–78. Wiener Studien zur Tibetologie und Buddhismuskunde 53. Vienna: Arbeitskreis für Tibetische und Buddhistische Studien Universität Wien, 2002.

Dreyfus, Georges B. J. *The Sound of Two Hands Clapping: The Education of a Tibetan Buddhist Monk*. Berkeley: University of California Press, 2003.

Dutt, Nalinaksha, ed. *Bodhisattvabhūmiḥ: Being the XVth Section of Asaṅgapāda's Yogācārabhūmiḥ*. Tibetan-Sanskrit Works Series, vol. 7. Patna: K. P. Jayaswal Research Institute, 1978.

Dutt, Sukumar. *Buddhist Monks and Monasteries of India: Their History and Their Contribution to Indian Culture*. 1962. Reprint, Delhi: Motilal Banarsidass, 1988.

Eck, Diana L. *Darśan: Seeing the Divine Image in India*. 3rd ed. New York: Columbia University Press, 1998.

Eckel, Malcolm David. *Jñānagarbha's Commentary on the Distinction between the Two Truths: An Eighth Century Handbook of Madhyamaka Philosophy*. Albany: State University of New York Press, 1987.

———. *To See the Buddha: A Philosopher's Quest for the Meaning of Emptiness*. New York: HarperCollins, 1992.

Egge, James R. "Interpretive Strategies for Seeing the Body of the Buddha." In *Constituting Communities: Theravāda Buddhism and the Religious Cultures of South and Southeast Asia*, ed. John Clifford Holt, Jacob N. Kinnard, and Jonathan S. Walters, 189–208. Albany: State University of New York Press, 2003.

Endo, Toshiichi. *Buddha in Theravada Buddhism: A Study of the Concept of Buddha in the Pali Commentaries*. Nedimala, Dehiwela, Sri Lanka: Buddhist Cultural Centre, 1997.

Faure, Bernard. *The Power of Denial: Buddhism, Purity, and Gender*. Princeton, N.J.: Princeton University Press, 2003.

———. *The Red Thread: Buddhist Approaches to Sexuality*. Princeton, N.J.: Princeton University Press, 1998.

Feer, M. Leon, ed. *Saṃyutta-Nikaya*. 6 parts. London: Pali Text Society, 1884–1904.

Filliozat, Jean. "The Giving Up of Life by the Sage: The Suicides of the Criminal and the Hero in Indian Tradition." In *Religion, Philosophy, Yoga: A Selection of Articles by Jean Filliozat*. Trans. Maurice Shukla. Delhi: Motilal Banarsidass, 1991.

———. "Self-Immolation by Fire and the Indian Buddhist Tradition." In *Religion, Philosophy, Yoga: A Selection of Articles by Jean Filliozat*. Trans. Maurice Shukla. Delhi: Motilal Banarsidass, 1991.

Fine, Lawrence. "Purifying the Body in the Name of the Soul: The Problem of the Body in Sixteenth-Century Kabbalah." In *People of the Body: Jews and Judaism from an Embodied Perspective*, ed. Howard Eilberg-Schwartz, 117–142. Albany: State University of New Press, 1992.

Foucault, Michel. *The Care of the Self*. Vol. 3 of *The History of Sexuality*, trans. Robert Hurley. English trans. 1986. Reprint, New York: Vintage Books, 1988.

———. *Discipline and Punish: The Birth of the Prison*, trans. Alan Sheridan. English trans. 1977. Reprint, Vintage Books, 1995.

———. *The Use of Pleasure*. Vol. 2 of *The History of Sexuality*, trans. Robert Hurley. English trans. 1985. Reprint, New York: Vintage Books, 1990.

Frank, Arthur W. "For a Sociology of the Body: An Analytical Review." In *The Body: Social Process and Cultural Theory*, ed. Mike Featherstone, Mike Hepworth, and Bryan S. Turner, 36–102. London: Sage, 1991.

Gayley, Holly. "Soteriology of the Senses in Tibetan Buddhism." Paper presented at the annual meeting of the American Academy of Religion, Washington, D.C., November 2006.

Gernet, Jacques. *Buddhism in Chinese Society: An Economic History from the Fifth to the Tenth Centuries*, trans. Franciscus Verellen. New York: Columbia University Press, 1995.

Gnoli, Raniero, ed. *The Gilgit Manuscript of the Saṅghabhedavastu: Being the 17th and Last Section of the Vinaya of the Mūlasarvāstivādin*. Part 2. Rome: Istituto Italiano Per il Medio ed Estremo Oriente, 1978.

Gokhale, V. V. "What Is Avijñaptirūpa (Concealed Form of Activity)?" *New Indian Antiquary* 1 (1938/1939): 69–73.

Gombrich, Richard F. *Buddhist Precept and Practice: Traditional Buddhism in the Rural Highlands of Ceylon*. 1971. Reprint, London: Kegan Paul International, 1995.

———. "Merit Detached from Volition: How a Buddhist Doctrine Came to Wear a Jain Aspect." In *Jainism and Early Buddhism: Essays in Honor of Padmanabh S. Jaini*, ed. Olle Qvarnström, 427–440. Fremont, Calif.: Asian Humanities Press, 2003.

———. *Theravāda Buddhism: A Social History from Ancient Benares to Modern Colombo*. 1988. London: Routledge, 1995.

Gómez, Luis O. "The Bodhisattva as Wonder-Worker." In *Prajñāpāramitā and Related Systems: Studies in Honor of Edward Conze*, ed. Lewis Lancaster, 221–261. Berkeley, Calif.: Berkeley Buddhist Studies Series, 1977.

———. *The Land of Bliss: The Paradise of the Buddha of Measureless Light: Sanskrit and Chinese Versions of the Sukhāvatīvyūha Sutras*. Honolulu: University of Hawai'i Press and Higashi Honganji Shinshū Ōtani-ha (Kyoto, Japan), 1996.

———. "Two Tantric Meditations: Visualizing the Deity." In *Buddhism in Practice*, ed. Donald S. Lopez, Jr., 318–327. Princeton: Princeton University Press, 1995.

Goswami, Bijoya, trans. *Lalitavistara*. Kolkata: Asiatic Society, 2001.

Gregory, Peter N., and Susanne Mrozik, eds. *Women Practicing Buddhism: American Experiences*. Boston: Wisdom Publications, 2007.

Griffiths, Paul J. *On Being Buddha: The Classical Doctrine of Buddhahood*. Albany: State University of New York Press, 1994.

———. *On Being Mindless: Buddhist Meditation and the Mind–Body Problem*. La Salle, Ill.: Open Court, 1986.

———. *Religious Reading: The Place of Reading in the Practice of Religion*. New York: Oxford University Press, 1999.

Gross, Rita M. "The *Dharma* of Gender." In *Contemporary Buddhism* 5:1 (2004): 3–13.

Grosz, Elizabeth. *Volatile Bodies: Toward a Corporeal Feminism*. Bloomington: Indiana University Press, 1994.

Guang Xing. *The Concept of the Buddha: Its Evolution from Early Buddhism to the* Trikaya *Theory*. London: RoutledgeCurzon, 2005.

Gyatso, Janet. "One Plus One Makes Three: Buddhist Gender, Monasticism, and the Law of the Non-Excluded Middle." *History of Religions* 43:2 (November 2003): 89–115.

Hae-ju Sunim (Ho-Ryeon Jeon). "Can Women Achieve Enlightenment? A Critique of Sexual Transformation for Enlightenment." In *Buddhist Women Across Cultures: Realizations*, ed. Karma Lekshe Tsomo, 123–141. Albany: State University of New York Press, 1999.

Halberstam, Judith. *Female Masculinity*. Durham, N.C.: Duke University Press, 1998.

Hallisey, Charles. "Buddhism." In *The Life of Virtue: What Do We Owe Ourselves?* ed. Jacob Neusner, 112–134. Belmont, Calif.: Wadsworth/Thomson Learning, 2001.

———. "In Defense of Rather Fragile and Local Achievement: Reflections on the Work of Gurulugomi." In *Religion and Practical Reason: New Essays in the Comparative Philosophy of Religions*, ed. Frank E. Reynolds and David Tracy, 121–160. Albany: State University of New York Press, 1994.

Hamilton, Sue. *Identity and Experience: The Constitution of the Human Being According to Early Buddhism*. London: Luzac Oriental, 1996.

Hardy, E., ed. *The Aṅguttara-Nikāya*. Part 3. London: Pali Text Society, 1896.

Harpham, Geoffrey Galt. *The Ascetic Imperative in Culture and Criticism*. Chicago: University of Chicago Press, 1987.

Harrison, Paul. "The Case of the Vanishing Poet: New Light on Śāntideva and the *Śikṣā-samuccaya*." In *Indica et Tibetica: Festschrift für Michael Hahn zum 65. Geburtstag von Freunden und Schülern überreicht*, ed. Konrad Klaus and Jens-Uwe Hartmann, 169–202. Vienna: Wiener Studien zur Tibetologie und Buddhismuskunde, forthcoming.

———. "Is the *Dharma-kāya* the Real 'Phantom Body' of the Buddha?" *Journal of the International Association of Buddhist Studies* 15:1 (1992): 44–94.

———. "Mediums and Messages: Reflections on the Production of Mahāyāna Sūtras." *The Eastern Buddhist* 35:1–2 (2005): 115–151.

———. "Who Gets to Ride in the Great Vehicle? Self-Image and Identity among the Followers of the Early Mahāyāna." *Journal of the International Association of Buddhist Studies* 10:1 (1987): 67–89.

Harvey, Peter. *An Introduction to Buddhist Ethics: Foundations, Values and Issues.* Cambridge, U.K.: Cambridge University Press, 2000.

———. "Vinaya Principles for Assigning Degrees of Culpability." *Journal of Buddhist Ethics* 6 (1999): 271–291.

Hedinger, Jürg. *Aspekte der Schulung in der Laufbahn eines Bodhisattva: Dargestellt nach dem Śikṣāsamuccaya des Śāntideva.* Wiesbaden, Germany: Otto Harrassowitz, 1984.

Heim, Maria. "The Aesthetics of Excess." *Journal of the American Academy of Religion* 71:3 (September 2003): 531–554.

———. "Shame and Apprehension: Notes on the Moral Value of *Hiri* and *Ottappa*." In forthcoming felicitation volume in honor of W. S. Karunatillake, ed. Carol Anderson and Susanne Mrozik.

———. *Theories of the Gift in South Asia: Hindu, Buddhist, and Jain Reflections on Dāna.* New York: Routledge, 2004.

Heimann, Betty. *The Significance of Prefixes in Sanskrit Philosophical Terminology.* Royal Asiatic Society Monographs, vol. 25. London: Royal Asiatic Society, 1951.

Hemacandra. *The Lives of the Jain Elders*, trans. R. C. C. Fynes. Oxford: Oxford University Press, 1998.

hooks, bell. *Ain't I a Woman: Black Women and Feminism.* Boston: South End Press, 1981.

Hopkins, Jeffrey. *Meditation on Emptiness.* London: Wisdom Publications, 1983.

Hopkins, Thomas J. *The Hindu Religious Tradition.* Belmont, Calif.: Wadsworth, 1971.

Hsieh, Ding-hwa E. "Images of Women in Ch'an Buddhist Literature of the Sung Period." In *Buddhism in the Sung*, ed. Peter N. Gregory and Daniel A. Getz, Jr., 148–187. Honolulu: University of Hawai'i Press, 1999.

Huntington, Susan L. *The "Pāla-Sena" Schools of Sculpture.* Leiden: Brill, 1984.

Huntington, Susan L., and John C. Huntington. *Leaves from the* Bodhi *Tree: The Art of Pāla India (8th–12th Centuries) and Its International Legacy.* Seattle: Dayton Art Institute in Association with the University of Washington Press, 1990.

Hurvitz, Leon, trans. *Scripture of the Lotus Blossom of the Fine Dharma.* New York: Columbia University Press, 1976.

Inden, Ronald. "Introduction: From Philological to Dialogical Texts." In *Querying the Medieval: Texts and the History of Practices in South Asia*, ed. Ronald Inden, Jonathan Walters, and Daud Ali, 3–28. Oxford: Oxford University Press, 2000.

Inden, Ronald, and Ralph W. Nicholas. *Kinship in Bengali Culture.* Chicago: University of Chicago Press, 1977.

Jan, Yün-hua. "Buddhist Self-Immolation in Medieval China." *History of Religions* 4:2 (Winter 1965): 243–268.

Jayawickrama, N. A., trans. *The Story of Gotama Buddha: The Nidāna-kathā of the* Jātakaṭṭhakathā. Oxford: Pali Text Society, 2002.

Johnston, E. H., ed. and trans. *Aśvaghoṣa's Buddhacarita or Acts of the Buddha.* 1936. Reprint, new enlarged ed., Delhi: Motilal Banarsidass, 1984.

Jones, J. J., trans. *The Mahāvastu.* 3 vols. 1949–1956. London: Pali Text Society, 1973–1978.

Jong, J. W. de. "La légende de Śāntideva." *Indo-Iranian Journal* 16:3 (September 1975): 161–182.

———. Review of *Aspekte der Schulung in der Laufbahn eines Bodhisattva: Dargestellt nach dem Śikṣāsamuccaya des Śāntideva,* by Jürg Hedinger. *Indo-Iranian Journal* 30:3 (1987): 230–235.

Karunatillake, W. S., ed. *Sinhala Thūpavaṃsa.* Colombo: M. D. Gunasena, 1994.

Kemper, Steven. "Wealth and Reformation in Sinhalese Buddhist Monasticism." In *Ethics, Wealth, and Salvation: A Study in Buddhist Social Ethics,* ed. Russell F. Sizemore and Donald K. Swearer, 152–169. Columbia: University of South Carolina Press, 1990.

Keown, Damien. *Buddhism & Bioethics.* New York: St. Martin's Press, 1995.

Kern, H., trans. *Saddharma-Puṇḍarīka or the Lotus of the True Law.* 1884. Reprint, New York: Dover Publications, 1963.

Khantipalo, Bhikkhu. *Bag of Bones: A Miscellany on the Body.* Kandy, Sri Lanka: Buddhist Publication Society, 1980.

King, Sallie B. "They Who Burned Themselves for Peace: Quaker and Buddhist Self-Immolators during the Vietnam War." *Buddhist-Christian Studies* 20 (2000): 127–150.

Kinnard, Jacob N. "Iconography: Buddhist Iconography." In *Encylopedia of Religion,* 2nd ed., ed. Lindsay Jones. Vol. 7. Detroit: Macmillan Reference, 2005.

———. *Imaging Wisdom: Seeing and Knowing in the Art of Indian Buddhism.* Surrey, U.K.: Curzon Press, 1999.

Klaus, Konrad. "Einige Textkritische und Exegetische Bemerkungen zu Śāntidevas Śikṣāsamuccaya (Kapitel XII und XIII)." In *Bauddhavidyāsudhākaraḥ: Studies in Honour of Heinz Bechert on the Occasion of His 65th Birthday,* ed. Petra Kieffer-Pülz and Jens-Uwe Hartmann, 397–406. Swisttal-Odendorf: Indica et Tibetica Verlag, 1997.

Klein, Anne Carolyn. "Buddhist Understandings of Subjectivity." In *Buddhist Women and Social Justice: Ideals, Challenges, and Achievements,* ed. Karma Lekshe Tsomo, 23–34. Albany: State University of New York Press, 2004.

Kosambi, D. D., and V. V. Gokhale, eds. *The Subhāṣitaratnakoṣa Compiled by Vidyākara.* Harvard Oriental Series, vol. 42. Cambridge, Mass.: Harvard University Press, 1957.

LaFleur, William R. *Buddhism: A Cultural Perspective.* Englewood Cliffs, N.J.: Prentice Hall, 1988.

Lamotte, Étienne, trans. *Karmasiddhiprakaraṇa: The Treatise on Action by Vasubandhu.* English trans. Leo M. Pruden. Berkeley, Calif.: Asian Humanities Press, 1987.

La Vallée Poussin, Louis de, trans. *L'Abhidharmakośa de Vasubandhu: Traduction et Annotations.* 6 vols. 1923–1931. New ed., Bruxelles: Institut Belge des Hautes Études Chinoises, 1971.

———, ed. *Prajñākaramati's Commentary to the Bodhicaryāvatāra of Śāntideva, edited with Indices.* Calcutta: Asiatic Society of Bengal, 1901–1914.

Levering, Miriam L. "The Dragon Girl and the Abbess of Mo-Shan: Gender and Status in the Ch'an Buddhist Tradition." *Journal of the International Association of Buddhist Studies* 5:1 (1982): 19–35.

Lewis, Todd T. "*Samsara* and the Soul." In *Buddhism: The Illustrated Guide,* ed. Kevin Trainor, 58–59. Oxford: Oxford University Press, 2001.

Lopez, Jr., Donald S. *The Story of Buddhism: A Concise Guide to Its History & Teachings.* New York: HarperSanFrancisco, 2001.

Ludowyk-Gyömröi, Edith. "Note on the Interpretation of 'Pasīdati.'" *University of Ceylon Review* 1 (1943): 74–82.

Mahoney, Richard. "Of the Progresse of the Bodhisattva: The Bodhisattvamārga in the Śikṣāsamuccaya." Master's thesis, University of Canterbury, 2002.

Majumdar, R. C., H. C. Raychaudhuri, and Kalikinkar Datta. *An Advanced History of India.* 3rd ed. New York: St. Martin's Press, 1967.

Makransky, John J. "Buddhahood and Buddha Bodies." In *Encyclopedia of Buddhism,* ed. Robert E. Buswell, Jr. Vol. 1. New York: Macmillan Reference, 2004.

———. *Buddhahood Embodied: Sources of Controversy in India and Tibet.* Albany: State University of New York Press, 1997.

Malamoud, Charles. "Cooking the World." In *Cooking the World: Ritual and Thought in Ancient India,* trans. David White, 23–53. New Delhi: Oxford University Press, 1998.

Marriott, McKim. "Hindu Transactions: Diversity Without Dualism." In *Transaction and Meaning: Directions in the Anthropology of Exchange and Symbolic Behavior,* ed. Bruce Kapferer, 109–142. Philadelphia: Institute for the Study of Human Issues, 1976.

Marriott, McKim, and Ronald B. Inden. "Toward an Ethnosociology of South Asian Caste Systems." In *The New Wind: Changing Identities in South Asia,* ed. Kenneth David, 227–238. The Hague: Mouton Publishers, 1977.

Martin, Luther H., Huck Gutman, and Patrick H. Hutton, eds. *Technologies of the Self: A Seminar with Michel Foucault.* Amherst, Mass.: University of Massachusetts Press, 1988.

Matics, Marion L., trans. *Entering the Path of Enlightenment: The* Bodhicaryāvatāra *of the Buddhist Poet Śāntideva.* New York: Macmillan Company, 1970.

McClintock, Sara. "Gendered Bodies of Illusion: Finding a Somatic Method in the Ontic Madness of Emptiness." In *Buddhist Theology: Critical Reflections by Contemporary Buddhist Scholars,* ed. Roger R. Jackson and John J. Makransky, 261–274. 2000. Reprint, London: RoutledgeCurzon, 2003.

McMahan, David L. *Empty Vision: Metaphor and Visionary Imagery in Mahāyāna Buddhism.* London: RoutledgeCurzon, 2002.

Miles, Margaret R. *Plotinus on Body and Beauty: Society, Philosophy, and Religion in Third-Century Rome.* Oxford: Blackwell Publishers, 1999.

———. "Sex and the City (of God): Is Sex Forfeited or Fulfilled in Augustine's Resurrection of Body?" *Journal of the American Academy of Religion* 73:2 (June 2005): 307–327.

Miller, Barbara Stoler, trans. *The Bhagavad-Gita: Krishna's Counsel in Time of War.* New York: Bantam Books, 1986.

Mohanty, Chandra Talpade, Ann Russo, and Lourdes Torres, eds. *Third World Women and the Politics of Feminism.* Bloomington: Indiana University Press, 1991.

Moraga, Cherríe, and Gloria Anzaldúa, eds. *This Bridge Called My Back: Writings by Radical Women of Color.* 2nd ed. Latham, N.Y.: Kitchen Table: Women of Color Press, 1983.

Mrozik, Susanne. "Cooking Living Beings: The Transformative Effects of Encounters with Bodhisattva Bodies." *Journal of Religious Ethics* 32:1 (2004): 175–194.

———. "Materializations of Virtue: Buddhist Discourses on Bodies." In *Bodily Citations: Religion and Judith Butler,* ed. Ellen T. Armour and Susan M. St. Ville, 15–47. New York: Columbia University Press, 2006.

———. "The Relationship between Morality and the Body in Monastic Training According to the *Śikṣāsamuccaya.*" Ph.D. diss., Harvard University, 1998.

———. "The Value of Human Differences: South Asian Buddhist Contributions Toward an Embodied Virtue Theory." *Journal of Buddhist Ethics* 9 (2002): 1–33.

Mukhopadhyaya, Sujitkumar, ed. *The Aśokāvadāna: Sanskrit Text Compared with Chinese Versions.* New Delhi: Sahitya Akademi, 1963.

Müller, Edward, ed. *The Atthasālinī: Buddhaghosa's Commentary on the Dhammasaṅgaṇi.* 1897. Reprint, London: Pali Text Society, 1979.

Ñānamoli, Bhikkhu, trans. *The Path of Purification* (Visuddhimagga) *by Bhadantācariya Buddhaghosa.* 1956. Reprint, Singapore: Singapore Buddhist Meditation Centre, 1997.

Nattier, Jan. *A Few Good Men: The Bodhisattva Path According to* The Inquiry of Ugra (Ugraparipṛcchā). Honolulu: University of Hawai'i Press, 2003.

———. "Monks in the Mahāyāna." In *Buddhist Scriptures,* ed. Donald S. Lopez, Jr., 269–277. London: Penguin Books, 2004.

Norman, H. C., ed. *The Commentary on the Dhammapada.* 5 vols. London: Pali Text Society, 1906–1915.

O'Flaherty, Wendy Doniger. *Women, Androgynes, and Other Mythical Beasts.* Chicago: University of Chicago Press, 1980.

———, trans. *The Rig Veda: An Anthology.* Harmondsworth, Middlesex, England: Penguin Books, 1981.

Ohnuma, Reiko. "*Dehadāna*: The 'Gift of the Body' in Indian Buddhist Narrative Literature." Ph.D. diss., University of Michigan, 1997.

———. "The Gift of the Body and the Gift of Dharma." *History of Religions* 37:4 (May 1998): 323–359.

———. "Internal and External Opposition to the Bodhisattva's Gift of His Body." *Journal of Indian Philosophy* 28 (2000): 43–75.

———. *Head, Eyes, Flesh, and Blood: Giving Away the Body in Indian Buddhist Literature.* New York: Columbia University Press, 2007.

———. "The Story of Rūpāvatī: A Female Past Birth of the Buddha." *Journal of the International Association of Buddhist Studies* 23:1 (2000): 103–145.

Oldenberg, Hermann, and Richard Pischel, eds. *Thera- and Therī-gāthā.* 2nd ed. with appendices by K. R. Norman and L. Alsdorf. 1893. Reprint, London: Pali Text Society, 1990.

Olivelle, Patrick, trans. *Saṃnyāsa Upaniṣads: Hindu Scriptures on Asceticism and Renunciation.* New York: Oxford University Press, 1992.

Orzech, Charles D. " 'Provoked Suicide' and the Victim's Behavior." In *Curing Violence,* ed. Mark I. Wallace and Theophus H. Smith, 137–160. Sonoma, Calif.: Polebridge Press, 1994.

Pagel, Ulrich. *The Bodhisattvapiṭaka: Its Doctrines, Practices and Their Position in Mahāyāna Literature.* Buddhica Britannica Series Continua V. Tring, U.K.: Institute of Buddhist Studies, 1995.

The Pali Text Society's Pali-English Dictionary, ed. T. W. Rhys Davids and William Stede. 1921–1925. Reprint, London: Pali Text Society, 1986.

Pāsādika, Bhikkhu. "Tib J 380, a Dunhuang Manuscript Fragment of the Sūtrasamuccaya." In *Bauddhavidyāsudhākaraḥ: Studies in Honour of Heinz Bechert on the Occasion of His 65th Birthday,* ed. Petra Kieffer-Pülz and Jens-Uwe Hartmann, 483–494. Swisttal-Odendorf: Indica et Tibetica Verlag, 1997.

Patton, Laurie L. *Bringing the Gods to Mind: Mantra and Ritual in Early Indian Sacrifice.* Berkeley: University of California Press, 2005.

Paul, Diana Y. *Women in Buddhism: Images of the Feminine in Mahāyāna Tradition.* 2nd ed. Berkeley: University of California Press, 1985.

Payutto, Phra Prayudh. *Buddhadhamma: Natural Laws and Values for Life,* trans. Grant A. Olson. Albany: State University of New York Press, 1995.

Peach, Lucinda Joy. "Social Responsibility, Sex Change, and Salvation: Gender Justice in the *Lotus Sūtra.*" *Philosophy East and West* 52:1 (January 2002): 50–74.

Pradhan, P., ed. *Abhidharm[a]koshabhāṣya of Vasubandhu.* Patna: K. P. Jayaswal Research Institute, 1967.

Prebish, Charles S. *Buddhist Monastic Discipline: The Sanskrit Prātimokṣa Sūtras of the Mahāsāṃghikas and Mūlasarvāstivādins.* University Park: The Pennsylvania State University Press, 1975.

Price, Janet, and Margrit Shildrick, eds. *Feminist Theory and the Body: A Reader.* New York: Routledge, 1999.

Pruden, Leo M., trans. *Abhidharmakośabhāṣyam.* 4 vols. Berkeley, Calif.: Asian Humanities Press, 1991. (This is an English translation of Louis de La Vallée Poussin's French translation of the text [see La Vallée Poussin].)

Rhys Davids, Caroline A. F. *A Buddhist Manual of Psychological Ethics of the Fourth Century B.C.: Being a Translation, Now Made for the First Time, from the Original Pali, of the First Book in the Abhidhamma Piṭaka Entitled Dhamma-Sangaṇi (Compendium of States of Phenomena).* 1900. New Delhi: Oriental Books Reprint Corp., 1975.

Rhys Davids, Caroline A. F., and K. R. Norman, trans. *Poems of Early Buddhist Nuns (Therīgāthā).* Oxford: Pali Text Society, 1989.

Ricoeur, Paul. *Freud and Philosophy: An Essay on Interpretation.* New Haven, Conn.: Yale University Press, 1970.

Robinson, Richard H. "The Ethic of the Householder Bodhisattva." *Bhāratī: Bulletin of the College of Indology* 9:2 (1965–1966): 25–56.

Rotman, Andy. "The Erotics of Practice: Objects and Agency in the Buddhist *Avadāna* Literature." *Journal of the American Academy of Religion* 71:3 (September 2003): 555–578.

Saito, Akira. "On the Difference between the Earlier and the Current Versions of Śāntideva's *Bodhi(sattva)caryāvatāra*, with special reference to chapter 9 (/8), entitled: 'Perfection of Wisdom (prajñāpāramitā).' " Research paper presented at the IXth World Sanskrit Conference held January 9–15, 1994, in Melbourne, Australia.

———. "Śāntideva in the History of Mādhyamika Philosophy." In *Buddhism in India and Abroad: An Integrating Influence in Vedic and Post-Vedic Perspective*, ed. Kalpakam Sankarnarayan, Motohiro Yoritomi, and Shubhada A. Joshi, 257–263. Mumbai: Somaiya Publications, 1996.

———. *A Study of Akṣayamati (= Śāntideva)'s* Bodhisattvacaryāvatāra *as Found in the Tibetan Manuscripts from Tun-huang*. A Report of the Grant-in-Aid for Scientific Research (C). Mie, Japan, 1993.

Samuels, Jeffrey. "Merit and the Heart: The Role of Emotions in Merit-making Practices in Contemporary Sri Lanka." *Contemporary Buddhism*, forthcoming.

Sanderson, Alexis. "The Sarvāstivāda and Its Critics: Anātmavāda and the Theory of Karma." In *Buddhism into the Year 2000: International Conference Proceedings*, 33–48. Bangkok: Dhammakaya Foundation, 1994.

Sāṅkṛityāyana, Rāhula. "Second Search of Sanskrit Palm-Leaf Mss. in Tibet." *Journal of the Bihar and Orissa Research Society* 23:1 (1937): 1–57.

Śāntideva (see also Cecil Bendall). *The Bodhicaryāvatāra*, trans. Kate Crosby and Andrew Skilton. Oxford: Oxford University Press, 1996.

———. *Śikṣāsamuccaya; Bslab pa kun las btus pa*. In the Sde dge Bstan 'gyur. Digital scans of Chengdu reproduction from facsimile edition published in Delhi. Vol. *khi*, Sde dge no. 3940, 2–388. New York: Tibetan Buddhist Resources Center, 2003.

Schmithausen, Lambert. "Die Vier Konzentrationen der Aufmerksamkeit: Zur Geschichtlichen Entwicklung einer Spirituellen Praxis des Buddhismus." *Zeitschrift für Missionswissenschaft und Religionswissenschaft* 60:4 (1976): 241–266.

Schopen, Gregory. "The *Bhaiṣajyaguru-Sūtra* and the Buddhism of Gilgit." Ph.D. diss., Australian National University, 1978.

———. "The Manuscript of the *Vajracchedikā* Found at Gilgit." In *Studies in the Literature of the Great Vehicle: Three Mahāyāna Buddhist Texts*, ed. Luis O. Gómez and Jonathan A. Silk, 89–139. Ann Arbor: Collegiate Institute for the Study of Buddhist Literature and Center for South and Southeast Asian Studies, The University of Michigan, 1989.

———. "Mūlasarvāstivāda-vinaya." In *Encyclopedia of Buddhism*, ed. Robert E. Buswell, Jr. Vol. 2. New York: Macmillan Reference, 2004.

———. "On Monks, Nuns, and 'Vulgar' Practices: The Introduction of the Image Cult into Indian Buddhism." In Gregory Schopen, *Bones, Stones, and Buddhist Monks:*

Collected Papers on the Archaeology, Epigraphy, and Texts of Monastic Buddhism in India, 238-257. Honolulu: University of Hawai'i Press, 1997.

———. "Vinaya." In *Encyclopedia of Buddhism*, ed. Robert E. Buswell, Jr. Vol. 2. New York: Macmillan Reference, 2004.

Schuster, Nancy. "Changing the Female Body: Wise Women and the Bodhisattva Career in Some *Mahāratnakūṭasūtras*." *Journal of the International Association of Buddhist Studies* 4:1 (1981): 24–69.

Sege, Irene. "Suicide or Sacrifice? *The Boston Globe*. July 15, 1993. Living/Arts Section.

Seneviratne, H. L. "Food Essence and the Essence of Experience." In *The Eternal Food: Gastronomic Ideas and Experiences of Hindus and Buddhists*, ed. R. S. Khare, 179–200. Albany: State University of New York Press, 1992.

Shastri, Hara Prasad. *A Descriptive Catalogue of Sanscrit* [sic] *Manuscripts in the Government Collection, Under the Care of the Asiatic Society of Bengal*. Vol. 1. Buddhist Manuscripts. Calcutta: Baptist Mission Press, 1917.

Shastri, Swami Dwarikadas, ed. *Abhidharmakośa & Bhāṣya of Acharya Vasubandhu with Sphutārthā Commentary of Acharya Yaśomitra*. 4 parts. Varanasi: Bauddha Bharati, 1970–1973.

Shaw, Miranda. *Buddhist Goddesses of India*. Princeton, N.J.: Princeton University Press, 2006.

Sherburne, Richard, S. J., trans. *A Lamp for the Path and Commentary of Atīśa*. London: George Allen & Unwin, 1983.

Silk, Jonathan Alan. "The Origins and Early History of the *Mahāratnakūṭa* Tradition of Mahāyāna Buddhism with a Study of the *Ratnarāśisūtra* and Related Materials." Ph.D. diss., University of Michigan, 1994.

———. "What, If Anything, Is Mahāyāna Buddhism? Problems of Definitions and Classifications." *Numen* 49:4 (2002): 355–405.

Sponberg, Alan. "Attitudes toward Women and the Feminine in Early Buddhism." In *Buddhism, Sexuality, and Gender*, ed. José Ignacio Cabezón, 3–36. Albany, N.Y.: State University Press, 1992.

Stearns, Cyrus. "The Life and Tibetan Legacy of the Indian *Mahāpaṇḍita* Vibhūticandra." *Journal of the International Association of Buddhist Studies* 19:1 (1996): 127–171.

Stone, Jacqueline I. "By the Power of One's Last Nenbutsu: Deathbed Practices in Early Medieval Japan." In *Approaching the Land of Bliss: Religious Praxis in the Cult of Amitābha*, ed. Richard K. Payne and Kenneth K. Tanaka, 77–119. Honolulu: Kuroda Institute and the University of Hawai'i Press, 2004.

Streng, Frederick J. *Emptiness: A Study in Religious Meaning*. Nashville: Abingdon Press, 1967.

Strong, John S. *The Experience of Buddhism: Sources and Interpretations*. 2nd ed. Belmont, Calif.: Wadsworth/Thomson Learning, 2002.

———. *The Legend of King Aśoka: A Study and Translation of the* Aśokāvadāna. Princeton, N.J.: Princeton University Press, 1983.

———. "The Transforming Gift: An Analysis of Devotional Acts of Offering in Buddhist *Avadāna* Literature." *History of Religions* 18:3 (February 1979): 221–237.

Sweet, Michael J., and Leonard Zwilling. "The First Medicalization: The Taxonomy and Etiology of Queerness in Classical Indian Medicine." *Journal of the History of Sexuality* 3:4 (1993): 590–607.

Takakusu, J., trans. *A Record of the Buddhist Religion as Practised in India and the Malay Archipelago (AD 671–695) by I-Tsing*. 1896. Reprint, New Delhi: Munshiram Manoharlal, 1966. 2nd Indian ed. 1982.

Tambiah, Stanley J. "Purity and Auspiciousness at the Edge of the Hindu Context—in Theravāda Buddhist Societies." In *Purity and Auspiciousness in Indian Society*, ed. John B. Carman and Frédérique Apffel Marglin, 94–108. Leiden: Brill, 1985.

Tatelman, Joel, *The Glorious Deeds of Pūrṇa: A Translation and Study of the* Pūrṇāvadāna. Surrey, U.K.: Curzon Press, 2000.

Tatz, Mark, trans. *Buddhism and Healing: Demiéville's Article "Byō" from Hōbōgirin*. Lanham, Md.: University Press of America, 1985.

———, trans. *The Skill in Means (Upāyakauśalya) Sūtra*. Delhi: Motilal Banarsidass, 1994.

Thapar, Romila. *A History of India*. Vol. 1. Harmondsworth, Middlesex: Penguin Books, 1966.

Thurman, Robert A. F., trans. *The Holy Teaching of Vimalakīrti: A Mahāyāna Scripture*. University Park: Pennsylvania State University Press, 1976.

Tin, Pe Maung, trans. *The Expositor (Atthasālinī): Buddhaghosa's Commentary on the Dhammasangaṇi, the First Book of the Abhidhamma Piṭaka*. 2 vols. in 1. 1920. Reprint, London: Pali Text Society, 1976.

Tiyavanich, Kamala. *Forest Recollections: Wandering Monks in Twentieth-Century Thailand*. Honolulu: University of Hawai'i Press, 1997.

Trainor, Kevin. "In the Eye of the Beholder: Nonattachment and the Body in Subhā's Verse (Therīgāthā 71)." *Journal of the American Academy of Religion* 61:1 (Spring 1993): 57–79.

———. *Relics, Ritual, and Representation in Buddhism: Rematerializing the Sri Lankan Theravāda Tradition*. Cambridge, U.K.: Cambridge University Press, 1997.

Tsong-kha-pa. *The Great Treatise on the Stages of the Path to Enlightenment*, trans. The Lamrim Chenmo Translation Committee. 3 vols. Ithaca, N.Y.: Snow Lion Publications, 2000–2004.

Vaidya, P. L., ed. *Aṣṭasāhasrikā Prajñāpāramitā with Haribhadra's Commentary Called* Āloka. Buddhist Sanskrit Texts No. 4. Darbhanga: Mithila Institute, 1960.

———, ed. *Daśabhūmikasūtra*. Buddhist Sanskrit Texts No. 7. Darbhanga: Mithila Institute, 1967.

———, ed. *Saddharmapuṇḍarīkasūtra*. Buddhist Sanskrit Texts No. 6. Darbhanga: Mithila Institute, 1960.

———, ed. *Śikṣāsamuccaya of Śāntideva*. Buddhist Sanskrit Texts No. 11. Darbhanga: Mithila Institute, 1961.

Vernant, Jean-Pierre. "Dim Body, Dazzling Body." In *Fragments for a History of the Human Body*, ed. Michel Feher et al. Part 1, 19–47. New York: Urzone, 1989.

Visweswaran, Kamala. *Fictions of Feminist Ethnography*. Minneapolis: University of Minnesota Press, 1994.

Walters, Jonathan S. "*Stūpa*, Story, and Empire: Constructions of the Buddha Biography in Early Post-Aśokan India." In *Sacred Biography in Buddhist Traditions of South and Southeast Asia*, ed. Juliane Schober, 160–192. Honolulu: University of Hawai'i Press, 1997.

Watson, Burton, trans. *The Lotus Sutra*. New York: Columbia University Press, 1993.

Wayman, Alex, and Hideko Wayman, trans. *The Lion's Roar of Queen Śrīmālā: A Buddhist Scripture on the Tathāgatagarbha Theory*. New York: Columbia University Press, 1974.

White, David Gordon. *The Alchemical Body: Siddha Traditions in Medieval India*. Chicago: University of Chicago Press, 1996.

———. "Why Gurus Are Heavy." *Numen* 31:1 (July 1984): 40–73.

Williams, Paul. *Altruism and Reality: Studies in the Philosophy of the Bodhicaryāvatāra*. Surrey, U.K.: Curzon Press, 1998.

———. *Mahāyāna Buddhism: The Doctrinal Foundations*. London: Routledge, 1989.

———. "Some Mahāyāna Buddhist Perspectives on the Body." In *Religion and the Body*, ed. Sarah Coakley, 205–230. Cambridge, U.K.: Cambridge University Press, 1997.

Williams, Paul, with Anthony Tribe. *Buddhist Thought: A Complete Introduction to the Indian Tradition*. London: Routledge, 2000.

Wilson, Liz. "Ascetic Practices." In *Encyclopedia of Buddhism*, ed. Robert E. Buswell, Jr. Vol. 1. New York: Macmillan Reference, 2004.

———. *Charming Cadavers: Horrific Figurations of the Feminine in Indian Buddhist Hagiographic Literature*. Chicago: University of Chicago Press, 1996.

Wimalaratana, Bellanwilla. *Concept of Great Man: (Mahāpurisa) in Buddhist Literature and Iconography*. Singapore: Buddhist Research Society, n.d.

Woodward, F. L., trans. *The Book of the Kindred Sayings (Saṃyutta-Nikāya) or Grouped Suttas*. Part 3. 1925. London: Pali Text Society, 1975.

———, ed. *Sārattha-ppakāsinī: Buddhaghosa's Commentary on the Saṃyutta-Nikāya*. 3 vols. London: Pali Text Society, 1929–1932.

Yearley, Lee H. *Mencius and Aquinas: Theories of Virtue and Conceptions of Courage*. Albany: State University of New York Press, 1990.

Zimmermann, Francis. *Le discours des remèdes au pays des épices: Enquête sur la médecine hindoue*. Paris: Payot, 1989.

———. *The Jungle and the Aroma of Meats: An Ecological Theme in Hindu Medicine*. Berkeley: University of California Press, 1987.

Zwilling, Leonard. "Homosexuality as Seen in Indian Buddhist Texts." In *Buddhism, Sexuality, and Gender*, ed. José Ignacio Cabezón, 203–214. Albany, N.Y.: State University Press, 1992.

Index